Mark Time has made overcoming adversity an art form. The Royal Marines was his first metaphorical Goliath, but with fortitude and resilience as his sidekick he became a commando by the age of 17. Camaraderie, adventure and the occasional bout of idiocy have become personal watchwords creating his unique style that reflects the alternate face of society. In battling his own mental health issues, Mark is keen to provide humour in all his work, and is passionate about painting the world with colour.

In addition to books, Mark writes for a number of satirical websites, is a feature writer for the national press and a bumbling tech biff trying to keep a travel blog.

Mark spends his spare time travelling, failing miserably to retain his six-pack and retrieving his hyperactive Jack Russell from rabbit burrows.

Mark grew up in Yorkshire but now divides his time between the UK and anywhere cheap.

Foreword

It may be unfair to say that the average immigration official isn't cut out for a second career as a children's TV presenter. I've often wondered what I've done wrong as I step up to their dais, the surliness received suggesting they've either forgotten to affix their nicotine patch or they're unimpressed by me approaching whilst eating a Scotch egg.

On occasion, though, one may discover a thin veneer of affability that can almost form a smile even in the roughest of places and, boy, have I been to some. I've walked through airports in Baghdad, Kinshasa, Kabul, Leeds. Despite their infamy, I've always received some form of geniality upon arrival.

In Baghdad, for instance, I thought immigration control was manned (as they were all indeed male) by a troop of simpletons, their inane grins never waning as I passed through dressed, as one does, with pockets full of *Fisherman's Friends* and mint sauce - delicacies one misses in such places of faded glory.

Kabul International Airport seemed to be teaming with immigration officers each eager in reminding us to have the correct documentation, waving a piece of paper Neville Chamberlain style. Here, peace in our time was still a dream.

In Kinshasa Airport I was pretty nervous. The Democratic Republic of Congo has been bloodying its own nose for too many years, so one could rate it pretty low on the list of welcoming nations. To reinforce this, I only had to look up at the huge picture of President Joseph Kabila staring menacingly over his subjects in the arrivals hall to make my arse pucker like lips in a brothel window.

I found a monster of a man at passport control with more sweat patches than a rugby scrum. Initially, I was a little intimidated by his 'come here now or be shot' wave, but upon noting my UK passport his eyes lit up. 'Ah Angleterre! Manchester United! Good oui?' he boomed in his pidgin Anglo/Franco attempt at communication.

I swallowed hard and gave the best false smile and comedy thumbs up I could muster. 'Ah oui, bien sur! Manchester United C'est fantastic,' I replied in my best year 9 French accent.

Being a Leeds United fan, I'd rather eat my arm than profess a love of Manchester United, however, all things considered the consumption of the aforementioned limb would be far more pleasant than spending time in an airport cell for upsetting an immigration official. Having previously spent a rather unpleasant 14 hours detained in a Sudanese cell the size of a size 8 shoe in 40°C heat, squeezed around a bucket of human shit with forty sweaty reprobates, I didn't care for a repeat performance. So with my footballing ethics as smashed as the pottery I'd bought in Nairobi the previous day, I sidled through without the slightest of hitches, not even declaring my excess duty free *Old Spice,* into the decadence of Kinshasa that satiated my lust for visiting places others may describe as a 'shithole'.

Experiences like these make me wonder why one of my favourite destinations in the world - the good old

United States of America sadly, for a while, created the atmosphere of airports similar to a gulag reception area.

Our first post 9/11 family holiday to the US was in 2003; our kids, aged 8 and 4, wearing all manner of Disney paraphernalia bought from a previous visit. Prior to landing at Orlando International Airport, we re-checked the world's most complicated landing cards for the fifteenth time ensuring we'd declared our innocence of terrorism, drug offences and stealing sweets when a child. We stepped off the plane, down the air bridge corridor and into the cacophony of the arrivals hall.

At this point I had to check whether I'd come on holiday or joined the US Marines. A rather unsavoury woman stood at the entry to the hall underneath a big motherfucking sign saying 'Welcome To Orlando International Airport', and barked like a Drill Sergeant at the hordes of tired and bewildered British tourists directing them to an appropriate immigration desk.

'That Line!' she pointed.

'This line?' pointed a confused tourist.

'No, that line!' she shouted at him. 'Did you not hear me? I said that line!' she screamed at a very suspicious looking 85 year old great grandmother with specialist macramé skills that would surely be of interest to the FBI.

This auditory assault continued until it was our turn to be shouted at from a distance of 30cm.

They say there is truth from the mouths of babes, and it was my darling daughter who approached the subject. 'Why does that gobby bitch keep shouting?' she asked, relaying language she'd often heard from her Irish grandmother.

All I could do was shrug my shoulders, pretend everything was OK, wipe the spittle from my face and wait in the line that I'd been so graciously screamed into.

When summoned to the control desk, we all cautiously approached together like a pack of dogs unsure whether the treats offered were poisonous. Trainee Immigration Officer Chad McJobsworth held out his hand, palms up. Whether this was an invitation for a 'low-five' hand slap I wasn't sure, so played on the side of caution and crossed his palm with passports. His expression, chiselled from the most miserable of grey stone, told me that this wasn't to be a pleasant experience.

'You guys on vacation?'

I turned my head and gestured towards my kids, one with an over sized goofy hat on his head and the other wearing a pink diamante Tinkerbelle T-shirt, and tried not to sound facetious in my reply.

As a trainee, Chad had a tutor looking over his shoulder, so he was damn sure that he wasn't gonna let any Al Qaeda into Orlando whether they were wearing Goofy hats or not. He scrutinised each page with utmost proficiency and seemed quite un-smilingly happy until he came to mine.

'You've been to Algeria?'

I wanted to pull a sarcastic, '*No, I just got the visa to fill up my passport*', but thought better of it. 'Yes.'

He turned over the next page slightly slower than the previous one. 'Tanzania, Sudan, Jordan. Interesting,' he nodded. I wondered in what context he meant 'interesting'.

I stood there like a startled rabbit for fear of saying the wrong word that could lead to a one way ticket back to the UK as had been reported in the news just prior to us departing.

'You've got an Afghan visa, oh and I see here you've been to Iraq.' I could see where he was going with this. I wondered whether the kids would prefer Guanta*nemo* Bay to Wet & Wild.

'Yes, with my work,' I stated confidently.

'What work?' Now it was the tutor who now hissed at me, I could swear I caught a glimpse of a serpent's tongue.

'I currently work under a US Government con-tract.'

'Yeah right,' sneered the ugly tutor.

Long-haired, unshaven, and wearing a Mickey Mouse T-shirt, I hardly looked like the stereotypical government employee. However, my patience was now running as thin as my smile. 'I'm working in Iraq for your Restore Iraqi Oil project.'

'Oh really?' the tutor replied, not in an interested way, but in a sarcastic tone, even placing her hand on her hip for added contempt. All that was needed for her to be a walking cliché was a sideward jolt of her head and a click of the fingers and to address me as 'girl-friend'.

With seemingly no alternative, I dug out my US Army Contractor ID card, packed only to take advantage of discounted attraction tickets.

The tutor grabbed it like a ravenous dog and stud-ied the features and hallmarks to check its veracity. Obviously disgruntled at not catching a terrorist, she threw the card back at me in a manner reminiscent of my son when a toddler and didn't want his sandwich.

'OK go,' she ordered. No please, thank you, or sorry for taking three fucking days to process you, just 'OK go.'

Even my wife, who is the most placid sweet creature on the planet, uttered the 'C' word at the baggage collection point.

While subsequent administrations seemed to have relaxed their attempts to frighten the bejesus out of tourists, the numerous times I returned to Bush led US, nothing changed. Not once was I smiled at, not once pleasantries exchanged, not once did I feel welcome; despite what the big motherfucking sign said.

Please do not think I am trivialising any of the atrocities that have happened in recent years and how this has impacted on changes in perception and values. However, I'd argue that courtesy and professionalism and the odd smile are not mutually exclusive from being security focussed, and if there is anywhere that these attributes should work hand in hand, it's at the airport where first impressions count. Of course, this didn't spoil my time in a place that I hold with great affection, and would certainly never define a country based upon some megalomaniac; yet for a time, the big motherfucking sign seemingly proclaimed:

'Welcome To Fortress America. Unhappy with our customer service? Call 1-800 EATSHIT.' *Have a nice day.*

Author's Note

This final instalment of the 'Bootneck Threesome' trilogy covers my final hurrah in the Royal Marines spending my last few months of military service cavorting through eighteen of the USA's States.

I wanted to remember the USA in different times. I'd prefer to reminisce about a country where wearing a beard without a moustache meant you were a twat and not necessarily a terrorist. I longed to recollect innocence, where shouting 'Bomb!' at the public swimming pool would cause a big splash and not a mass evacuation. I rejoiced for a country where the president just fucked his aides, not the whole world over, allegedly.

So this book deviates, like the river it mainly features, from my 'green time' in the Royal Marines to a trip I was honoured to be part of, where haircuts were optional and bland galley food yearned for, in those halcyon days prior to 9/11.

With their kind permission, for the first time in the series, names, other than mine, are real. This does not indicate a lessening of buffoonery, merely redemption of men who once swung regularly from the debauchery tree then developed into mature adults who would shy away from rule bending and irreverence, preferring the sedation of societal norms and responsibility.

And if you believe that...

Mark Time

Acknowledgements

Without resorting to Oscar-esque clichés:

To the military and emergency services along the Mississippi River who offered gracious hospitality to four scruffy arsed foreigners.

To the many 'river rats' we met who offered us food, shelter and friendship. You will never be forgotten.

To those friends closest to me - your creativity, benevolence, and friendship inspire me every day.

To the readers - I thank you for supporting my work but apologise for being rubbish on social media.

To Jo, Connor and Finlay - you are the reason I wake every morning.

'The collective human mind shrivels without frontiers.
The longing for odysseys and faraway adventures is in our genes.'

~ Edward O. Wilson, biologist, author

I AM THE ETERNAL TRAVELLER. I may sound like some tree-hugging, lice-laden hippy when I say I class myself not as a citizen of a country, but of the world. I'm proudly British but live in Australia, and see far off lands as my backyard. Vietnam is my flower garden, Ireland my lawn. I see the Caribbean as my entertainments area and Moldova is where my dog shits.

I have a strange homesickness for places I've not yet explored, and often daydream of distant destinations yet to be discovered or reminisce about random regions I've ruined. There will never be a time when I think I've seen enough and every opportunity I can I will don my day sack and take a flight, preferably to somewhere difficult to spell.

I've been honoured to stand in silent wonder at the foot of structures humanity's talented have crafted, and awestruck by some of nature's most dramatic gifts. I've witnessed feats of both unquestionable bravery and unimaginable horror. I've met those who I'd marry tomorrow and people who I wish would die painfully the day after. Whether good or bad, these experiences have made me further yearn for travel, even if my weak stomach can't handle anything spicier than a cinnamon doughnut. It was due to this fervent wanderlust that I'd become rather frustrated at how my career in the Royal Marines had turned out.

I'd been drafted to Security Troop at RM Poole. The troop was a stockpot of vagabonds, ne'er do wells, and others who were just biding their time prior to leaving the Corps. Amongst these was a sprinkle of keen lads who'd just had the misfortune to be plucked from a hat when personnel were needed.

My role in Security Troop was Guard Commander meaning a protracted period of incessant guard duties in a box of boredom that would see me drinking acrid coffee at unearthly hours, play pool on a table with less felt than my leaking shed roof, writing serials with the aid of ruler to ensure the daily occurrence book was neat enough for the RSM to read, and listen to the spring countdown of the ubiquitous *Dualit* toaster that could constantly toast umpteen loaves to feed the lads who ate just to forget the drudgery of their existence.

At least I could get home regularly, which was vitally important seeing as though I was preparing for discharge from the Royal Marines.

Leaving the Corps had been a conscious effort, one easy to make with my son on my knee, even if I'd just recently passed my Senior Command Course for promotion to sergeant. At the age of 25 it was a jagged pill to swallow and confirmed me as a victim of my own success. I'd passed the course on the Friday and reported to my Company Commander on the following Tuesday to inform him that I was submitting my notice to leave the Royal Marines, much to the shock of both he and the Company Sergeant Major. Both called me an idiot. It wasn't the first time.

Since the birth of my first child, Connor, two years previously, my purring to the sweet caresses of family life had coincided with my career hitting a speed bump. MOD had tightened the purse strings and 'fun', it seemed, was a luxury it could ill afford. Tours of duty seemed to have dried up, so too tours of duty free. A recent strategic defence review ensured plenty of redundancies but a reduction in overseas trips. I'd managed to squeeze in another Northern Ireland tour but, in general, life had slowed from driving in the Lamborghini Diablo of life to a being the passenger in a rusting old Lamborghini tractor belching its way over a ploughed field of Chantenay carrots.

If I chose to accept promotion, life as a General Duties Sergeant could see me stagnate in dreary positions that were 'gap' fillers' in a unit: PRI Sergeant, Quartermaster SNCO and other appointments meant for much older sergeants who were looking forward to their pension.

I'd lost control of my future that, as family man, I needed. Professionalism is intrinsic to Royal Marines proficiency, but it was becoming a creeping definition of doing something I didn't want to do, including overriding my own family's needs for the sake of someone else's.

While it would've been short sighted of me to make wholesale decisions based upon my next appointment, I also had doubts about becoming an SNCO.

Being an SNCO meant I'd be expected to buy into a 'system' from which I was becoming more rebellious. As soon as I stepped over the Mess threshold, I joined a regimented boys club governed by the unit RSM. I feared I would prematurely age, losing my penchant for designer clothing to instead carefully browse through the sales sections of gentlemen's outfitters looking for brogues, cords and pin striped shirts. I may even take up golf - a sure admission of middle age. I'd socialise with men probably ten years older with whom I had little connection other than our beret, and while I would know some, I didn't really want to give up my youthfulness and unconformity, which would guarantee the ire of any RSM and see my career festooned with extra duties.

So, with such a personal conflict, I found it only fair to abdicate my responsibilities to someone who would be eager to impress. As Euripides said, 'the wisest men follow their own direction'. While I couldn't say I was necessarily wise, I knew that the route the Royal Marines wanted me to take was not of my choosing.

Of more concern was my dark twin. He was still there and his presence was becoming harder to hide. My regular darkness was becoming a spreading coffee stain on my CV and while it didn't yet define me, I feared it may spill further to a position where not only my life but those of my colleagues were in jeopardy. It was time to go.

In those days, when submitting a notice to discharge, 18 months notice had to be given - a long time when seeking a new direction. This period sees many preparing to leave feel in limbo, a sort of military purgatory where their motivation for the military has waned yet their keenness to start again is hampered by the tyranny of time. I was determined not to let my standards slip in my final period, hard to do when trying to implement orders to subordinates or question orders from above as the answer would always be, 'What do you care? You're leaving.'

But I did care, I cared for personal standards that had been engrained by the Corps, and I also was aware of letting down those lads on Security Troop who were still keen. They already had a hard time staying motivated when surrounded by lads who clearly couldn't wait to leave. Yet 18 months was going to be a long time to wait. I needed to seek something to keep me motivated, to prevent me slipping even further away from positivity. It came in the form of Sean.

I knew Sean from my time in 40 Commando. Due to his unimpeachable professionalism, he'd forged a career in the Special Boat Service, so I saw him on occasion along with a good mutual friend Rob who, although wasn't a Special Forces operator, was attached to SBS doing something secret with secret boats that were always being secretly towed around Poole under a big tarpaulin marked 'Secret'.

They were keen on fund raising for Ashley, Sean's Godson, who'd been diagnosed with cerebral palsy. Being a fervent Yankophile, Sean's idea was to kayak the length of possibly the most famous ribbon of water in the world - the mighty Mississippi River.

Lacking the necessary finesse for something so life changing, Sean popped his head through the small guardroom window hatch that forever smelled of acrid bleach. 'We need a safety team. I can't find anyone who can get time off. You fancy doing it?'

'Do bears shit in the woods?' I replied. They do. I have photographic evidence.

So despite the likelihood of me being near the bottom of a very long list entitled 'Blokes I Trust With Admin', here was I, a support crewmember of Expedition 'Mississippi Madness'. It'd be fantastic to recreate the hedonism of my previous visit to the USA, only this time it'd be preferable not to get nearly murdered.

'When are we planning on going?' I asked, hoping that we'd have about a year to properly prepare.

'I was planning on next September…' Sean replied.

Good, I thought. *That's a year.*

'…But two lads in my squadron are rowing the Atlantic in September. The only time I can get off is in May.'

'Oh,' I replied, trying not to sound too despondent. 'That sounds achievable?' With a purposeful questioning that mirrored my uncertainty.

This was mainly due to us being members of the Armed Forces that raises its own unique set of problems, the first being getting permission to do it.

The chain of military command is so long, by the time you find the person who will actually give you the required permission, you will have retired and started to enjoy gardening. Danny, my boss, was more than happy to give me time off, as it transpired he couldn't wait to get rid of someone who questioned his every decision. Officially getting 14 weeks off may present more difficulty.

I submitted my request to see the HQ Company Commander, Captain Martin Grixoni, a great man who perfectly blended affability with leadership.

He pondered my request with a smile. 'OK, it sounds a great idea. Why should I give you that amount of time off?'

Under the circumstances it was a fair question. My argument was simple. 'Well there are many benefits of the expedition, Sir.'

'Yes, you've explained that perfectly well already. Go on, I need more than you repeating yourself.'

I'd shown all my cards. It was time to go all in. 'Well I've been in the Corps eleven years, Sir…'

'…Well done, I'll wait 'til the end to give you a medal.'

'Well, amongst the myriad of military directives is one that states that personnel are allocated two weeks adventure training per year. So far I haven't had any.'

'Stop showing off with big words. Didn't you say in your preamble that you'd been on a rock climbing exped?'

'Ah yes, but that was with the army so doesn't really count, so I'm still owed 22 weeks,' I explained, my speech quickening with every word. 'Take away the three weeks summer leave we'll be away, I'm only asking for half of that and I'm happy to forfeit the rest that I'm owed as a gesture of goodwill.' I hoped my garbling would confuse him into submission.

Captain Grixoni rocked back in his chair and pondered this with a smile. Whether he actually agreed, was overwhelmed by my cheek, or just saw this as an opportunity for a fellow Royal Marine to do something positive in his final year rather than slip into a coma of negativity, he gave permission for me to go.

It was game on.

***

The next hurdle to jump was to get official permission from the departments who oversaw adventure training and the such-like. This required a plan. Not just a plan, a failsafe plan.

Since a group of British soldiers became lost in the valleys surrounding Mount Kinabalu in Borneo, the safety plan for even a visit to a coffee vending machine would equal that of a presidential space shuttle mission. Therefore, Sean and I submitted a proposal that covered every eventuality including being attacked by an overly aggressive catfish.

On such an expedition, funds were needed. As ours was somewhat further afield than a picnic over the Purbeck Hills, our budget was substantial even with our own contributions. There are numerous service funds out there all designed to assist service people. Like all funds, they too required budgets and plans submitted before releasing any monies. Unfortunately, when we needed such assistance, a number of these funds suddenly became 'Top Secret' organisations, hidden from view to keep their money locked away under a mattress in a locked room behind a secret panel in a safe house only known to a few. We were going to have to do some sweet talking.

I was the only one that had a job with a telephone, heating, lighting and general modern day necessities. As such, I commandeered the pass office, renaming it the 'Expedition Office' to sound grandiose and even the resident pass office lance corporal became my improvised secretary with no recompense other than belt fed wets and a promise of a tacky fridge magnet upon our return. Therefore, my unofficial job title for the expedition expanded from 'support crew' to 'organiser'. Sean and Rob did their utmost to help when time allowed but were often overworked with their own military commitments. By the time January arrived, we'd organised a few things here and there, but as far as I was concerned, we were on a snakes and ladders board and had hit too many snakes for my liking.

Through various tantrums that would have put my toddler to shame and the uninterested organisations that turned down our requests for sponsorship, we'd got as far as... well, nowhere, we'd not even confirmed a vehicle. The type needed was expensive to hire for three months, so success depended on how much we could extract from the various Forces funds that were our main source of income. The more helpful funds, such as the SBS Cockleshell fund and the Royal Navy Sports Lottery were keen to assist but we'd have to await the next allocation meetings with no guarantee of success.

To pile more problems into the in-tray, I had to find a new man to partner me in the support crew. Steve Rooney, part of Driver Training Wing at RM

Poole, was a close friend back in my 40 Commando days. We'd shared a grot and many nights out, including the infamous 'Battle of Corfu.' With him being a heavy goods driver he seemed the perfect choice as a partner. He'd taken to the expedition preparation with gusto and as a logistics expert was forging ahead with route planning. But now, in mid February, he had a new boss who wanted to stamp his authority on things, enjoyment being one.

He told Steve, 'Because of some totally trivial reason, it gives me great pleasure in telling you, that indeed after careful consideration of nothing other than my sense of self importance I, in my infinite wisdom, have decided that you cannot go.' Admittedly, I'm paraphrasing a bit.

Steve was obviously threaders and was close to challenging his boss to a morning duel, or failing that, a naked oil wrestle. I too was gutted, now even more so, as it would have been my last time spent with him. Although we always kept in touch, we never managed to meet up in civvy street. He died of a heart attack aged 42 when working in Saudi Arabia as a driver trainer.

With twelve weeks until departure, we'd progressed nowhere and my zeal was flagging. In fact nowhere now seemed an attractive place to get to. Our problems were mounting and whenever I passed on my concerns Sean suggested reassurance by saying 'it'll be alright.'

What wasn't alright was my mood that swung from gleefully planning the intricacies of time/distance/speed calculations of the journey taking into consideration food, water and shelter, to struggling to decide whether I wanted two or three slices of toast. The debilitation of normal function was becoming harder to disguise in the goldfish bowl of the guardroom and often in such circumstances, my frustration at not being able to process the simplest of tasks would result in ill aimed anger at confused victims, including one sergeant major who I told 'Get your subnormal head down', when he rang to complain of some utterly trivial reason. My gold stars that I'd built up in my career were dropping swiftly from the wall...

***

I still couldn't get hold of Captain David Wilson, the Liaison Officer at the British Embassy in Washington DC. It was imperative that we contacted him as soon as possible to get final permission to undertake adventure training in the USA. Forever away on trips, he seemed as busy as a bee to a demanding queen. So were we, but he was probably getting honey from the hours he worked. We were weakly hovering around the stalks of dead dandelions.

'Luckily' I had the benefit of working after 6pm most days, so I could get away with phoning the Capt Wilson at not too much cost to the taxpayer, psychologically timing it so I would get hold of him after a large lunch, where his decreasing sugar levels would ease him into drowsy contentment. I eventually got hold of him exactly nine weeks to D-Day on the same day that Sean booked the flights: Depart 28th May - Return 31st August - a total of 94 days (why I mention this will become apparent later on). We were finally making headway.

Capt Wilson was initially guarded about the expedition getting approval within the necessary time frame. All the necessary paperwork took at least seven weeks to process, meaning the best case scenario would be receiving approval only two weeks before deployment. That was if the paperwork was processed promptly, or the postal service on each side of the Atlantic got their act together, or any other anomaly designed to hamper us, such as a revolt in Tristan De Cunha or the CO needing his fishpond cleaning. But, despite my initial doubts, the paperwork was expedited thanks to our man at the embassy, who was probably fed up with me phoning every two minutes.

With confidence growing, I thought it'd be a good opportunity to get something from this period of awaiting decisions, so Rob and I went to a couple of boat shows to promote our venture with high hopes of securing a multi million pound sponsorship deal. We succeeded in getting some free snazzy paddles from 'Lendal' and some free sandals from Teva.

Just as welcome were the two tickets I managed to blag to Washington DC in the name of 'reconnaissance' for the main expedition. Sean was again away doing something strenuous, secret and sweaty, so it was down to Rob and I to sample the delights of the capital city.

David Wilson sounded suitably surprised when I phoned him to book a meeting for the following week, but not half as surprised as Rob, who, when told that I had a ticket for him, luckily wasn't standing one-legged on a gymnast's balance beam holding an over filled urn of boiling tea, whose instant delight would have surely caused him to spill a splosh and sustain minor scalding. Needless to say, he was as pleased as punch to be going to the capital of the USA on a freebie in six days time.

***

We set off to the capital with impending excitement in a hire car that made us look like a pair of 1970's gay prostitutes. It suited me very well; Rob, however, wasn't so keen.

We looked at our courtesy map, trailing our fingers to our destination - Henderson Hall US Marine Corps barracks overlooking the Pentagon, in a military wing for service people in transit. Being one of the largest buildings in the world we thought making the Pentagon a reference point would be a good idea. However, we seemed to get slightly confused in the contra-flow system that was in operation and ended up actually going to it. An overbearing building, if not vaguely drab, from the ground it looked comparable to a sand-coloured biscuit tin. It seemed slightly menacing with CCTV cameras at every uniformly rectangular window, security both overt in their obvious patrolling, and most definitely covert surveillance from men hiding in drain pipes to 'Police-a-likes' eating chilli dogs from the dashboard of a '77 Thunderbird.

'Yes Sir, what can I do for you?' asked the man wearing 'Pentagon Security' patch on his shirt, stood in a booth stating 'Pentagon Security', that sat across from a number of signs stating 'Pentagon' something or other.

'Ayup mate, are we near the Pentagon?' asked Rob.

'Yes Sir,' the guard replied, not biting on Rob's sarcasm. He then pointed us towards the barracks not hearing my childish hubris at his helpfulness as we drove off. It then transpired that Rob hadn't been sarcastic. He hadn't realised we were at the Pentagon. I made a mental note to check his eyesight.

At the accommodation office sat four men without a single crop of hair between them. The first noticeable difference between a US Marine and a Royal Marine is hair. We don't feel the desire to shave our heads just leaving a small tuft the size and thickness of Melba toast on our bonces. The first sergeant we addressed, who looked about 21, didn't really understand how such lowly corporals had managed to get here without an officer. We were summarily palmed off to another sergeant.

'I'm Sergeant Morris,' he glared, his head as shiny as his toecaps.

'Alright mate, I'm Mark Time, this is Rob Tweddle.' We stuck out our hands. After picking himself up off the ground from the informality, he returned with a bone-crushing handshake.

After formalities, he led us up three flights of stairs. 'OK guys, try and keep up with me,' he demanded. 'Running up stairs keeps you fit.'

He obviously thought sprinting up a flight of stairs carrying luggage was the running equivalent of '6 second abs'. Rob had just completed the Devizes to Westminster International Canoe Marathon and I could still crack a sub 38 minute 10K, which wasn't quite as impressive as my sub 1 minute eating five rounds of guardroom toast.

'It's OK, we'll give it a miss thanks,' said Rob politely, before carrying on our leisurely stroll up the concrete stairwell. The ever more confused Sgt Morris gave us a quick orientation of the camp emphasising the direction to where we could find a barbers. We nodded solemnly.

'Do the barbers do shampoo and sets?' I asked. They didn't.

Our room was a cell of grey walls and a stone floor; all that was amiss were window bars. Upon the rickety bunk beds sat grey blankets, a brilliant grey sheet and 40 year old unwashed pillows that probably contained enough skin to reconstitute a human head. It was perfect.

Also like prison, we had en-suite facilities, totally unheard of in British barrack rooms of the day. Rob, somehow, struggled to come to terms with the intricate pulling of the toilet flush lever. I can't ever recall seeing a toilet lid on an American loo and this one was no exception, so when clearing up after him, I would eyeball his floaters before being swallowed in the bowl's whirlpool. At first the job wasn't too bad, nice sturdy logs that had to have their backs broken with a stick before succumbing to their Wet-n-Wild adventure. Healthy, firm, and not too pungent, as quality faeces as I'd ever seen, I commended Rob on his bowels.

Once we'd sorted ourselves, it was time to make a mandatory visit to the PX - the especially inexpensive shop for military personnel, eager to spend $40 to save $10 on shit we didn't need.

Heeding our jetlagged bellies we sauntered to the pizza parlour where we clocked eyes on the big guy behind the counter stacking cups, rearranging condiments, and wiping down the worktops in a very house proud fashion. He turned to face us; regaled in a green apron, cherry red polo shirt and baseball cap. It was Sgt Morris, the steely-eyed skinhead with shiny boots.

'Yes Sir, can I help you?' he asked, as if he'd never laid eyes on me.

I was gobsmacked. This man, who not more than an hour ago eyeballed me in a fashion that suggested he wanted to see me crawl naked through barbed wire mud flats, within a flip of pizza dough was now subservient, wearing an ill fitting apron.

'Err...' I managed to burble, still trying to come to terms with the identity of Pizza Man.

'You Sergeant Morris?' said Rob, never one to duck from asking a stupid question.

'Of course, Sir. Who did you think I was?'

'Not fucking Sgt Morris, that's for sure.'

It transpired that many of the guys working in our accommodation block did a stint in the pizza parlour as an extra bit of cash and a free bit of scran. It still didn't make things easier to comprehend and throughout my meal I was positive Sgt Morris was eyeballing me to ensure I ate in a military fashion.

It was, however, a good fill, and as we were both tight fisted Northerners we worked out how to wangle cheap drinks. It is a method I urge you to use if you as miserly as we are:

The sodas were offered according to your thirst, i.e:

Small (UK large) - 90c

Medium (plant pot) - $1.15

Large (window cleaner's bucket) - $1.40

Unlimited Refills - free.

If the refills are free, why buy a large? We could buy a small and still leave with our brains floating in cola and save a whole 50c into the bargain, Brilliant! We congratulated ourselves on our unashamed penny pinching and to celebrate our combined profit of a dollar, we decided on a night out.

Those from both sides of 'The Pond' had told us that 'M Street' was the best place to go for a beer, so we pinned the tail to the Georgetown Donkey and dialled a cab.

The April evening air was pleasantly humid, the breeze blowing into our faces most agreeable. Waiting for a taxi we caught our first real glimpse of Washington DC. From our vantage point the fire of an electric red dusk silhouetted the picturesque low-rise skyline. Over the left shoulder of the Pentagon, the angelic obelisk of the Washington Monument; over the right, some would say, the devilish Capitol Building. The serenity of the cityscape belied the power of the dealing and decision-making within. Perhaps the fire in the sky was telling us something.

Once in a 'Washington Taxi', the taxi driver negotiated Washington's new contraflow system with embarrassing ease, taking us onto Washington Boulevard, which then merged with the George Washington Memorial Parkway (yes, we also noticed a pattern developing). We then passed the highly impressive USMC War Memorial. Up-lighters exaggerating to gladiatorial proportions the height of the six brave men hoisting the Stars and Stripes on Mount Suribachi, the familiar landmark on the South Pacific island of Iwo Jima which gives the memorial its more commonly used name.

Over the Francis Scott Key Memorial Bridge we travelled. I wondered if it was in memorial of Francis Scott Key or Francis Scott who had many a memorial bridge named after him, but this was the most important. It was an irrelevance; we had a poorly planned trip to undertake.

After crossing the bridge, we turned right to see 'M' Street. Apparently 'M' Street wasn't named thus because it was alphabetically placed northbound away from Capitol Hill. The M stood for 'morgue'. Wednesday was obviously Sabbath to the local drinkers; I expected tumbleweed to blow from one bar to another.

We entered a sports bar recommended by a US Marine and asked the barman why it was so quiet.

'It's always quiet tonight, who else but alcoholics come out to drink on a Wednesday?' It was a fair point, I could recall staying in at least five times on a Wednesday, 'Sportsnight' was usually on.

It was typical of the sport bar that now dominates the theme pub market, not only killing traditional pubs, but also irreverent conversation. I can't think of anything more pointless than going to a pub to sit gawping at a TV screen for four hours. Usually the screen is so high that after the first bit of action the neck seizes and one spends the rest of the night ordering a beer to a fluorescent light directly above the bar staff. Shallow as it may be, the pub/bar/club was the meeting ground for many bootnecks to try and get a bit of 'tit and kipper' by the end of the night. So it perplexes me even more when blokes are sat watching TV screens of some 1974 second division football match commenting on sideburns and tight shirts when underneath there could be a bus load of naked nubile Nordic nurses rubbing each other down with strawberry jam, totally unnoticed. Admittedly, it was unlikely to happen here on a Wednesday night.

Back into the balmy night we wandered, and in the hour holed up in the sports bar people had decided to take to the bars and cafes that lined the road. It seemed quite a lively place after all, and wealth was evident. Young men cruised the streets in cars that I could never afford, trying to look cool nodding and winking suggestively at anything in a skirt. I was hoping that they'd end up ramming into the back of psychopathic serial killer's pick-up at the traffic lights.

As is typical in city life, beggars counterbalanced affluence. Whether they were double jointed and able to conveniently hide limbs or they'd actually been chopped off in some burger factory machinery was irrelevant. They all seemingly had overdosed on medicine stronger than paracetamol and so we did the British thing and tried to avoid guilt by ignoring them the best we could. Most were novices at this begging game - they were negative some sort of canine accomplice. My sympathy for animals far outweighs that of humans so Mad Mick the Mormon Murdering Maniac from Morecambe could be knelt there with a grimy hand outstretched, yet as long as he had a scruffy, flea-ridden mutt with alopecia sat looking sad through foggy eyes, I donate whatever coin I have, naïvely insisting that the dog gets fed first.

As we walked, the street bobbed along to different music, rap, rock, and worst of all, the ear bleeding tones of 80's American heartbeat. Put off simply because 'Toto' blared out benign chorus lines, we couldn't resist taking a peek through the window and, as expected, saw what looked like a fantastic Brian May look-a-like contest - all white shirts and perms drinking sugar free white wine spritzers and talking about the nutritional benefits of a quinoa and goji shake while playing organic tennis.

Turning left onto Wisconsin Avenue we saw the 'Third Edition' bar that the sentry had suggested. Apparently many scenes from the film 'St Elmo's fire' were filmed here. I hoped the smell of Demi Moore's farts still lingered. It didn't. It smelled of sweet cash, patronised by the sons and daughters of society's upper echelons. The men dressed uniformly in a style that said 'hey girls I know I'm a complete twat, but I'm rich' - a sweater draped over the shoulders, the sleeves in a loose hitch high on the chest purposely positioned to avoid covering the designer logo; the girls all tanned, slim and impressionable. We drank and talked and ogled brilliant white teeth. I certainly prefer to nestle within the bosom of carefree evening dialogue, free from corporate convention that stifles free expression. Unfortunately here, the materialistic genes created from this melting pot had passed from generation to genera-tion without natural selection lending a helping hand, the conversations distinctly status driven, bouncing from what car they drove to the salary they earned - all before I'd offered my name.

Wearing our working class heads we headed off to the 'Cellar Bar', made attractive by having the same name as a place frequented when based in Taunton. Comfortingly, it was just like being at home with balding, overweight doormen frisking everyone, glaring particularly at the goon saying 'ooh yeah down a bit', as if he was the first person ever to say it. Inside, it was antithesis to a British club. The music, the way everyone danced, the way they dressed, and the drinks were nothing like a British club. Perhaps the carpets were similar - sticky and of obscure colouring. It closed at 3am and we thought it would be a little ignorant to leave early whilst watching recorded British football...

'Life's city ways are dark. Men mutter by.'

~ F. Spencer Chapman, adventurer, war hero

It's comforting to know that doner kebabs are crap worldwide. With the stale taste of poor quality food on our palettes, we woke to a knock on the door. Rob immediately stumbled to his favourite seat - the loo, so it was up to me to open the door with my morning glory a tent pole for my towel. With surprise only surpassed if a farting Demi Moore herself had knocked, I was confronted by a bootneck with whom we'd both worked. Currently employed at the British Embassy as the admiral's driver, Si had heard of our presence, living only three rooms away. Fortunately, due to the admiral's propensity for holidays, Si had three slack days so rather than sitting in his room discovering the endless catalogue of adult websites on this new phenomena called the internet, he offered to drive us to the various people we needed to meet. It was better to be chauffeured by someone rather knowledgeable than self-driving into South East Washington and becoming rather dead. So while I went to scrounge anything from the USMC for our trip, Rob and Si returned our rental cackmobile.

Rob had a smile that made him look as though he'd swallowed a coat hanger. 'Have you seen the car we're in?'

Obviously I hadn't, so I too smiled like the proverbial cat from North West England when found we had at our disposal a state of the art Lincoln Town Car, pimped up to diplomatic standards to chauffeur only the most important government officials, and us. From being over age rent boys, we now looked important. Standby when we pulled up in M Street in this mofo.

Si had to go to Quantico USMC base to drop off some documents. It nicely coincided with our need to visit to see the Morale Welfare and Recreation Department (MWR) to assess their rental RVs' suitability.

The worst thing about standing on the main gate of a military camp is the approach of a VIP. There will be the mandatory presence of some junior officer who will panic as if his hair is on fire to ensure you can stand properly and salute perfectly as if a poor salute will besmirch the professionalism of an operationally experienced unit, so it was wholly predictable when we observed the Quantico sentries brace up in anticipation of our approaching VIP car. The sentry saluted smartly and peered in nervously when Si produced his Embassy ID, and looked quite confused when he saw us two hungover tosspots in the back.

'Thank you Marine,' I called in my best attempt at the Queen's English from behind my jet-black sunglasses - totally unnecessary within heavily tinted car windows; however, coolness always comes with a hint of twatishness.

'Thank you Sir,' he replied, uncertain as to whether I was some mysterious aristocrat or a very young ambassador with a stash of *Ferrero Roche* hidden in the seat pocket. He was wrong on both counts. I was just a scraggy arsed bootneck on a jolly.

I gave a rather regal wave as we pulled off carrying on where we'd left off, by seeing who could wipe the biggest bogey under the limousine's plush rear seats.

Upon investigation, the MWR's heavily subsidised prices were still more expensive than the RV we'd provisionally booked back in the UK as cover, so intent on it not being a wasted trip we rode the Marine Exchange escalator to see if it was as quick as the one at Henderson Hall. It wasn't. We left heartily disappointed.

The rest of the day was taken with organising the final details of our forthcoming meeting with David Wilson at the Embassy, and as importantly, getting ready for our night out. Because of the previous night's activities, Rob's stools were less cohesive than before, and through the door his morning evacuation sounded like a council gritter preparing for icy conditions. My moonlighting as his personal toilet flusher was now becoming a less tolerable occupation.

Once I'd got myself ready and his Lordship suitably cleansed, we decided on Georgetown again as we'd heard that the sports bar was kicking, for the simple fact was that you paid a $10 entrance fee then beer was free for the night.

'Corking,' said Rob. 'Tight Northerners + free beer = heaven.'

At 7pm, heaven is a place on Earth. At 7am, hell is pulling at the end of your bed.

The trip to the embassy took us back through Georgetown. Different in the daytime, the characterful streets to the north of 'M', where star spangles bounced from all well-buffed surfaces offered calm to the nearby mayhem. Not one fish and chip smeared newspaper blew onto the windscreen, not one speed bump scraped the car, not even an errant shopping trolley littered this enclave of respectability. Red brick Victorian styled townhouses rubbed shoulders with wooden clad buildings straight from the set of 'Gone With The Wind', only now it was the enviable sight of Stars and Stripes that fluttered gently through the quiet breeze. Many a house proudly flies a star spangled banner from a gleaming white pole stuck in a rhododendron bush contrary to the wishes of the progressive fascists, disguised as liberals whilst besmirching its good name, confusing patriotism with right wing nationalism, often embarrassed to fly the nation's flag in order not to offend other cultures who really couldn't give a rat's arse.

We followed a confetti trail of cherry blossoms that made us feel like Asian royalty. Hungover Asian royalty it has to be said; a small spiky ball bounced energetically around my skull.

Even grander houses welcomed us onto Massachusetts Avenue. We passed the home of the Vice-President, the 'Naval Observatory' looking like a piece of grey Wedgewood pottery. It stood high on a small hill behind a barrier of trees and razor wire, guard dogs, and overweight security guards with laser guns positioned to zap any tourist who loitered too long or looked hungrily at their sandwich.

While I couldn't consider myself an architectural expert; after all, I struggle to spot the difference between the Blackpool and Eiffel Towers, the British Embassy itself was aesthetically odd. Stuck on the front of what I assume was the original grandiose Georgian building, like a comedy wart, was a circular glass structure similar to a fancy greenhouse looking as if some posh Yorkshireman was trying to impress his neighbour. I muttered my disapproval to an uninterested guard at security before entering the annals of power. We'd made a concerted effort to look professional - I'd spent a whole £12 on a PVC briefcase - and dressed accordingly, although I felt by wearing a suit and tie I was dressing for the funeral of my unconformity.

Traipsing up three flights of stairs, we passed various important sounding departments such as 'Quoits Legislation', 'Centre of Benolyn Distribution' and the ultra secretive 'Pontefract Cake Experimentation Laboratory'.

David Wilson greeted us at the entrance of the Defence Department. It was nothing like a James Bond film. Instead of retina scans allowing passage through sliding doors secured by diligent guards, we just walked around an energetic tea lady. Like all military establishments, pictures of warships, jet fighters and steely-eyed soldiers hung on corridor walls painted in colours refused by the more discerning departments.

Our meeting went well. We answered all questions to an acceptable level and we had to admit we actually sounded as though we knew what we were talking about. But all good things have to come to an end. Towards the end of our appointment, David asked, 'So, you have your visas sorted?'

Before answering, I tried to take stock of the question *visa? Do we need a visa?*

He noted our hesitation. 'As you're staying longer than 90 days you need visas.'

Knowing that bullshit baffles brains, I confidently lied, 'Oh of course.' Even adding a slight laugh to add to our authenticity.

'When did we get the visas?' asked Rob, when we finally left the meeting.

'Next week,' I replied.

We hadn't yet seen the sights of DC. With our tasks complete, there was no time like the present to start. Leaving the Embassy we thought better of leaning out of the window to wave wildly at the oiks on the sidewalk as there may have been some Carlos the Jackal type wanting to take out British dignitaries, although I wouldn't suspect that dignitaries picked their nose while putting two fingers up at passing pedestrians.

Downtown had the aesthetics of a sterile office corridor, where men in starched collars ate lunch on the hoof and women in pencil skirts talked sternly into mobile phones. We noticed exchanged waves weren't a social 'hello', just a hand movement to acknowledge social position - an *ubermensch* culture of American business where life moved in small kindred circles.

'I told you you'd miss it,' laughed Si from the front seat.

'Miss what?'

'The White House.'

Si had previously said it isn't this monstrous building that expectantly dominates the locale. We strained our necks looking through the back window noting a few people stood gawping through its wrought iron fence.

We drove round the Ellipse, a grassy area evidently used as an afternoon football ground. Goals made from T-shirts littered the floor like mole hill cosies, de-vested men kicking balls around often getting mixed up in an adjacent game, bringing an almost irresistible urge to sit down and watch around a picnic hamper. Some had succumbed and I'm sure we would have, if we had in our possession a wicker box of outdoor delights. We instead gorged out on $1 hot dogs with extra onions, mustard and ketchup just to enhance thrift.

We parked at the Washington Monument and were mightily impressed. It truly is a striking centrepiece. A 555ft marble obelisk can't be described as the world's most technical piece of architecture, yet in its day was the world's tallest building and is still the tallest all-masonry structure on earth.

It was built to commemorate the 1st President after whom the city is named. George Washington's grandparents emigrated to the New World in 1656 from their home in northern England. Unfortunately they didn't have a typical northern English name. I'd have loved the world's superpower's capital be called 'Hegginbottom DC'.

Work began in 1848. The monument's cornerstone laid on July 4th and finished in 1884 after a 25 year suspension in construction. Before assuming it was a typical builder's tea break, it was actually suspended by a persuasive local anti-Catholic group. Called the 'Know Nothing' movement, they halted the building in 1853 at the 153ft mark in protest at the gift of marble given by Pope Pius IX from Rome's Temple of Concord. After that pathetic episode was sorted, one assumes by the members of the 'Get A Life' movement, lack of funds prevented further construction and the area became neglected. Surrounded by cattle awaiting slaughter next to the foetid Washington Canal, Mark Twain likened it to a "factory chimney with the top broken off". While his literary genius cannot be argued, I do think Mr Twain must have been going through his 'say what you see' phase influenced by Roy Walker and his visually themed game show 'Catchphrase'. Once complete, the monument was equipped with a steam-powered elevator solely for the use of men. Sexism did play a part in this decision. It was feared too dangerous for women and children to board, so only the brave male guinea pigs avoided the safer 897 step hot, dark, claustrophobic toil to the top.

The Washington Monument would have been more enjoyable had we a few millennia to wait until we could head the never-ending queue to reach the top via the new internal unisex elevator, so we carried on our trek around the monument area noticing memorials for anything and everything:

'This monument commemorates the wearing of wrong
sized shoes by immigrants in 1786'
'On this spot in 1865, Sheridan V Gitface Jnr III was in
the most northerly position ever to mould marzipan
into comedic animal shapes'
'These stains signify a specific area of interest for
urinating tramps'

There are more busts here than in a nurses' hall of
residence, but not quite as visually exciting. We scurried
on through the Ellipse, careful not to interrupt the
games of football, one in a titanic struggle tied at 21-21
with the next goal the winner, until we reached the
barriers guarding the White House alongside visitors of
various nations conferring in different tongues, all
probably saying, 'It isn't very big is it?'

We stood at the wrought iron fence, fully clothed
unlike a bootneck years later. Getting naked in a pub in
Taunton is typical bootneck fare. Doing it in front of
the White House would be great for dits back home,
unless over the phone from a jail cell.

Set back from the fence, a pair of opera glasses
would be welcome to get a decent view of the building,
although it'd be likely they'd be confiscated by the
plethora of police that patrolled the area who'd also
prevented us from making a suitably ostentatious, if not
cheesy, opening scene to the trip's video diary.

All historical accounts are questioned and sometimes rewritten, but we considered the version that best
suited our past was the one reciting that during the war
of 1812, it was the Royal Marines who burnt down the
President's Mansion, possibly in a game of 'Zulu
Warrior' gone wrong. In an attempt to cover up the fire

damage and keep up morale of the defending forces, the building was painted white, hence its current name.

We finished off the day, or should I say, saw in the new day in a club called 'Polly Esters', an alternative club that we'd been told by a Marine was full of 'faggots, weirdos and hippies.' It sounded perfect. Also considering myself an outsider to 'normal' society, the only difference between me and the other clubbers was their ability to dance and my ability to booby trap a car. Everyone we talked to was friendly, many were extremely interesting, and most had a sense of humour, a quality that was sadly lacking at Henderson Hall where seemingly there had been a contagious outbreak of misery.

DC's plethora of attractions meant a day was never going to be enough to fully explore, so peeling ourselves from the beds that we'd fallen into only four hours before ensured we'd not waste the day. We needed to get shit, showered, shaved and have a decent fill before 9am to get to the Pentagon Metro. The shit part of this morning ritual was now gut retching. The last thing to look at first thing in a morning is someone else's snot-like diarrhoea. I now had to fish for the knob at an extended arms length with my neck stretched like a tortoise out of the bathroom to negate having to eyeball Rob's insides, now sprayed like a Damien Hirst painting around the bowl.

The Metro underground rail system was refreshingly clean - no walls adorned with grammatically poor graffiti above layers of dried urine that so elegantly stain the sticky floors. The maps didn't require knowledge of calculus to understand and the roomy platforms supported the mandatory scraggly haired young couple, both wearing stretched sweaters with sleeves too long, and external framed backpacks especially designed to nudge anyone holding a sandwich to their mouths.

With a hastily formulated plan to glaze past as many attractions as we could, we emerged like casually dressed moles to heavy traffic before walking along Independence Avenue, past the weird and wonderful plant pot of the Hirshorn Museum, towards the US Capitol Building where we found people mulling about looking in large rooms full of posh furniture that didn't really warrant standing in a queue for. We stood silently, admiring the grander view down the Mall. Straight as a die, it swayed with a lawn of camera-clad tourists. Along the grassy area we moved towards and past the Capitol Reflecting Pool and a rather imposing statue of Ulysses S Grant on horseback. Considering his infamous drinking, it was small mercy that he was moulded to his horse.

The air smelled of hotdogs and academia. There are nine museums within a mile lining the Mall, diverse in their content to cater for all but the most ignorant. We chose the National Air and Space Museum as we'd been drawn in by Si's interweb thingy on his computer. While the computer was surprised not to be displaying pornography, the website's homepage opened with:

'The National Air and Space Museum is due for a renovation. Among the most visible things that need to be replaced are the skylights and "window walls", the large exterior panes that give the museum its distinctive look. The sealant around the glass has dried and the double-glass thermal panes have lost their effectiveness as an insulating barrier.'

We'd dressed hurriedly as if there'd been a bomb threat and rushed out just to see the effectiveness of any new sealant.

Even with ongoing renovation, we entered expecting to pay an extortionate fee to see all these silvery flyey things and sealant. Surprisingly, we found it free, which was nice but for the fact that the city was bankrupt so I'd have gladly paid $1. The museum was fantastic, especially for air enthusiasts and tight Britons. I'm not the former, but willingly absorbed the information and exhibits chronicling the history of flight from a US perspective. The 'Spirit of St Louis' was of special interest, as we'd be passing through on our forthcoming expedition.

We found other places of interest that interrupted our continual shuttle sprints to the loo after drinking too many free coffees, so left reasonably happy that we'd had a few hours entertainment without spending a dime.

Now eager to nick free entry anywhere, we headed to the Museum of Natural History as in London it's my favourite - Romanesque assertiveness draws one inside its massive doorway, the ambience whisking a patron on an imaginative journey of formaldehyde and dried animals, expectancy imagines a myopic scientist around every corner carrying a test tube of prehistoric sperm, and halls haunted by the ghost of a Victorian porter crushed by the stuffed carcass of an Indian Elephant brought back from the Raj. The Washington version elicited equal inquisitiveness, yet Disney obviously disagreed or else they would have lost one of their dinosaurs here, yet there is nothing finer than looking at a load of prehistoric arses for free.

Aesthetically, the Lincoln Memorial stands like a modern day Acropolis swarmed by a constant buzz of tourists and sellers of cheap white T-Shirts with a crest printed centrally surrounded by 'Washington DC it's a city', just in case we didn't already know. The eastern steps gave us an opposite view of the Mall all the way back to Capitol Hill. Appreciating the scene for a second time with President Lincoln looming down our necks was especially difficult when constantly knocked by tourists trying their hand at trick photography by 'leaning' against the Washington Monument in the background.

To contemplate the fallout of war, the Vietnam Memorial is the place to visit. Unlike everything else that is high and mighty in its memorial of something or nothing; this 250 ft long wall of unassuming polished black granite stands low, dug sub-surface as a dog leg into Constitution Gardens. The names of 58,191 casualties listed in chronological order are etched deep not only into the granite, but into American hearts, remembering names in a war that some want to forget, a war that many cannot. Sobered by rows of tearful souls, we walked amongst other war memorials, many with more overtly military styling therefore, to me, less symbolic.

After traipsing around the majority of monuments we felt it apt to finish the trip in front of another - the Iwo Jima Monument. It was our own personal pilgrimage to pay respect to those who'd earned the title 'Marine'. Still impressive by day, the surrounding pristine gardens were in keeping with the US Marine Corps tradition of regimentation. Just a hop, skip and a jump away stood the Netherlands Carillon; a strangely shaped bell tower given in thanks to the Americans by the Dutch in thanks for their liberation from the Nazis. Just over the other side a monument to journalists who lost their lives in the line of duty. Proof enough that Washington DC had a memorial for everything.

***

Back under the dour grey skies of England, we finalised the expedition planning. Things, at last, were gaining momentum. We'd now found a bootneck to join the support team. Rob knew him, I didn't. His name was Fitz and was currently dossing about at 45 Commando in Scotland. According to Rob he was a 'good blerk', which would be encouraging but for the fact that due to his benevolence of spirit, Rob thought everyone, including women, a 'good blerk'.

Rob is nice. Too nice. Gooey nice. My wife and every woman I know love him. It makes me sick. He's just so nice. He could murder a pregnant hedgehog and everyone would forgive him with one swoosh of his perfect hair and pearly white teeth. But sickening as it is, he himself is a 'good blerk', so I love him too.

Finally, we had a team. The only problem left was the approval of visas. Information suggested it was unlikely we'd receive the visas in time should we apply by post. This would mean a personal visit to the US Embassy in London. Fitz had waffled his way into getting extra time off, so was an ideal choice to do the embassy run. It ended up being an exercise in embarrassment as he'd forgotten to remove the stash of porn from his bag before entering the US Embassy security point.

I'd spoken to Fitz on the phone. He could only join us a few weeks before departure. To say we were going to be sharing a vehicle for the next fourteen weeks, we needed to hit it off, so I invited him to my house. I vaguely recognised him. No small talk or polite introduction, we started as we meant to carry on, by taking the piss out of each other. After only being in each other's company for ten minutes I realised he was a good choice. Even though the twat nicked the last jam tart as he left.

Fitz was also leaving the Corps; indeed only Sean of the expedition team wasn't 'going outside'. This made us even more determined to show that while the Corps sculptured us into the men we were, it now longer defined who we would become. We could take on this challenge without the need of the military structure. How naïve was I.

With only a few weeks remaining, I discovered we needed an officer as part of the expedition to gain approval from the necessary powers. With all the effort we'd so far expended, I was loath for an officer to bask in reflected glory. With barefaced manipulation of the rules, we assigned Captain Grixoni, my Company Commander, with the desktop appointment of 'Liaison Officer', one that he readily accepted.

Whether someone had intentions to see us fail or not, I don't know, but once we'd overcome that problem we were thrown another 11th hour edict stating one of the expedition crew also had to undergo some formal adventure training instruction. Using all the friendships I'd built up over the years and a crate of beer, I managed to wangle myself onto a Unit Expedition Leader's course within a week. How seven days amongst the beauty of Snowdonia learning to lead a day's hill walking and organise a campsite was to assist a kayaking expedition down the Mississippi River was anyone's guess, but with the qualification we could gain approval.

***

Our transport finalised, we'd kindly been given grants to help fund our trip, we possessed valid visas and I could identify the flora of North Wales. We were on our way.

After so many hassles, it seemed strange dropping off our freight at South Cerney Royal Air Force base. No problems, no overzealous bureaucrat; just a young man signing a form before putting our cargo into hold labelled 'Washington DC'. He bid us goodbye wishing he were coming with us. We were glad he wasn't, he had horrendous halitosis.

The sadness of leaving loved ones vanished once under the tartan of white vapour trails crossing the cerulean sky that signalled our proximity to Heathrow airport.

Standing at the departure gate, our three months odyssey 'Mississippi Madness' was now ready to depart.

*'Somewhere on the freeway
the instructions got confusing or I became confused.
I have a great dislike both for freeways and for instructions'*

~ Charles Bukowski, poet, novelist

Our Stateside timetable was hectic - Pick up mini-bus. Drive to St Andrew's Air Force base. Collect and check freight. Get to Henderson Hall. Eat pizza. Drink cheap soda. Shit, shower, shave. Go ashore. Hopefully wake up.

Our friend Sgt Morris was still employed in the block, still smart as a guardsman, still too serious. However, on this occasion, he initiated the handshake. He'd realised we were here to do the business and not just some scrotebags out here for a holiday. He still managed to get in a verbal Venn diagram about hair length and discipline; but as we'd previously ignored all his well-meant advice, he knew it was a futile exercise.

Our admin wasn't totally complete. We now had to buy shorts to match our Mississippi Madness polo shirts that we'd managed to sell at a loss for charity. This seemingly trivial task brought on our first argument.

'We've had nine months to sort this out, why do we need matching shorts all of a sudden?' I asked.

'They're cheaper here,' replied Sean correctly.

Normally such thriftiness would have been welcome if it wasn't for the fact that the Marine Exchange stocked shorts only for tall old men who admired plus fours.

Sean chose a pair. 'What you think?' he said looking in the mirror.

'They suit you like a officer on sentry,' replied Fitz.

'I think they're alright,' said Sean .

'You got shit in your eyes?' I said, probably too aggressively. 'You look like an extra in 'It Ain't 'Alf Hot Mum.'

'They're the best here,' replied Sean. Sadly, it was true.

We all tried on a pair, I begrudgingly more than the others. They were the world's baggiest shorts. The size of clipper sails, they made Fitz's thin legs look like string. Rob looked OK, but he could make a bin liner look like an Armani suit. On donning a size 'small' I found they weren't 'shorts' but 'longs'. I looked a twat. My legs are renowned for their poor length, anything longer than swimming trunks and I look rather top heavy. But these were excruciatingly bad. I rolled the hem up until it looked like I had a roll of carpet wrapped around my thigh. I noted the accompanying sniggers.

'Fuck off, I'm not going to look a bell end in these.'

'Stop being a girl and get them bought,' said Sean.

But I was adamant. Even Don Estelle would laugh at me, and I wasn't about to pay money to look a total idiot.

'Come on, mate, buy them. Yep you look like a twat but you usually do anyway.' Rob's attempt to lighten the mood worked slightly but my blood was at 98°C and rising.

I decided to pretend to go to the loo to calm down. If it had come to blows, Sean being as handy as an octopus called Andy with a talent for DIY would have left me looking like mashed potato with a sausage for an unhappy mouth. So it was with a slight cloud we left the exchange, short-less and returned to the accommodation to check our kit and equipment. Day 1 wasn't going as expected.

If jetlag was to rear its head it would be better fought by a night in Georgetown. For once it was sensible for Fitz and I not to go mad, as we were driving early the next morning. It was the first time I'd ever really drunk with Fitz so wasn't aware that his flash to bang time between sobriety and turbo mingbats was about thirty seconds. One minute he was eloquent, the next it was if somebody had hit him with a comedy mallet, and had suffered some form of delirium. I thought it wise to get him back to the accommodation so left the bar getting light-hearted grief from Rob and Sean for going back early. It was only 6am back in the UK after all.

I awoke early and noticed Fitz in a pair of strange boxer shorts. On him waking, I asked about his new attire. He looked equally confused before realisation dawned. He was prone to the occasional bout of sleepwalking and he'd found himself at 5am out on the parade square naked as the day he was born. It goes without saying that it wasn't where he'd laid his head a few hours earlier so was distinctly disorientated. Not having a clue how to retrace his noctambulation, he ran like the wind with his tackle swaying like a tiny bag of washing to the nearest block. Fortunately, as he walked along the walkways, he'd found an early bird with lights on in his room. Fitz peered in and heard the sound of shower spray and so crept in a nicked a pair of stars and stripes boxer shorts that were laid invitingly on the floor. Their cleanliness was irrelevant, covering his embarrassment was his only concern. He could get away with walking round in just boxers, naked would have probably meant him spending the rest of the day in cells explaining his streak to a po-faced Military Policeman called Chuck.

It set the day up on a happy note and we soon set off to the embassy for a Marine Corps Times interview with Gidget Fuentes and a final brief from David Wilson. The British Embassy was easy to find when we'd been chauffeur driven a few weeks earlier. On this occasion we found ourselves passing a 'Welcome To Maryland' sign. I felt, at this point, it was time to turn back. With the others and I questioning my navigational skills we took in the suburbs once more. It was Fitz who actually said what we'd all seen but had taken for granted, probably because we were more interested in finding a sign saying 'This way to the embassy, morons'. Washington DC is very green. Not in an ecological, but in a botanical sense. Washington DC really is the City of Trees. Avenues and streets were all lined with maple, oak and cherry trees giving the city a soft welcoming look and made the inconvenience of travelling 16 miles in the wrong direction slightly more bearable.

Our first ever press interview went swimmingly well until Sean interrupted Gidget and said that I thought she fancied me.

The redness of her face gave the impression that:

a) She didn't really appreciate the joke

b) She fancied me

I am without question, the most handsome being ever to rear up on two legs, so you make up your own mind.

We retired to the embassy and fed upon traditional English fare, as one would expect from this most British of enclaves. I had Barbecued Chicken, the rest had ribs. The only thing not American about the meal was that the ribs didn't hang three feet over each side of the plate.

Our vantage point overlooked the rear of the Naval Observatory and the Vice President's gardens. I must admit, I'd seen better-kept grounds and government funds must surely stretch to a strimmer or a pair of shears at least.

After refreshment and a trip to RACAL to collect our communications equipment in a suburb so mazy I thought we'd run over a minotaur, we said our farewells and gave thanks to David Wilson.

It was 3pm. Ahead of us lay a cramped journey from Washington DC to Chicago. On a map it doesn't look far - it was only about a fifth of the way across the US. But when four men are crushed in a van accompanied by a bumper book of equipment - three canoes, six paddles, two tents, four bergans, radios, bags and various boxes of miscellaneous gear; a laugh a minute it's not.

I looked at the map from my uncomfortable position and realised that Chicago was indeed a bit of a way. In fact, counting the mileage on my 'Transcontinental, Mileage and Driving Time Map', the 760 miles suggested it was about the same distance as from Thurso in the far north of Scotland to Plymouth. On roads, where the speed limit was 50 or 60 mph, it meant that we were in for a long 13 hours 26 minutes according the aforesaid map. And that didn't include time out for eating, toileting and general getting losting. After my mess up trying to get the four miles to the British Embassy, travelling 190 times the distance was certainly unnerving to the others.

'I've driven around theM25 hundreds of times,' I explained trying to administer a degree of confidence.

'We're not on the M25...' replied Rob.

'I was voted top navigator 1983 at school,' I lied confidently, and hoped, as we left RACAL in the labyrinth of Rockville, that we were indeed going the right way on Interstate 270.

Taking the interstates, although about as stimulating as counting chips in woodchip wallpaper, was the only way to get to the Mississippi Headwaters in time for us to sufficiently prepare for paddling to commence first light on the Sunday morning. The van seemed less happy at travelling at maximum speed as we rose in altitude, our eardrums convexing. Through a red mud gorge we rose until we came out on top of the world. The 360° sylvan vista suggested we were steaming along in a sea of foliage. As far as the eye could see tree covered hills rutted the landscape like an ill-fitting carpet. In the far distance the Appalachian Hills exploded to mountains. The lowering sun extended the highs and repressed the lows exaggerating the scenery to a panorama of camouflage. To the left, the Potomac River gave us all an exhilarating view but signified we hadn't really travelled all that far.

A few Taco Bell's and toilet stops later we were on Interstate 68 and due to hit Interstate 79 towards Pittsburgh. While this sounds easy, on many Interstates positioning is approximated not by mileage markers, but by hoarding boards advertising fast food outlets, motels, truck stops, and new real estate developments:

Dying soon?

You need to spend your last few miserable years at

Pearly Gate Park

An exclusive development of 20 apartments especially designed for people who dribble.

*All Deposits taken before April 1st receive free
gravestone of their choice!*

After unsafely negotiating the concentric circles of
Columbus Ohio's road system, we left the Interstate
and State highways and found ourselves on the less
direct single carriage provincial highways, in the middle
of Indiana, in the dark, and in serious need of some
shuteye. While navigation appeared pretty straightfor-
ward, at the centre of a small town called St Mary's,
Highway 33 decided it wanted to play hide and seek by
pretending to carry on straight ahead under the clever
disguise of provincial Highway 29 while quickly sneak-
ing around a sharp bend towards Chicago looking like
the dead end of a narrow alley. After weary confusion,
we managed to find a small sign the size of a water
biscuit directing us to continue our less-than-merry way
along the crap road from hell.

Americans are unfairly stereotyped as boastful in
that they have everything bigger and better than anywhere else. In certain circumstances it's true, potholes
being a case in point. I'm not saying for one instant that
you drive elsewhere as if sliding along a slick linoleum
travellator, but here in Indiana the pot holes were so big
every other advertising hoarding board displayed shock
absorber repair services, and the owners of Highway 33
should be extremely proud of their ability in producing
an exact replica of a bombed-out runway.

Chicago loomed as daylight tried to fight its way
out of the duvet of smog that belched from the concrete bamboo of industrial chimneys. Stopping at
another gas station to buy coffee and refuel our van, the
service counter clocks showed 5am. I was sure it'd been
5:30am when I'd last looked at my watch. Fitz was

equally confused. Being worldly wise and exceptionally quick at this questionable time in the morning, I asked the counter assistant whether the clock was right. This young man could have appeared on a talent show as a chewing gum ventriloquist as he spoke without once changing his cow like mastication. We squinted and turned our ears to try and decipher his slurred mumbling but all we understood was, 'Easterrrrrrn.'

We looked at the map and straddling a dotted line in the faintest red pen through the turquoise of Lake Michigan we saw the words Central T.Z and Eastern T.Z. Since we were both abbreviation experts we reckoned we could suss it quite quickly.

Nearly every phrase in the armed forces is condensed into ridiculous brevity: TBC, TTBC, FIBUA, OBUA, DIBUA, MLRS, GPMG. I once wrote out Daily Orders for the troop adding as a footnote: 'One place available for CAMPN course. First come first served'. There are numerous short military courses offered that are designed to indulge in strange pleasures and possibly learn something. So when a course is offered, nearly everyone applies. Even if, as on this occasion, many didn't know what the course was. Older guys knew to ignore strange sounding courses, after all, many had heard of young lads volunteering for 'Introduction To Underwater Fire Fighting', 'Ship's Snooker Table Supervisor' acquaint or the infamous 'L75 Flamethrower' course that sends men to run around camp each armed with a fire extinguisher covered in black masking tape pretending to burn down the cricket pavilion as taught by the pan-faced instructor. So I knew it would be a young keen bloke in his late teens who'd be the first to knock at my door asking if they could put their name down.

'Of course,' I answered to the first and lucky applicant, a young spotty Marine called Smudge.

He looked slightly bemused as I held out a pound coin.

'Do you know what CAMPN is?' I asked as he took the coin.

'Is it something to do with parachuting?'

'Go on, explain your rationale.' I was looking forward to this.

'Doesn't CAMPN stand for Combat And Military Parachuting...' he paused to show he hadn't really thought the whole thing through. 'At Night?'

'Close, but no cigar. Chicken and Mushroom Pot Noodle. I'm starving. Go get us one from the NAAFI shop. Keep the change.'

So it was with ease we understood T.Z to be 'Time Zone' and we being international jet setters had just passed through one.

To locals it must be a way of life, but it struck us as weird should we have to cross a time zone everyday to commute to work. Would we rather wake late to arrive at work at the same or earlier time if we lived east of the time zone? Or would we rather come home at the same time we set off if travelling from the west? Such a conundrum was too complex after driving all night; the only thing we could understand was caffeine.

If Highway 33 was the reigning champion of pot-holed roads then it should relinquish its title forthwith. As we got carried along on the commuter conveyer belt it seemed that the Borman Expressway had more potholes than the Yorkshire Dales. Some were not just holes; some were pot caverns, pot craters, pot abysses. Their regularity woke both Rob and Sean, frightened they were in a vehicular earthquake. We could only apologise and to prevent vibrating white body syndrome, we pulled into the next service station to consume a timely breakfast.

Now would be as good a time as any to phone home and tell my good lady how we were getting on. I bought a phone card from a vending machine written primarily in Spanish with English translation underneath. I unwrapped the card and then proceeded for the next twenty minutes to swear at both it and the phone, as the PIN number wouldn't work. I also directed many expletives at the phone operator who couldn't understand me, at the piece of wrapping plastic that had now statically lodged itself on my shoe, and at anyone who even dared glance at this insane idiot using the handset to hammer imaginary nails into the phone booth. Conceding defeat, I tucked into my omelette, which I described as tasting of poor quality polystyrene that shit furniture is packed in, accompanied by a rasher of bacon that took the form of the plastic twisty thing that takes 3 hours to untwine from a card-backed toy.

'Are you tired by any chance?' said Sean.

I absorbed his smile and my mood lifted. The paddlers kindly took over the reigns of driver and navigator allowing us to kip until we picked up our Recreational Vehicle.

I was woken at the RV collection point in the suburb of Bartlett. Despite spooning a tent valise with a paddle blade for my pillow, other than a severely stiff body and a flip flop that had somehow lodged its foaminess in between my tongue and palate, I felt quite lively.

The sales office was bedecked in camping accoutrements that looked tacky yet expensive, like a Middle Eastern jewellery store. I raised a cheek-cramping smile when it was explained that our designated RV was out of stock so we would be upgraded to a C27. The prince of the RV fleet, only second in size to the C30, it was an oil tanker on wheels (and far less flammable). We were due a break and as we stepped into the glorious daylight, we stood in awe at our home for the next 89 days - the 'Californian Flyer', glinting in all its 27ft glory.

After cramming in every last item, I returned to the sales office to sign the paperwork. Having pre-paid almost everything, we expected to simply pick up the RV, hand over what was due, then drive off into the sunset singing gaily. The cashier was a lovely smiling woman, a smile that widened when she asked for $1853.51. I chuckled. Surely there was some mistake? I was told that everything was paid for, but the $500 deposit and $375 one way drop off charge. She then read a list the length of the Magna Carta describing all charges that were payable on site. I was fuming. The UK travel company had said everything had been taken care of and here was I forking out an extra $1000 because of sales taxes, CT1s, VDKs, CU-OFFs, RTSMs and other abbreviations that my befuddled brain couldn't fathom.

I left the sales office with a black cloud over me as if I'd just exited the bookies with a palm full of torn up betting slips.

This sudden financial crisis caused much bickering and I felt rather guilty as the transport organiser. Yet I felt more aggrieved by the fact that only Fitz and I stumped up the extra cash and therefore was no need for the other two to continue squabbling especially when it was suggested we shouldn't have accepted the free upgrade, the logic of which I couldn't fathom but it at least kept up the argument's momentum.

We'd been gravely naïve supposing that Chicago was only a hop, skip, and jump away from our destination of Bemidji, Minnesota, the nearest town to the Mississippi Headwaters. This triple jumper would have had to extract over 860 miles to land in the sand pit of Bemidji, so another journey equivalent to driving the length of Great Britain was something to really look forward to. It also meant that after the endurance drive of the previous day/night we were still not even half way there. So it was with less than a sudden purge of over eagerness that we took to I90 and another extended period of death by driving.

Since we'd nothing better to do for the next 865 miles it was time we got acquainted with our new toy to see what new gadgets we could find and subsequently break. First it was discovered that the power steering was so light it led to frequent over steering causing us to swing waywardly like an ill aimed bowling ball thrown across adjacent lanes. The next twiddly knobby thing we came across was the cruise control button. A totally new concept to the owner of a string of shit cars and oh how I took to it. Having the aforementioned leg length of a small child with rickets, I am always pulling the seat so far forward as to crush my chest on the steering wheel, just so I can tickle the accelerator with my tippy-toes. In this behemoth it was most divine to sit back and chill with my leg tucked up on the central console and not suffer from prolonged achilles-tendonitis. At the flick of another switch we were plunged from the concrete jungle humidity of the Chicago environs to the arctic tundra. With what we were experiencing when it was fully turned on, the word 'conditioning' in air conditioning was reference to the conditioning of our bodies to sub zero temperatures.

Some friends of ours were in training for an expedition to reach the North Pole unaided, a feat so extraordinary that they'd just returned from a practice trip to Prince of Wales Island far into the Arctic circle for a month, a severe test on its own. I cast my mind back to them as I sat shivering my tits off in the cab and wondered whether it would have been cheaper and easier for them to acclimatise for the North Pole by setting up a tent on the passenger seat. At least the cold would keep us awake, unless of course we slipped into a hypothermic coma.

Behind the cab was a living quarter that was larger than the majority of new buildings that are passed off these days at extortionate prices as a 'two bedroom townhouse'. It was equipped with all mod cons that Americans demand including a refrigerator the size of a double wardrobe. The rear bed was so wide that apparently it was designed to accommodate the average American couple - and as American gluttony is a much written about subject I'll say no more aside from the fact that I could be spun 360 degrees on the bed and not touch the edges. The over cab double bed wasn't quite as wide, and the dining table and chairs could be folded down to make an uncomfortable sleeping area for small children, or me.

The RV took me back to the early 80's when my 'parents' were the proud owners of a caravan. A working class status symbol showing the world that although you couldn't afford a second home in Monte Carlo you could at least reside in a flimsy wind break on wheels at a number of dreary seaside resorts at any chosen time of the year. I, as the child in our modest three berth, would loath these trips as even a weekend away would cause me to suffer from spinal compression sleeping on a bed 2'6" long cleverly converted from the dining table the size of a tea tray. Twenty odd years later, not only did the dread of sleeping there take me back but also the upholstery, that was totally out of style with its contemporary surroundings. The RV's brown flowered velour was reminiscent of the lining of that condensation filled coffin I had to call home in thunderstorms from Glencoe to Perranporth.

A certain pattern had developed as we started our engine for another 200+ mile leg. Coffee had become our lifeblood and their containers became of interest. I'd only ever noticed the one style - the one that leaves you with the uncertainty of the lid being properly attached, where you press down to confirm only to tip over the first two fingers of scolding sludge. The US has turned the humble takeaway hot drink lid into an art form. The first one we sampled was designed with two small holes at opposite sides of the circular lid. On a scale of 1 to 10 we only rated the 'doll's mouth' a poor 4. Invariably we had to suck from the hole to get a decent drink, and as it was like swapping spit with a small plastic toy designed for maternal 6 year olds, somewhat disturbing. The most popular it seemed as we trundled on through Wisconsin was the 'nose protector'. Designed like a soft drink can you would pull the triangle from the outside to the centre of the lid creating a shield, hence its name. We gave the nose protector a 6. It would have been 7 but as any sudden movement would cause unnecessary spillage, we decided to dock a point.

Going over the border from Illinois to Wisconsin was akin to the three Billy Goats gruff trip trapping over the bridge to pastures new. It is known as the Dairy State and as the land flattened to endless horizons, all that separated us from total isolation and loneliness was a parade of farms. All sprouting numerous siloes, like cigar shaped bodyguards they towered above and around the often hidden farmhouses, threatening anyone to come close if they though they were hard enough. Fitz and I often taunted them as we drove past but would drive off if we thought they'd seen us. This, literal dancing to tunes like 'Monkey on my back', planning to buy Battersea power station and turn it in to a nightclub for woodlice, and penning stupid limericks kept us mildly amused. We concocted classics of circumcision-based rhymes such as:

After circumcision the fear is compelling

But no more cheese, no more smelling

When I took a first look

I screamed 'Oh fuck'

'Nurse take away the pain but please leave the swelling!'

Continuing onto the more bizarre:

Alan Whicker

Ate a snicker

But his aversion to nuts

Played havoc with his guts

And caused him and his wife to bicker… as it was she who had inadvertently bought him the aforementioned chocolate bar forgetting about his Irritable Bowel Syndrome.

It made the seemingly endless trip towards Duluth pass a whole lot quicker.

Rob and Sean were getting some well needed shut eye. Their trip hadn't yet begun so both had to make the most of their rest while they could. To a degree, their slumber was blessed relief as it removed the bad feeling of the last few hours. The previous altercations were surprising as we'd never argued before, so I hoped once they awoke it'd be with renewed vigour that we could amicably continue our journey. Thankfully it did, as our stomachs decreed we should eat at yet another gas station cum truck stop.

We all subscribed to the 'All you can eat for $10' offer to gauge how much we could actually eat. Rob ate about $400 worth. He was positively picky compared to a trucker on an adjacent table who'd taken the sign too literally. From his mouth he pulled a femur that was thrown half gnawed onto a plate piled high with a cemetery of condiment wrappers, cups, and entrails from assorted road kill. He spat paper and plastic out of his machinegun mouth and, in the opposite direction, I'm sure he swallowed a spoon as he shovelled both main course and dessert at a speed that blurred to a Supermanic swirl. It was quite the most disgusting, animalistic display of gluttony I'd ever seen, and was truly impressed. In between his bucket-like mouthfuls we managed to talk to him on of his life as a trucker. We tried to impress him by telling him we'd just come from DC on our way to Bemidji, a distance of 1700 miles. This was his equivalent of driving to the local shop for a paper. He was en route from Indianapolis to Anchorage, Alaska a distance of only 3850 miles. He'd drive constantly for a month, then take two weeks off.

'That's a good routine to keep a family going,' I said.

'Don't need no wife when you got prostitutes in nearly every god damn stop.'

He seemingly made good money so, apart from spending plenty on oily sex, we wondered why he dressed like an unfashionable tramp from the 80's and smelled like he'd just been dragged through the bowels of a cattle barge's sewerage system. It was clearly a solitary life, and long distance driving was clearly his unhygienic vocation.

Through the darkness we continued over a bridge on the south eastern tip of Lake Superior and looked from our position high over Duluth towards the blackness that wouldn't touch dry land for another 320 miles; similar to dipping your toe in the sea in South-ampton and waving north at your friend who was dipping his foot in different water in Whitley Bay.

Finally in darkest Minnesota, we drove on smaller, poorly signposted roads, so it was with great relief when we joined Highway 2 to take us on our carefree way to our destination.

By now, my eyelids felt like I had a small rodent clinging onto each flap of skin trying to save themselves a perilous fall onto my lap. Fitz felt the same, and only my high pitched code word 'mince pie' would wake him from his nodding dog syndrome to rectify his veering off to the right. 'Monkey baby' was a warning should he veer towards the central reservation, but as the balance of the wheels was slightly awry it meant that we had more 'mince pies' than 'monkey babies'. Once the time between a 'monkey baby' and a 'mince pie' was down to around five minutes, like a somnological midwife it was wise to find assistance in the form of another coffee stop.

Amongst the darkness appeared an oasis of dim neon that hung over a wooden shack on the outskirts of Floodwood. It was 1:15am. I expected the gas station to be manned by a young guy behind a grill watching cable erotica while picking grime from under his oily nails. This gas station was markedly different, masquerading as a late night meeting place for all the young kids with nothing better to do on a Friday night than to meet at a gas station in the middle of nowhere.

Talking abruptly ceased as we walked in. This was no place for two men who had no better things to do than eat microwaves savoury pastries at early o'clock on a Saturday morning. The crowd looked as us rather strangely, as if we were normal people. We smiled at each other knowingly and dithered about pretending to decide whether we should choose chocolate covered pretzels or a cheese and ham sandwich, just so they could think of something to say to these two interlopers. The counter assistant looked as though my head had spun 360° and oozed green pus from my armpits when I opened my mouth. It was obviously the first time he'd ever confronted an Englishman, and as expected some young guy, sat at one of the Formica tables, asked the most frequently asked question a Brit will get from an American: 'You guys from Australia?'

Why do Brits always get asked that? I know the US can be labelled insular but surely it holds more ties with the UK than Australia, so why do they assume anyone with an odd accent is Australian? Rarely is an Aussie accent heard on US TV, so why, when they often hear Brits playing evil geniuses, do they confuse us? There are over 67 million people in the UK compared with around 22 million in Australia, so why expect an Aussie when it's three times likely that they'll meet a Brit who lives half the distance away? Explaining the concept of population comparisons to a young guy hanging out in a gas station in the middle of a forest could be deemed a futile exercise.

One redeeming factor of this visit to Floodwood's equivalent of Stringfellows was their selling of the god of all coffee lids, the supreme sipper - the 'Sheep Palate'. Next time you come across a sheep, chase it into the corner of its field and, trying not to kill it from shock, prise open its jaw and get your hand in its mush.

Hold out your hand palm up then give its palate a good rub while looking out for a farmer wielding a 12 bore shotgun approaching in a rather hostile gait. You'll find the palate as a corrugated patch of skin that could if necessary be used as a washboard for otters, badgers or other similar sized woodland creatures. This particular coffee lid had a similar corrugated area in plastic to minimise 'lip-slip' indented with three holes for optimum flow. Truly a marvel of drink dispensing engineering, it was a unanimous decision, the 'Sheep Palate' was the best hot drink takeaway lid ever, and of that there surely was no doubt. We sat quiet for a second both letting the moment sink in. We drove off still not thinking straight, and after collecting our thoughts gave the 'Sheep Palate' a perfect 10 out of 10, remembering to tell all on our return of our time using such a container top.

At 3:30am we wearily pulled into Bemidji. The matchsticks had been replaced by RSJ's to keep our eyelids separated and our caffeine buzz was now a haze caused by sleep deprivation. On a complimentary camping guide, one page was headlined with the sentence 'Paul Bunyan does exist, and is alive and well in Bemidji Mn'. So with a welcoming sign beckoning us into its warm bosom and boasting that it was the first city on the Mississippi River, we pulled into a more than welcoming supermarket car park. Falling into such a deep sleep, we didn't even question who the hell Paul Bunyan was.

'A journey is best measured in friends, not in miles'

~ Tim Cahill, author

With a crooked head, I awoke to fruit kindly bought by Sean on his return from the store. On this mildest of Saturday mornings, Fitz and I would stock up on provisions, leaving Rob and Sean to stretch their legs around this most picturesque setting.

'Food 4 Less' was our first real experience of American supermarkets and found it exciting in a 'visiting a supermarket' sort of way. Having escaped the clutches of RV hell we rode like pre-pubescent teenagers on the sides of the trolley, skidding around corners and causing general annoyance to Saturday shoppers who love to dominate the aisles with Blitzkrieg efficiency. We crossed the Maginot line of fruit and vegetables bumping into the trolley of a pervert absorbed in fondling a pair of stacked melons.

Women are supposedly the most adept bargain hunters but I reckon we men could give them a run for their well-saved money. We searched like forensic scientists for the elusive '2 for 1' bargains, the sacred 'Buy 3 get 2 free' slogans and the rare 'we'll pay you to take some of our crap' pleas to rid the shop of unwanted crap. Finding a splendid deal on pizzas and bananas, we stocked up accordingly, and left the shop with a trolley laden with fruit and the cheapest processed rubbish one could store in an RV.

Time pressed, so we took the final drive through pine lined roads through Beltrami County to Itasca State Park - the home of the Mississippi Headwaters. Fresh, but warm, it was a truly awesome morning so let the wind blow through the RV, sending paperwork and window blinds across the furniture. The sweet pungency of pine filled our nostrils and we cared not a jot at receiving strange stares for our preference to fresh air over aircon. Our hearts beat faster as we turned into the side road welcoming visitors into the fifty square miles of Itasca State Park.

We then saw it. Shimmering pearlescent in the morning sun, through the curtain of trees, Lake Itasca sat alluring. We cheered with lifted hearts. Birds sang sweeter over the pumping introduction of Oasis' 'Columbia' as we sidled on.

We pulled over for a quick map check. A vehicle pulled alongside. Inside the battered old Chevy, three small kids sat silently in the back, a petite woman peered up alongside the driving seat in which sat a big, big man, with cropped hair. With a booming voice he told us we needed to take a right at the next fork to the campsite.

At the car park we pulled alongside other boats, trailers and RVs. Jumping out of the vehicle we ran to the lake like Israelites to the Promised Land. We were here. At last, we were here. And we hadn't even started.

Sean and Rob's first task was to organise the kayak and ancillaries. They'd be paddling an old Klepper kayak, a Special Forces military kayak that has the shape and drag of a bedroom ottoman. This obviously made the paddling harder. That was the whole point. Anyone could paddle down a river, no matter how long, in a sleek modern, fibreglass arrow with a light prepeg hull. This monster weighed 110lbs dry, 120lbs wet (it was so old it didn't have a metric weight). With a coarse rubberised canvas shell covering a wooden and steel frame construction, its main advantage over a modern kayak was due its similarity to a miniature barge it could carry up to 1000lbs of stores. Since Sean and Rob may have to portage the canoe some distance in places, it was wise not to carry such weight. They planned to carry enough stores solely for each leg, plus emergency kit to cover any event that may extend their time on the water.

While they organised themselves, Fitz took some camcorder footage. The rightful intention of Rob hounding us all for the past three months was to ensure we filmed plenty for posterity.

'Fitz, tell everyone how hard it is and how good we are for doing it.'

Fitz laughed. 'OK, as long as I can say you told me to say it.'

'No I'll sound like a nob. And say how it's a world record.'

'But it's not' replied Fitz.

'Why isn't it?'

'It may be a precedent to kayak the Mississippi in a Klepper.'

'Well it's a world record then.'

'Hmm not sure,' Fitz replied with sarcasm seeping from every syllable.

However, despite his longing for a glorified video diary, Rob suddenly became as unspeakably camera shy as a defendant leaving court when Fitz sought some feedback. Upon seeing the sweep of the camera come his way, he'd either involuntarily run out of shot or hide his head, much to the amusement of everyone. Once we'd taken some decent video of Sean, and some pretty awful stuff of the back of Rob's head, Fitz and I tried to get a spot to pitch the RV. Trudging off to the Park Warden's office we inhaled the sweet, tangy woods of White and Red Pine, sprinkled with Aspens and dots of Birch. On finding it, we explained our situation, pro-moting the fact it was for charity in the hope he could waive the overnight camping fee. He duly obliged, so thanking him for his kindness, donated him a signed expedition photograph. We walked away thinking how pretentious we'd been to sign it, so annulled any future autographs there and then. Besides, the real stars of the expedition, Rob and Sean weren't present. Glad to get our site sorted we returned to the paddlers, but feeling like spare parts, decided on hiring out a couple of Mountain bikes to ride the trails.

Former home of the Ojibwa people, Lake Itasca is ineffably stunning - 32,690 acres of eye catching pine woodland surrounded the lake's transparent beauty. The first and most important State park in Minnesota, Itasca contains trees over 200 years old stood high like Grandparents watching dutifully over their younger saplings.

We rode over rutted trails, vibrated down uneven slopes, bumped over raised roots, and shook any bones that were connected to the bike as we crashed speedily over dips and through burial mounds. We noted on the trail maps how many areas still possessed Native American names: 'Ozawindib Heights', 'Peace pipe Vista', 'Indian Mounds', and the romantic sounding 'Bison Kill Site'. These were slightly grander than the modern day equivalents that also dotted the area, including the memorable 'Landmark Interpretative Trail'.

The area oozes history like sap from a tree wound. I decided on creating some impromptu chronicles for a young couple sat at a bench carved from a tree stump.

Pointing at the wishbone shape of the lake on their map I recounted, 'It's in local folklore that on the 7th day, God had a lovely roast chicken dinner cooked by Mrs God. With only the wishbone left, they all look longingly. Mrs God has been wishing for some new curtains, God himself had always wanted a set of golf clubs now he had a bit of time on his hands. Jesus wanted world peace. So Jesus grabs hold of it, Mrs God, of course, gets overly upset as she's set her heart on the curtains. God sends him to his room for being selfish. Jesus has a tantrum and storms off upstairs throwing the wishbone to earth, creating the wishbone shaped hole that now is Lake Itasca. Mrs God tuts, 'I don't know what'll become of that boy I really don't,' and clears the table, God reminding her not to give the chicken bones to the dog.'

'Really?' the girl replied, after pondering my rendition.

I wasn't sure whether she meant 'Really? That's so interesting,' or 'Really? You're such a dick, piss off.' I'd prefer it to be the former, but in reality…

'Can't stop,' I said. 'We are on a secret government mission of the highest importance and have to go before the baddies get us. If you see two British guys one with a really big head and the other, a miserable looking Welshman, phone the FBI.'

We sped off, Fitz considerably speedier than I on my pink teenage girl's bike I'd picked to compensate for my shit legs.

We carried on our merry way full of joy at such wondrous scenery towards the Mississippi Headwaters tourist information building whose purpose in life, it seemed, was to promote the tackiest of trinkets at 'you can only buy here', prices. I suppose there's only one source to any river, and this being the Mississippi there had to be money made. We took in the information on the boards outside, giving its history.

Dependant on origin, the river's history has changed many times. In another case of colonial pantomiming:

'We saw it first!'

'Oh no you didn't!'

'Oh yes we did!'

The historians now acknowledge Hernando De Soto as the first person from the New World to find the river.

A serial conqueror and bounty hunter, De Soto managed to ravage indigenous civilisations from Peru to Tennessee and still manages to get a memorial for landing in Florida. Fortunately, he died from a fever and was buried in the depths of the Mississippi mud banks. So if you ever find a hair while eating Mississippi mud pie it may be a remnant of this murdering bastard.

Parts of the river were discovered at different times during the 16th, 17th, and 18th centuries, all nationalities claiming rights to each piece. None even considered the Native Americans who had used the river for generations.

It wasn't until 1832, when Henry Schoolcraft sourced the river back to Lake Itasca, was the whole river pieced together.

History aside, we disagreed with the caption explaining that the Mississippi was the world's third longest river. Our research discovered the Missouri/Mississippi, which takes 3,740 miles to run, is the fourth longest flow in the World behind the Nile, Amazon, and the Chang Jiang (Yangtze) in China. On its own the Mississippi is only a paltry 14th in the world. Let's not slight the Big Muddy, it still is one big mother but we wondered why it needed to jump up the league table of river lengths. Possibly to justify the tourist center's 'you can only buy here' prices. Even so, we bought postcards, after all you could only buy them there, then saddled up to ride the short distance past the 'cyclists dismount here' sign to the Mississippi Headwaters.

Nestled in a pine grove stood a 10ft high tree stump. In yellow lettering, it proclaimed:

HERE 1475FT

ABOVE

THE OCEAN

THE MIGHTY

MISSISSIPPI

BEGINS

TO FLOW

ON ITS

WINDING WAY

2552 MILES

TO THE

GULF OF MEXICO

Thankfully, the inscriber had managed to spell it right. What a nightmare carving 'Missisipi', to then wait another twenty five years to grow a girth thick enough to re-write it correctly.

Next to the marker spanning the river's Headwaters lay a stone causeway that played a soothing tinkle as water rushed over from the lake to the stream. It is the start line of the Mississippi River. People stood on the causeway shouting, 'Look I'm walking across the Mississippi! Whoo hoo yee haa!!!'

'It takes thirteen steps to cross,' another added before continuing across swaying and swinging as if on a tight rope over the Niagara Falls.

Of the many that have ever visited the source, most have likely walked these thirteen or so steps into history. But how many have ridden piggy-back on a pink girl's bike across it? Fitz and I declared that we were the first ever to complete such a feat and took mental notes to contact Norris McWhirter immediately on our return just to annoy Rob that, although it was only a precedent, we too could pretend it was a record. We came to an awkward end, getting bogged down half way up the shallow bank opposite, before sliding clumsily back into the six inches of clear water with a splash. Only we, out of the dozen or so people there, didn't think we were twats.

Twats had a prefix of 'useless' as we returned to the lakeside car park to see how the lads were getting on. They'd been for a paddle and were now waiting for our return eager to complain. The RV position was too far to carry the kayak - a whole 200 yards. Our offer to carry it didn't appease them and brought up the irrelevant argument that the RV didn't have a roof rack and was too big. The fact the kayaks could be stowed under the cab and that even if we were in a Mini Moke we would still have to camp in the same place that we'd been kindly given for free didn't seem to have the slightest effect, so more bickering ensued. Nevertheless, we set up the RV in its designated spot.

We started to store the extra kit and ancillaries. Rob couldn't find a green bag that the cookers were in.

'I definitely took it from the van in Chicago,' he said. 'I didn't see it go in the RV.'

'You mean the RV that Fitz and I packed.' I wasn't overly pleased with his insinuation, but I bit my tongue reticent to uphold further bad feeling.

'Well, all I know is I took it out and I didn't see it go in.'

We searched high and low. We searched quite high and quite low. We even searched very high and very low. There was no sign of a green bag.

Sean had also developed a form of alarm as he'd lost something as well. It all developed into a blinkered panic. We wondered what he'd lost as he turned the RV upside down. Credit cards? Money? Sight?

'No, it's my Welsh flag.'

We laughed that it wasn't as important as the cookers, but wished we hadn't, it only inflamed the Welshman, which was ironic considering the other lost item.

They didn't have a Welsh flag, they didn't have a cooker. The lack of cooker, it transpired, didn't really matter anyway as they had nothing to cook. Their earlier shopping trip was just a quick stop for snacks without the foresight that it would be the last time they'd see a place selling general provisions for the next four days. Fitz and I again found this funny. They didn't. As the equation read: F+M(piss take) = S+R(pissed off). It led to more arguments.

Fitz found a red bag. 'Is this it?'

'No, it's green.'

'You sure?' asked Fitz.

'Yes, definitely green,' replied Rob.

'Not red?'

'Stop taking the piss, Fitz. It's green.' Rob swore blind it was green. Maybe he should have sworn colour blind.

'So this can't be the right one then.' Fitz pulled from the red bag, like a rabbit from a hat, a nice shiny cooker.

Rob still couldn't take this in. He was positive it was green.

'Perhaps its taken on a chameleon quality as it's been stored next to you red bag.'

'Or your head,' I added, with no regard for Rob's obvious embarrassment. Again Rob didn't find it particularly funny.

Later, I, being the unoriginal character that I am, again jumped on the bandwagon, when on testing the 'lost cooker of Atlantis' Rob found it not to be working.

'Surely you tested it prior to our departure?'

'I didn't have time.'

I burst into laughter. 'You've had it four months.'

'And? I've been busy.'

'Mate seriously, I pity you not having 5 minutes to test the most important bit of kit you'll have for the next 3 months.'

'Oh, just fuck off.' It was the first time I'd ever seen Rob flash. I'd certainly never seen him flash at a hot spoon, even when depressed hard on the back of the neck. While it was pretty pathetic, it certainly made me realise he was more threaders than I'd ever known him. I decided to back off and bin the idea of rimming his mug of tea.

The sealant of friendship between the kayakers and the support party seemed to have dried and started to crack, which was quite appalling considering our long friendships. A clear-the-air meeting was required. We all agreed that blame lay everywhere, the kayakers admitting edginess due to the pressures of the quest before them, in contrast to our arsing about. We'd managed to get this far by 'arsing about' but admitted we'd been too eager to take the piss. Sean and Rob would loosen up, Fitz and I would calm down from our excitable states and quilt our words so as not to seem so harsh, unless they were being nobs. We were all friends again.

Night closed in, Rob and Sean planned a trip back to Bemidji to 'Food 4 Less' for a proper shop and to take in a well deserved slap up meal. Fitz and I, after our first RV cooked meal, accepted the generous offer to join the couple who owned the battered old Chevy we'd bumped into when first approaching the campsite.

Darkness grew to the crescendo of the insect night chorus. Campfires ignited irregularly around the site casting weird shadows around the forest. Tangy wood smoke carried along the cooling air along with the sound of laughter and chatter. The couple were called Lee and Sandy, Lee immediately informed us he was an Ex Navy SEAL.

Oh dear, I thought. We were gonna be burned by a flamethrower of testosterone. He informed us that he was now a computer engineer, *'good that's better'*, something we knew nothing about. Yet conversation flowed quite easily and I was quite chuffed that northern US folk call fizzy drinks 'pop' as well as their UK counterparts.

In between jovial dialogue, Lee would bark military style orders at his three young children who were the best-behaved 5, 6 and 8 year olds I'd ever seen. Sandy, silent and observant, would just nod in congruence with all Lee's accomplishments over the years. 'I was Scott Russell's chief mechanic,' he said.

I didn't know Scott Russell from Jack Russell but as Fitz wees his pants at all motor sport he pointed out that Scott Russell was a world champion, so sat like a puppy at Lee's stories.

'I'm the great-great-great-great-great-great-great grandson of General Lee,' he continued, counting the seven greats for added accuracy. Even though he had the build of a Panda I certainly hoped that he wasn't called Lee Lee as that would just be too ridiculous to contemplate and we would have had to promptly walk away. Thankfully he wasn't, but his conversation, machinegun like it was, grew more eccentric as the full moon floodlit the brush floor. His children, sitting upright as if at an infants debutante ball, would receive a bark from their father for the slightest misdemeanour i.e. slouching, unsynchronised breathing or the swatting of mosquitoes that buzzed around making repeated and often successful dive bombing attempts on us. The Citronella candles could hold them back for so long before they would hyperventilate and manage to hold their breaths for two minutes while sucking claret from our skins.

Katie, the only girl, was a sweet thing but embarrassed me by asking me to sing her a song. Not quite Pavarotti, I chose something simple and tried 'Baa Baa black sheep' that she found so enthralling she wanted the second verse. Fortunately, there is no second verse (is there?). Unfortunately, she wanted an encore of the first, so reluctantly I carried on singing nursery rhymes in a campsite next to a Royal Marines Commando who, while sniggering, was noting all for future reference. The kids happily chatted until Lee barked. Obviously he was of the opinion that children were to be seen, not heard. Threatening them with his belt, he asked Fitz and I whether we could see a stick. Not wanting to be involved in transacting implements of child torture we quickly scoured the area purposely ignoring the size of anything larger than a tooth pick.

It was all becoming notably too serious for camp-fire chat as he ranted on about the USA's decline due to the Democrats in power.

Attempting levity through satire I said, 'It's just been in the paper back home that an infamous graffiti artist has become a millionaire at the age of 19 through reporting his own crimes.'

'How's that?' replied Lee.

'In the UK, the fine for committing acts of graffiti is £200, yet the reward for reporting graffiti is £500,' I joked.

'So?' He wasn't clicking on.

'Over a 5 year period he reported his own crimes three times a day and bagged himself over £1.1million. He's now retired.'

'What? That's mad! No man, I'd shoot that mutha-fucka.'

It wasn't the expected reaction. I tried more frivoli-ty. 'But I suppose if he no longer commits crime it shows the system works.'

He was apoplectic, threatening murder on any criminal, even those who had dodged their train fare. I'd clearly underestimated his desire to kill undesirables. I turned to the only subject that would calm such a person - guns.

We asked about the problems of weapons as all we hear of in the UK was the continual shootings of this, that, the other. He agreed that too many people had them and nearly all of them should be certified. We agreed, especially when he carried one.

'I've only got three guns in the house,' he said nonchalantly. 'I hold a Desert Eagle, the most powerful handgun in the world. That sucker would drop an elephant.'

'Do you get many elephants in Minneapolis? asked Fitz.

'No, but if I had the justification of shooting one we'd be OK,' he laughed, so did Sandy on cue, so did the kids fearful of a thrashing for not finding father funny.

I just wondered what justification one would have in shooting an elephant with a handgun. In Minnesota.

'You want to get yourself a Berretta 92F like I have, 'cuz when you get to Missouri you'll need it.' He described Missouri as a cross between the Gaza Strip and Baghdad, and if we were to believe what he was saying it would be wise to take corks to stop our rear orifices being invaded by baseball cap wearing rednecks.

'I got my service M16 too. I managed to smuggle it bit by bit through the post from the SEALs while I was in Haiti.'

I just hoped he hadn't needed it while in Haiti, it'd have been quite embarrassing turning up on patrol holding only a firing pin.

We were now finding his stories decidedly hard to swallow, unlike the succulent Mauritius-sized steak Sandy was throwing down our necks. The children ate like dystopian robots, dipping their bread into the cheese fondue by numbers, rods still firmly bolstering their backs. We finished the feast with 'Schmorrs' - a tower of chocolate on fire-melted marshmallow and biscuit.

The orchestra of buzzing insects and our burping serenaded the calm night. Both covered in melted chocolate, we decided we could easily get used to this. Lee was a genuinely good guy, if not altogether eccentric. A twig snapped. He bolted upright then, with a tantric stare, slowly sat back down with the aid of Sandy.

'You know, when I'm out here every time I hear a noise it takes me back to Haiti.'

Fitz and I cringed. This guy needed help.

'On Earth there is no heaven, but there are pieces of it'

~ Jules Renard, author

At 6am we rose wearily, sweating more than the inside of an international squash player's jock strap. We must have been appetisingly tender having stewed in our own juices overnight. It would be truly be a magnificent day when we finally got an electrical hook up to initiate our living area's air conditioning.

Sean and Rob, like excited youngsters on Christmas morning, dragged the two less excited parents, called Fitz and Mark, out of bed. To be truthful, we were quite excited about getting started, and a pang of pride washed over me. Preparation finished, all the tantrums and arguments were forgotten. For the first time since Sean first asked me to join the expedition, I felt sadly redundant as the paddlers did their last minute stretching. There was nothing I could do to help them other than film Rob scurrying from shot. It was now up to Rob and Sean to fly the flag - note the singular; Sean still hadn't found the Welsh flag, leaving a lone White Ensign to flutter in their wake.

An early morning fisherman made up the crowd to cheer them off from the chilled waters of a sleepy Lake Itasca, more concerned with their paddles getting caught in his line than celebration of embarkation.

'How far ye gown?' he asked lazily, as he reeled back his line. His words dragging in a Southern drawl and not in the more clipped local accent.

'From source t'sea,' answered Rob in his equally laboured northern tones.

'Where?' answered the fisherman slowly.

We feared running out of daylight if these two continued their drawn conversation.

'All the way to the Gulf of Mexico,' answered Sean swiftly.

'Sheesh,' he exclaimed slowly, shaking his head and scratching his whiskered chin as sluggishly as his speech. He paused before speaking. Usually this pause could be construed as deliberating upon some profound answer. 'That's a long way.'

I did say usually.

That 'long way' was actually as accurate as anyone could put it. The Headwaters marker stated 2552 miles. However, during research I'd read of differing lengths from 2300 miles to 2552 miles. The US Army Corps of Engineers, who administer the river, use mileage markers to chart the river, so it was from them we took the true length. At the Headwaters, the DNR charts, which were derived from the Engineers' record, showed the Upper Mississippi starting at mile 1349. Since the Lower Mississippi started at mile 953 at Cairo Illinois, we took it as gospel that the river was currently a rather disappointing 2302 miles long. The river never runs the same from one year to the next. The US Army Corps of Engineers' continual redirecting of the flow and flood precautionary measures ensure that the river's length constantly changes. Sean and Rob somewhat deflated by the fact that they hadn't chosen this year to extend the river by another 500 miles.

After completing a quick photo shoot, off they paddled, a small cuddly toy of Sean the Sheep from 'Wallace and Gromit' tied to the bow of the kayak became the craft's cuddly guardian and figurehead.

We met them by the causeway adjacent to the tree stump marking the headwaters. More photos were taken, then after the shaking of hands and a chorus of 'good luck', they were off. As we had dreamt of starting the paddle with the sunrise guiding them into the intrigue of the Big Muddy, it was somewhat of an anticlimax that they waddled through the 12" of water, dragging the canoe along the pebbly bed, shifting plankton, reeds and driftwood. But as the saying goes, a journey of a thousand miles must begin with a single step.

For the first time, Fitz and I were now alone. We bid our farewells to Lee and Sandy before returning to Bemidji. Sunday mornings here are typical of small town USA - spots of people milling around with only leisure or prayer on their minds. We followed the crowd, namely a man and a small child, hoping they'd lead us to Paul Bunyan. Miraculously they did. What a sight stood before us - an 18ft glazed paper mache statue of a bloke in a bobble hat wearing a lumberjack shirt next to a dozy blue ox looking as if his cattle feed had been spiked with benzos.

Paul Bunyan continues as a boy's own hero. His fable passes from generation to generation like a faulty gene. His deeds of bravery and adventure amaze the same children that nowadays sit enthralled by promiscuous 6 year olds in *Toddlers and Tiaras*. Some cynics say Paul was created by the logging companies keen to promote their business in a family friendly way. But as all children know, Paul, just like Santa and the tooth fairy, exists as much as you and I live and breathe.

The 18 stone baby Paul was delivered to his parents, carried by five giant storks working shifts to get him to mum, who would have been relieved not to have delivered an 18 stone baby; my wife is a midwife and she reckons mum's perineum would have been ripped open as if a blood orange.

By the time he was a week old, he wore his father's clothes and eventually grew so large wagon wheels were used as shirt buttons, which must have created plenty of melted chocolate every time he dressed; his mom's laundry bill must have been horrendous. Food bill too, he ate forty bowls of porridge just to whet his appetite.

His pushchair was a lumber wagon drawn by oxen and his cradle was a raft off the coast of Maine. It is said that his rocking caused tidal waves that sunk ships.

His first toys were an axe and a crosscut saw. Amazingly his parents were never placed on the social services register. As a first birthday present he was given an ox named 'Babe'.

Together they grew so large that the tracks they made by gallivanting around Minnesota filled up and made the 10,000 lakes that the State is famous for.

He was soon the strongest man in all America and he single handedly cut down forest with one fair swoop of his axe, Babe dragging away the logs down to the Mississippi from which he drank dry when thirsty.

His right hand men were the seven axe men, all called Elmer so when he called they would all come running, much to his annoyance I imagine. They were all over six feet tall when sitting and all weighed over 300 pounds and probably liked dancing to the Spice Girls (read on to see what I mean).

Amongst his friends was Lucy the purple cow, a cow it is claimed, that was the finest dairy cow of them all. I would say it was the most stupid of them all, as Paul in the winter would give it green tinted spectacles to wear, so she chewed on the snow thinking it was actually grass, even the yellow patches.

His associates also included an army of giant ants. Weighing over 20,000lbs each they ate nothing but the finest Swedish snuff (is this getting more bizarre by the minute?) and wore padded mackintoshes in the winter to keep warm.

He also had his faithful dog 'Spot the reversible dog'. Chopped in half by one of the less careful Elmers, he was sewn back together by an evidently shit veterinarian, his rear half upside down to his front, so that his hind legs stuck up into the air. However he seemed happy enough and would just flip over when his front two paws got tired.

Although we never saw Paul, we heard his cough as thunder rolls as he still apparently walks the northern forests helping the lumber companies decimate the landscape, the bastard.

Behind the Paul and Babe statues was a fairground of sorts. The sort of fairground you would find travelling around the UK hired especially for garden fetes in and around the Home Counties. Old, rickety pulleys squeaked in pain as they operated the peeling wooden roundabout with Fire Engine, bus, and a stereotypical US taxi, resplendent in fading yellow. The children had spurned the taxi, and I wondered if it was due to children knowing that being a taxi driver was the most dangerous occupation in the US.

According to a study carried out by the National Institute for Occupational Safety and Health. The 140 murders per 100,000 workers meant that taxi driving was more than twice as dangerous as being a County Sheriff and you were three times more likely to be murdered in the front seat of a taxi asking for smaller notes than being a police officer. Frightening indeed, and therefore the kids were rightly cagey about manning this one in case an infant shot them from the following pimped up wooden sports car.

Amongst others in this list of dangerous occupations were gas station workers, security guards, bartenders and car salesmen (although is that a bad thing?). So, if like many people in the US, you may hold down two jobs e.g work at the local gas station by day and, as you're saving up for that holiday in Mexico, a night job in a bar, you might as well go down the local gun store and blow your own head off to cut out the middle man.

Scant of items to keep any self-respecting kid over seven amused, we noted the fairground's proximity to Lake Bemidji, making it aesthetically more pleasing, and perfectly placed for any adventurous toddler to drown in its tempting waters. Surrounded by infinite Pine, interrupted occasionally by small beaches that played host to the watersport fraternity, the calmness of the lake and was cut by the spray of Jet skis. Small boats bobbed restfully on the gentle swell, the faint silhouette of fishermen reeling and casting. Needing to know what would keep us amused for the next three days, we entered the Chamber of Commerce.

A rather business-like name for a tourist information office, it was quite a grand affair; clearly a lot of money had been recently invested. Presumably the marketing strategy being if they could afford to spend such sums to build these state-of-the-art buildings, the area would be absolutely saturated with awe-inspiring wonders. So its vortex sucked us through its double doors. I think they were aiming for a hunting lodge atmosphere with a tongue and groove pine ceiling over a stone grey floor. A huge fireplace dominated the right hand wall made from bricks brought from every State in the US. Being the ugliest fireplace that you'd find outside of a seventies council house it had to have some redeeming feature. If you could call having bricks from every State a redeeming feature, which actually was the crux of the problem. They made it the monstrosity that it was. Around it lay the detritus of commercialism where Paul Bunyan had 'donated' to the town a barrel sized Coca-

Cola can next to a needle the size of a javelin and 2-man saw that looked like, well, an over-sized 2-man saw.

Behind the counter, two young women happily answered an elderly lady with their lilted 'ya' emphasising the Scandinavian influence of the local accent. Their names were Anna and Claire, the latter a very intelligent lady who'd sustained a serious 'soccer' injury and was now undertaking rehabilitation. What physiotherapist would prescribe sitting behind a counter handing out leaflets on pine trails and church tours was beyond me, but there she was. Anna was more chatty and scatty, and her attractiveness wasn't constrained to her character.

Her eyes lit up like the proverbial Christmas tree when we opened our mouths and after telling her, 'No, we're not Australian,' asked if it was worth going to International Falls, as we considered visiting Canada. Not wanting to drive another yard more than necessary, we asked about a train service. It was undoubtedly naïve to think there'd be a passenger service that stopped here en route to the Canadian border, but my innocence paled in comparison to Anna's.

'There are trains here,' she added. 'But they're all freight wagons. Do you have passenger trains in England?

Trying not to sound sarcastic we answered yes and we had travelled frequently on such modes of locomotion.

'You mean you've been on a train?' she gasped with the incredulity more appropriate for the question, 'You've been on the Space Shuttle?'

'Err yes,' Fitz answered in a deadpan tone that specifically didn't make him sound a facetious motherfucker.

If being on a train impressed the local ladies, Bemidji was a trainspotter's paradise.

We scanned the calendar of events pinned to the information board to see if there was anything worth a look should we choose to spend a whole year here.

We'd missed the Junior Midget Tournament in Nymore Gardens. Presumably a competition for under developed infants to test their mettle against others of similar stature. I asked when the Senior Midget Tournament would be and could I enter.

'Why would Bemidji pre-plan an outbreak of stomach illnesses in early March?

Anna looked confused. 'I'm sorry, I don't follow.'

'Well how do you explain 'Girls Squirt competition?' He could have been more sexual with his definition, but gladly resigned himself to a modicum of decency.

'Is the Diversified Dogs Day Regatta on the 10th of August a rowing race for dogs?' I asked.

Anna's furrowed brow suggested she was slightly unsure on how to handle such ridiculous quick fire questions.

'I've never seen a poodle in a numbered vest and towelling head-band scull before,' added Fitz, furthering Anna's confusion.

With no events in the next three days, we satisfied ourselves that Mother Nature would be our entertainment, although the snow shoe workshop would definitely on our 'things to do' list should we return in December.

Intelligent conversation was slowing and came to an abrupt end when, for the second time in two days, I was asked to sing. This time Anna asked for some local rendition. She didn't think she'd heard English music as she only listened to 'I Love Baby Jesus' radio. I doubted Ozzy Osbourne was on the playlist.

'Setting Sun' by the Chemical Brothers was the last song we'd listened to on our mix tape before pulling into the car park so was still rummaging through my mind. Claire's mouth dropped in unison as I launched into the opening bars.

'Naaa na na na Naaa na na na Naaa na na na. Chum chum chuggy chuggy chum. Chum chum chuggy chuggy chum.'

Fitz followed with well timed bass of, 'Bum bum… jiggedy jiggedy bum.'

Fitz continued air drumming as I became hoarse screeching 'Eeeaaa. Eeeaaa Eeeaaa Eeeaaa.'

'You like it?' I finally asked expectantly, clearing grommets from my aching throat.

'What was that?'

'English music.' Fitz answered, and not like it sounded - the bombing of Dresden.

'Oh.'

It was a perfect conversation stopper. I noted this phenomenon for future reference when confronted with a potential carpet salesman stalking me with a book of samples at an incredible £8.99 an acre. A few bars of Setting Sun would soon send him on his way.

After bidding farewell to the bemused pair we elected to walk round the town to shake away the Sunday morning cobwebs.

It boasts being the first city on the Mississippi but I wondered what criteria a place had to fulfil to be classed as a 'city'. In the UK I believe you have to have a cathedral, but here in Bemidji it seemed having a totally surreal folklore figure as a figurehead constituted grounds for citydom.

We walked along Bemidji Avenue, lined with Native American edifices and detoured amongst the fish heads and discarded fishing gear that mingled with the shingle on the lake shoreline towards Bemidji State University, where we hoped our casual scanning of the windows wouldn't meet the stares of a 21 year old naked cheer-leader practising her dance moves.

We sauntered lazily, like everyone should on a Sunday, before driving to a small lakeside beach to have a chilled lunch and listen to someone else's radio playing country songs on 'Pointy Head FM'. It was here we reaffirmed that Bemidji's beauty didn't lie in its urban boundary, but in its unbridled scenery and endless capacity for outdoor activities. Drinking plastic tainted water, we couldn't have been happier.

We guessed the best place to park overnight was the police station. It was safe, convenient to the bars, and hoped they'd hook us up to their power supply for the air conditioning.

The long drive had started to take its toll. Thus at around 4pm, a nana nap was declared to prevent us falling asleep into our evening beer. We were awoken at 8 by a knock at the door by a builder asking us to move as the car park was being dug up. Confused, with dribble dried down my left cheek, I wondered why they would start on a Sunday evening. With the deductive skills of Sherlock high on cocaine, it seemed that we'd slept sixteen hours. It was now 8am. We were the last of the fast living high rollers.

Our mission now was to check on the guys' progress. We had pre-planned rendezvous points along the river at approximate timings. On visiting Stumpage's Rapids to see the lads we were told by a veteran USMC guy; obvious from the fact he wore a 'I'm a USMC Veteran' baseball cap with matching number plate insignia, that they'd passed through an hour ago and were doing fine. So, off to Iron bridge we headed where they'd planned to stop for their early afternoon break.

The campsite was within throwing distance but didn't have vehicular access, which we thought totally absurd for a campsite. We asked a woman called Mrs Lindsay if we could cut through her land so we could get to the site. I thought politeness greased the wheels of human interaction. If this was the case she was in dire need of some duck fat to remove the stiff brush she obviously had up her pontificating arse - a walnut-faced harridan with the mouth of a Calcutta sewer telling us in no uncertain terms to 'Go fuck'en git before I set the dogs ontya.'

We bid the miserable witch farewell hoping she wouldn't accidentally fall in front of our RV. That's what we'd tell the coroner anyway.

The only option was to wait at certain points, so we leap frogged back to Bemidji, skirting and waiting for an hour or so at each point. It was fruitless. We'd had no radio contact; as expected, our radios didn't operate too well in the rolling forestry blocks and the mobile phone up here was about as much use as tits on a fish. This was in the days when dropping a mobile phone on your foot could lead to severe injury. I don't know what this phone was made from but I guessed it was an amalgam of lead, osmium and gold and I curled it as a improvised dumb-bell while watching the world go by through the passenger window.

Not having comms wasn't too worrying. We had back up plans should no contact be made within an allotted time. As long as they turned up in Bemidji by the following noon we'd be happy.

Returning to Bemidji by nightfall we each volunteered to wait by the lake to watch for their arrival knowing Sean would want to press on to Bemidji if possible. By 10pm their paddling would have turned into sleeping in some mosquito-infested riverside dyke. Our only RV-friendly vantage point to watch for their unlikely arrival was a lay-by we named Fish Alley, named due to the thousand of fish bits laying about.

Prior to one summer leave, a Marine friend placed a frozen fish, stolen from the galley, into his mate's pillowcase. We returned three weeks later to retch at an odour that even the strongest of constitutions struggled with. Fish Alley was full of such fish that had putrefied to an afterbirth-like disposition. Jellied and melted like rotting blancmanges, the smell was totally unbearable. Fitz has an affliction of preference, where he finds difficulty in smelling. He must have realised it wasn't pleasant as when the cool breeze wafted the smell of a 1000 fish carcasses the way of the RV, it sent me retching like I'd just slipped head first into a fresh patch of doggy diarrhoea. It was the only place where we could park up and they see us, so we were stuck. Once settled, as much as anyone could settle in a sea of fish giblets, we rested.

It started as a faint rumbling in the distance, then the siren, honking far, far away. Slowly it got louder, the rumbling getting stronger. The earth started vibrating, the honking piercing our eardrums. Still it got louder. Our senses were being smothered until we thought we were going to get crushed by this moving earthquake of foghorns and engine noise. The pressure wave rocked the RV like a baby's cradle. We held hands over our ears as the honking continued on, and on, and on. Eventually, the swaying stopped as the rumbling faded along with the banshee horn. Pity we'd not seen the rail line when positioning ourselves.

Thankfully, only another six freight trains passed through during the night, each one seemingly louder and nearer, a catalyst to my ticker to jump into overdrive. I held the pillow over my head shouting fruitlessly at the top of my voice. No one could hear me, not even Fitz snoring 15 feet away. I sincerely hoped the paddlers were having more luck.

We awoke at 6am. Fitz was as fresh as a daisy. I wasn't. After a listless night, still tired, my head throbbed with the sound of monster trains banging on my eardrums. His accusation of me being a fanny was well founded.

The morning became a case of 'will we won't we' go to the shop to buy milk and bread for breakfast. Since waking, we'd waited five hours for them. Surely they'd see the RV on their arrival, so we edged our bets to nip off for ten minutes to get provisions. We returned twenty minutes later and asked Mr Literal on the riverbank if he'd spotted two men in a black canoe.

'Nope,' he answered scratching his unshaven chin slowly, it seemed a popular mannerism in these parts.

As we walked to the nearby bridge where Mr Literal was sitting, Fitz noticed the kayak tied to the bank and would have had to pass the prosaic old bastard who still scratched his chin when speaking to another fisherman.

'I thought you said you hadn't seen them?' I asked, somewhat nettled.

'I ain't,' he replied slowly.

'Well what's that there?' I pointed towards where I could see Sean and Rob's feet.

'That ain't a canoe,' he explained, stretching his words to the limit of drearification. 'That's a kayak.' Technically he was correct.

'Couldn't you have said "no" but you'd seen a kayak?'

He pondered with another chin scratch. 'Yup.'

Fitz rightly pointed out that sympathy not anger should be my recommended reaction to unshaven simpletons.

We expected to get shit from the paddlers, but they greeted us with some light-hearted grief. We apologised to relieve our guilt. It was sod's law that we'd waited eighteen hours for them and when we nip out for ten minutes they'd arrive.

It was good to see them. They looked knackered, as though they were 57 miles from the finish not the start. Sean the sheep looked most upset, dirty and dishevelled, his head hung heavy from a necktie of forlornly dangling weed, staining green his white woolly jumper. Admitting it had been horrendous, paddling had been impossible so they'd mostly dragged their kayak and stores - in these parts the meandering watercourse should be named the 'Mississippi Reed Bed'.

Sean had an 'Elephant Arse' disfigured beyond recognition where he'd been ravaged by insects on the first night. On the upside, they'd seen deer, otter, moose, beaver, and muskrat along the way, but no sign of Deputy Dawg. We were impressed, and not just because they'd waded nearly 60 miles, bent over, through algae. Being a casual wildlife enthusiast it was quite breathtaking to spot such animals in the wild. We ourselves had seen a female elk and young feeding in a tree line and had noticed numerous unrecognisable rodents slipping in and out of the river. It was even more impressive when Rob boasted they'd been five feet from a Bald Eagle and had taken photos for proof.

Communications were still a problem due to the terrain. With radio checks still ringing in our ears we trudged off towards the box shaped buildings of the town to see if there was anything open. We peered into antique shops, or as my elderly aunt would call them - 'knick-knack' shops.

As I've the expertise of a badger when it comes to distinguishing a Ming vase from a Tupperware potty I considered anything and everything in these shops cast offs from Granny's house not worthy of being kept after she snuffed it while feeding the goldfish. They were filled with artefacts such as matching porcelain King Charles Spaniels, chairs from circa1984, statuettes of Bing Crosby and 19th Century American figures whose prominence had passed me by.

Pottering through the shops we passed a curiosity. The 'Headwaters Science Center,' looked like a shop, but as the sign read 'Headwaters Science Center', it aroused interest. Inside was a jazz odyssey of improvised oddities with a tenuous link to science.

To be frank, any place that has a Newton's Cradle as an attraction is poor. The 'Air Cannon', that gave the impression it was there to dispense novelty items within plastic eggs at the turn of a rusty knob, was basically a kitchen roll tube that on the press of a button would shoot a jet of wind to startle unsuspecting visitors. What fun. My favourite was 'Science through Stamps' where we marvelled through six volumes of science related postage stamps organised into categories of equal boredom.

To a 5 year old, this assortment of improvised experiments was a veritable cavern of wondrous phenomena. It's amazing how over the years we become less and less impressed by more and more. Maybe cynicism is part of the ageing process, where a puddle is an obstacle rather than an opportunity and a party invitation is greeted with questions about the other attendees rather than unbridled glee.

Of all the features that lay round the Center, only one caught our eye. Perched in a cage, this fake red parrot was special. For a start it was called Humphrey, but that wasn't all. Humphrey was the 'All Knowing Parrot'. Ask him a question and he would squawk the answer right back. Impressive stuff especially when you consider you couldn't even see the room where a rather smart person would listen to the question through the parrot's intercom frantically flicking through the pages of an encyclopaedia before answering the question through a microphone in his best parrot impression.

'Ask me a question, ask me a question,' Humphrey would squawk annoyingly. 'Ask me a question, ask me a question.'

A young child asked wondrously, 'Where are you from?'

Humphrey paused before squawking, 'I'm from the rain forests of the Amazon.'

The boy looked puzzled. His mom added, 'It's near Mexico where we headed for vacation last year.'

Now incorrectly educated, the young lad walked away full of vague geographic information. He couldn't remember seeing any parrots on his holiday, mainly because parrots didn't spend all day in fast food joints and ice cream parlours.

'Ask me a question.' Humphrey's mechanical wings flapped slowly. 'Ask me a question.'

'Where's a good night out in Bemidji?' I asked.

Humphrey paused. Longer than before, the silence now amplified by his wings not flapping as if he should whisper such a non-academic question. 'Stats Bar ain't bad.'

Duly noted, we wandered once again, Fitz buying a guitar from a Christian music shop owned by a musical Ned Flanders. However, while chatting, as one often does over a newly bought guitar, we discovered he was a pious Attila the Hun of hunting.

'Every self respecting Christian in these parts is a hunter,' he informed us, adding that the Moose was the easiest to hunt due to its ambivalence of humans point-ing guns.

'Doesn't it take the fun out of it if there's no skill involved?' I asked, wondering whether the word 'fun' was appropriate in the killing of docile animals.

'There's nothing more fun than emptying your shotgun into one of those dumb sons of bitches. They'll just stand there 'til they can take no more shot, then just fall to the ground.'

It would be easy to castigate such bloodlust. So we did, we castigated the murderous cunt.

Here's a highly interesting fact for you to digest at bedtime:

What is the USA's most dangerous animal? Sabre toothed bears? Knife-wielding rattlesnakes? Vengeful elks? No, oddly, it's the poster deer for Disney's 'Bambi' - the white tailed deer.

Vehicular accidents caused by hitting white tailed deer as they vault across a road cause more fatalities than any other animal in the US. They also carry ticks that spread Lyme disease and they'll probably poison your tea given half a chance. So as we drove into 'deer country' I donned binoculars, started a deer watch and grew sympathy for murderous Christians.

'I'm unboreable in the great outdoors.'

~ P.J O'Rourke, satirist

Because of our new-found fear of deer it was all the more disturbing to see their warning signs dotted plentifully along Minnesota's highways. UK road signs have a red bordered triangle within which stands a graceful stag. Over here a yellow diamond contains a horned devil beast rising up on its hind legs ready, one assumes, to rip out the throat of unsuspecting virgins.

The meeting at the next checkpoint was to capture Rob and Sean's first scheduled portage of the trip and gave opportunity to talk to a Native American for the first time. Sitting at a pontoon with his three kids, they were totally oblivious to the swarms of mosquitoes and gnats, unlike us who waved as if lost at sea. He directed us to a campsite that was just a hole in the woods. Still wary of blood thirsty deer creeping up on us we decided that as Bemidji was only thirteen miles away, we should take up Humphrey's advice and go to the Stats Bar.

A short cut that looked like a road on the map took us onto dusty dirt tracks where we ran the gauntlet of pine trees that scored both sides of the RV as we bumped and lurched over clumps and dips of dried mud. The pines parted to a clearing of derelict shacks. Wood smoke billowing from chimneys hung heavy in the air mirroring the despondency of the drab dilapidated sheds that were home to Native Americans who sat on their neglected porches. Nearly all dressed in rags, they hardly noticed our colossus of a vehicle swaying over the ruts swerving round wrecks of 1970's rust buckets containing numerous children jumping over torn leatherette seats. It was sad to see people who we'd acknowledged as being of noble heritage looking for the remnants of their pride at the bottom of a brown paper wrapped bottle. As quickly as we came across them, we left and felt strange relief as we hit tarmac back to Bemidji.

Our return to Bemidji had actual relevance. The lads needed a couple of bits of extra kit, so after a night sweating in the 'Food 4 Less' car park, we drove to Paul Bunyan Mall.

We entered a Wal Mart for the first time - it's a rite of passage for bargain hunters either side of the pond. We stumbled across the gun counter that held an array of weapons that would make a Royal Marines armoury look positively inadequate. We'd mistakenly thought that weapons were only sold at specialist gun shops, not run of the mill supermarkets. Our shock heightened, when lying on a shelf low enough for a child to pick off, was an air rifle. Even worse, next to it was a box of air rifle pellets. The thought of a young child getting hold of a gun and ammunition was incomprehensible but certainly likely. Putting both on the top shelf was the only sensible short-term measure we could think of before advising the gun counter assistant. However, he was busy engaged in small talk with a Native American about a shotgun.

'I love the black, it makes it look a mean mother fucker.'

He was right, it did.

He then turned to the counter assistant. 'Is it still accurate if I cut the barrel down to the fore end?'

'Err, that's not strictly legal, Sir,' answered the assistant nervously.

Brandishing the gun with gay abandon, the Native American was in no mood for the trivial issue of legality of sawn-off shotguns. 'Yeah, yeah I know, but will it be accurate?'

'I... I... I... couldn't say, Sir.'

He turned to his wife and muttered something like 'I'll go somewhere else where a fellow homicidal maniac may be able to help us.' He tutted and walked away with a shake of his head before presumably checking out half price balaclavas and the timings of the security van entering and leaving the nearby bank.

Leaving Bemidji was quite a wrench. It had nuzzled our hearts. Because it was such a simple place we simpletons found it so appealing. Passing Paul and Babe for the last time, we noted him smoking a pipe on our 'you can only buy here' postcards. He no longer smoked it. We wondered whether it was a politically correct gesture to make him an ex smoking forest destroyer or some similarly sized geezer had nicked it and being of such monstrous build no one dare contest his pilfering.

***

Out onto Highway 2 we stopped at a road bridge overlooking the Mississippi now it had opened up into something resembling a river. We sat on the hard shoulder, basking in the morning sun eating shop brand Corn Flakes, camera equipment primed to get some action footage of the lads. The air temporarily turned black when a Bald Eagle eclipsed the sun as it swooped overhead onto a pine branch it shared with another beast of a bird. It was so impressive that I dribbled corn flakes.

We were now in the region of the Chippewa National Park - home to the highest density of breeding Bald Eagles in the Continental USA. Any British ornithologist would have creamed their knicks as these two sat majestically on a branch bent by their weight. I tried to catch a couple of photos but my zoom wasn't long enough but still took a couple of shots that I hoped would look a living version of the US emblem.

It wasn't long before Rob and Sean paddled into view. When in ear shot we got a honk of the bike horn as a welcome from Sean and a whinge from Rob that we'd given them dead batteries. Communications were still a problem and we'd not yet made any radio contact. I couldn't understand how their batteries were flat and readied spares to give them as they pulled over for a pit stop. These radios were of the same make and model that is widely used in the British Armed Forces, nothing fancy apart from an extra mode allowing communication to be sent securely through coded transmission.

'You sure they're dead?' I asked genuinely confused.

'Yeah, listen, I've had to put up with this squelching for the last day.'

Listening to the intermittent noise Rob had suffered, Fitz and I shared glances.

'It's not the batteries Rob,' said Fitz.

Rob became hazed with confusion.

'You've got it on the secure frequency channel.'

Rob's face became redder than his cooker bag but still the blame lay firmly with the radio. Oh how we laughed as he wriggled and squirmed trying to make an excuse while firmly taking hold of a grave robber's shovel and digging himself even further into the earth. Leaving them with Sean babysitting 'beep beep' Tweddle, it wasn't long before we managed to get underway to reach our next town of Cass Lake.

***

Thankful of the 50mph speed limit, California Flyer's throaty roar powered us up and around the heat hazed roads lined with wooden houses, the odd farm and endless pine. With vibes and shades on, we tapped fingers, with our legs akimbo on the dashboard. We conformed to RV etiquette by offering a cursory wave to fellow Road Trekkers. We were now fully trained RV veterans. All we now needed were 'I heart somewhere' stickers all over the windscreen. Cruising was meant to be like this.

Just short of Cass Lake we pulled into the car park of what was once a diner full of bouffant wearing males in crepe souls and drainpipe trousers. Frankie Vallie would have blared from a 1950's Chevy convertible as the chain smoking driver tried to get 'tops' with his puff ball skirted girlfriend who wanted commitment and another stick of gum. Now it stood forlorn. Sprigs of unkempt grass, like errant pubes in speedos, stuck out from the concrete standing that hosted a flea market. It was more of a junk sale, some items seemingly the reward of a weekend scavenging the local dump. Record players negative arm but three cracked 33's, a pink board game, originally designed for 2-4 players but now with missing pieces, perfect for a spoilt only child with victory the sole option sat in stalls also offering books, which is always of interest to me, but was disappointed when these were the five year old sort - Mills & Boon type rejects that cost 5p at a garden fete and not the relics of a grander age. One stall held a selection of machinery that would have Heath Robinson reaching into his trousers. Whole diesel combine harvester engines stood rusting next to dairy cooling generators that could be powered by pigeon poo. Odds and ends that could only be used as odds and ends sat waiting for the day some oddball in need of a 1963

Studebaker piston ring would whisk them away to a new life. Embarrassed by the riches on offer, we approached a tiny stall manned by an old fellow sporting the longest beard I'd ever seen since Mrs Llewellyn in 3rd year Religious Studies. I was sure I heard a rustling from within the hair so I peered in and unless I was mistaken, clocked eyes on a pith-helmeted hunter in plus fours, porting a blunderbuss. Around the bearded man's neck, or what I saw of his neck, was a Crocodile Dundee necklace made from teeth. To add to his skeletal collection, a band of bones circled his hat that adorned his greying hair. He welcomed us warmly and explained his wares to us, dream catchers sat next to warning symbols, all hand made with fantastic dexterity. He had jumbo sausages for fingers yet had woven the most delicate and difficult of materials into wonderfully weird ornaments and decorations. We could have cleaned him out but for the problem of overloading the RV, so we settled for a single item apiece. I chose a protection sign, two crossed arrows pointing upwards astride a turtle breast bone. Fitz went for a welcoming pendant similar to mine but with the arrows pointing downwards. Chuffed with our purchases we rolled into Cass Lake in need of chocolate milk and bananas. Making a bee line for Teals - 'The One Stop Shopping Center' we found a Cass Lake Vacation Guide to help us find our way around this smallest of towns that would be our home for the next 24 hours.

Cass Lake's location made it an ideal retreat should you enjoy fishing. We didn't. I tried fishing once with an over enthusiastic uncle who baffled me with science when describing the finer points of roach poles and reel tensions. Notwithstanding he warmed maggots under his tongue, his lectures on bait management were boring in the extreme. This man, who had paint come round to watch him dry, then had me there sitting by a motionless pond for seven hours, the highlights being he tensing his line or casting out to a different spot. My mind raced with non-thought that then meandered into the thoughts you only scrutinise when in limbo. Situations like on a long train journey without a book, headphones or £30 to take away the boredom by buying 6 tins of McEwan's 'Red Death'. Situations like being sent to the silent corner at school after proclaiming at the top of your voice that Mr Hunt's name rhymed with his character.

People recommend fishing as a release from the stress and strains of work, yet sitting for hours on end doing an impression of a garden gnome truly freaks me out. And as for those who decree fishing as 'pure recreation' and put back their catch I say 'is there anything more pointless?' You wait an absolute eternity to catch a fish that wouldn't feed an anorexic, and then after the thrill of success you then throw it back. It's like making a martyr's pilgrimage to Lourdes walking 1000 miles in bare feet swathed in rags of glass then on reaching the shrine deciding you'd like to try a bit of Islam.

Despite my disinterest, fishing is still the number 1 participant sport in the UK and would imagine it's up there in the US. In Minnesota for instance, 97% of children fish, a figure so deplorable one Northern Minnesotan commented 'What on earth went wrong with the other 3%?'

This pastime is what drew the majority of these check-shirted children and their similarly dressed parents here to Cass Lake. The Vacation Guide recognised this, so basically became a fishing magazine with a few other bits thrown in, RV park adverts, lake homes and casinos in the Indian reservations.

Maybe this explained why they had to fill the re-maining space with a map pinpointing important businesses in the town itself. Amongst those advertised were important vacationer hot spots such as Clem's Ace Hardware, Waabooz Embroidery and, more worryingly, both the 'Thomas' and aptly named 'Cease' Funeral Homes. I didn't know whether it had an imperceptibly high rate of vacation deaths, but won-dered why such a tiny place had two. Perhaps that explains the fourteen churches necessary to accommo-date the continual funeral procession that blighted this part of the world. Because of the approaching storm clouds Fitz and I had decided to make an unscheduled meeting with the paddlers at Knutson Dam to give them shelter during the imminent downpour. They'd reached the dam before us. In a moment of immense bravado/stupidity they'd tried to negotiate the dam by paddling straight through it rather than the usual portaging of the vessel around the obstacle. In doing so they'd capsized. As Sean rightly said, 'When you plan a route stick to it,' and with his usual dark humour, 'At least the capsize drills have been weighed off.'

The incident had left a tear in the hull of the boat too large for the puncture repair kit to handle. So thank you Cass Lake Vacation Guide for leading us to Clem's Ace Hardware shop where we cheerfully munched through piles of free popcorn while browsing through 'fixings and attachments' and noticing that taps were called faucets and how many Native Americans shopped here. All, bar none, were shabbily dressed, dirty and bedraggled making me wonder how low was the poverty line they were obviously living under to leave them in this condition. My mind raced back to the previous day where we'd seen families huddled around faltering fires on their porches. Also noticeable was their size. Not fat, although a couple could have done with getting down the gym to work off excess abdominal insulation, but *big*. Big boned, the proverbial brick shithouses, and that was just the women. Years ago when fighting to save their land they should have challenged the people from the New World to arm wrestling competitions as an alternative method to deciding land rights. Not one person I saw in Cass Lake would have had much trouble twisting off the arm of some puny Frenchman and could have even made it an entertaining spectator event by slapping him over the head with the soggy end for good measure.

We eventually bought tractor tyre repair kits, an invaluable addition to any man in this neck of the woods. Luckily the storm skirted around us, but left the scorched air kneaded by humidity creating an even more uncomfortable atmosphere.

The next morning we woke apprehensively. Today the biggest challenge yet awaited the paddlers - crossing the 14 miles of Lake Winnibigoshish - 91,475 square miles of water as unpredictable as the recent weather. From the relative calmness of the river, the lake could swell to a coaster of white frothed rollers that could overturn vessels in a flash. This was made all the more pertinent by the fact that weeks before, two experienced canoeists attempting the same feat were drowned when they capsized.

We wished them more luck than usual and promised to meet them on the eastern side. Our concern soon faded as we returned to the RV. The interior had apparently suffered a well-aimed attack by grenade wielding maniacs. The paddlers had taken over all available space, left their rubbish strewn around the cab and managed to empty a castle worth of sand on the floor, all in their 10 minutes 'admin' stop.

Our trip to the east side was interrupted by having to dump our waste for the first time. We were undeniably disgruntled that a charge was levied for anyone to empty their tanks of 'grey water' i.e. washing up water, shower water and what we would call 'piss and shit' i.e. piss and shit. However, we were fast becoming experts at receiving things gratis, our promotional booklet the passport to fee waiving. Chuffed we'd dumped for free and saved $5, we continued our merry penny pinching way.

We were cruising through the Lakes Country. Minnesota is named the 'Land of 10,000 lakes' originally by someone who'd lost part of the list. There are actually over 15,000, giving this landlocked State more coastline than California, Florida and Hawaii combined. The weather was how it was back in the British summer of '76. The heat haze on the melting tarmac was rising so high it made driving seem like a passage through transparent smoke, the air unstable, quivering beyond the windscreen altering the view ahead. Wind burned my arm as I tried to look cool hanging it out of the open window finally retracting it when my skin started to resemble a pork scratching.

Upon arrival at our destination, we pulled up at the side of the road. With time to spare and energy to burn, we decided to pump some iron after buying some cheap weights in the Wal Mart in Bemidji. Opening the box and getting them out would be a start. Our vanity took over, so before long we were bench-pressing while lying on a roadside log, receiving wolf whistles from motorists zooming by. We felt as chad as your dad's cardigan, but as this was the land of the bulging bicep we didn't give a toss.

'Chad', now there's a word I first used in the military and I have no real experience of it being said outside of the Royal Marines' culture. The nearest word that springs to mind that is used in civilian circles would be the word 'naff'. In a nutshell, 'chad' is something that is embarrassingly bad e.g. if I tried to seriously show off by doing 100 press-ups in a pub, that would be 'chad'. If I hung dice in my windscreen, that would be 'über chad'. Conversely, if you knowingly do something 'chad', it is cool to do so. In fact, there is a saying that 'chad is good'. So if you tried to chat up a woman by reflecting on her eyes being like diamonds cascading from the waterfall of beauty knowing you were being a total twat that would be 'good' and your street cred would rise exponentially. I have a very good Royal Marine friend Mick, who bought a Reliant Robin and removed the roof replacing it with tent canvas to give it a cabriolet effect. As if this wasn't enough, he bought leopard skin seat covers, dice and any other kitsch accessories he could purchase before painting a naked lady on the bonnet and flames up the sides to make the ultimate 'chad mobile'. Because he knew it was 'chad' it was the best car on camp. People would beg Mick to let them ride to the beach in it, despite the fact that it didn't have a starter motor therefore needed a gang to push him just to get going. Indeed it was about as roadworthy as 99% of tractors that you get stuck behind on the way to work when you're running ten minutes late. Knowing we were chad by lifting weights, meant we were cool, especially with shorts tucked up our arses à la sumo wrestlers.

By the time Rob and Sean reached us on the east bank they were exhausted. It had been a 'ball bagger' and both needed to lie down to cool off.

It had come to note that Fitz and I were spending a lot of time shuttle running up and down the river looking for the paddlers to keep a check on their progress. Now communications were better it was not only an inefficient way of contact but also an unnecessary draining of both fuel and our mileage allocation. Sean rightly said they were big boys and didn't need mothering and as a consequence the routine was changed where instead of trying to rendezvous everyday at certain checkpoints we would propose to meet at a nominated town every few days. This made things far more flexible for both teams and therefore once the paddlers had sufficiently rested, Fitz and I set off to search for somewhere that sold cheap bananas and chocolate milk.

***

So named because of the 3 1/2 miles of river cataracts, Grand Rapids crept up on us. As shooting and fishing stores became concentrated, we eventually found ourselves in the middle of town while 'Judge Fudge' by the Happy Mondays blasted the air. Whether it was the strangled vocals of Shaun Ryder or that two scruffy twats were in charge of such a vehicle that caused stares at the traffic lights we didn't know or care.

The Tourist Information Office was a modern well-lit building with an obligatory drinking water fountain. I have always found these thirst-quenching contraptions somewhat disconcerting. However hard you seem to depress the button, the jet will pathetically loop back into the bowl compelling you to lower your lips a whole lot further than you'd care to. Sufferers of herpes, leprosy and people that slaver profusely could have used the same fountain spout, yet we share it. No matter how carefully we are, we purse our lips and bob just that inch too far and end up kissing the spout. If I did it, sufferers of herpes did it, lepers did it, and human St Bernard dogs definitely did it. So even if I had been crawling through the Sahara for a week with only my concentrated urine as a source of refreshment I would possibly think twice before using a water fountain to re-hydrate. And so as I walked passed it, giving the button a cursory push just to see how inadequate it was, I found a rather powerful stream, not quite a fire hose jet but one certainly to prevent spout kissing. Against my better judgement my thirst took over and I succumbed. The ice cold gush shattered my teeth, running messily down my cheek as if I'd just had a dental anaesthetic. In my eagerness to get a good guzzle my neck reflexed to lower my head and in an instant kissed the lips of a 1000 herpes carriers, of a 1000 lepers, of a 1000 people that couldn't say 'resuscitate' without covering you with spittle.

Here we found what I'd expected to see in such a place, General Eva Braun of the Blue Rinse Brigade marshalling people to the places that she wanted them to see with an itinerary planned down to the last detail. Detraction from the route would be discovered by the tracking signal attached to the guide, the miscreant hunted down then given a concrete bathing costume to swim in. Handing us a Grand Rapids Resort Guide, ignoring our initial request for a nearby campsite, the tourist information lady systematically filed through each article and advert with such detail that by the 3rd hour we knew that Eugene and Betty Screeslope owners of the Southland Lodge often had wife swapping parties. Eugene having a passion for edible crotchless knickers that Betty carefully made from her own recipe using dried apricots, parma ham, and fruit pastilles. Betty herself loved being bound in cellophane then smeared in Swarfega and ball bearings then to be beaten with a high-tension tennis racquet by two petite women.

I tried to tell the tourist info lady that both Fitz and I had undertaken twelve years of education and in that time had managed to acquire a reasonable proficiency in reading and didn't really need her pointing out each word explaining that Amoco Service Center provided:

'Tune ups.'

'Hmmm, right but...'

'...Brake jobs.'

'Indeed. However...'

'...Drums and rotors turned. My husband Jerry had his tuned there and felt as if he'd got a new ve-hi-cle.'

'Excellent, we just need...'

'Mufflers, and Lord knows, some of the kids around here should get something done. Only yesterday I heard a pick up truck of...'

It didn't seem right to interrupt her so I just grabbed her purple hair and banged her head repeatedly on the counter in a vain attempt to shut her up.

Startled, she drew breath. We thought that the end of her jabbering. We were wrong. Inhaling a volume of hot air that could take a balloonist from Darwin to Jakarta (winds permitting) she continued her resume of page 29. This was the final straw. Fitz pulled from under his T-shirt an Uzi and promptly emptied a magazine of 9mm rounds into her face.

Sparks flew from her shiny cheeks, chunks of flesh flew from her forehead and scorch marks tattooed her chin. She was an automated tourist information android, her armour-plated coating deflecting the bullets. Smoke billowed from her high frilly neck line as she took twice as long to promote the 'Plaza Laundry and Cleaner' with its coin operated laundry, non-smoking facility and on-line tailor.

'If you turn to page 40,' she continued, 'You will note the facilities of Cedarwild Resorts including a store on site.'

Now only half operable, she endured the next magazine as round after round bounced from her tungsten skull. The only damage sustained appeared to be below her left bionic eye where a small tear of oil dribbled down her metallic cheek.

Still she ranted on. Her robotic voice monotone, as statistics ad infinitum were reeled off unabated from her precision-engineered lips, 'Itasca Lumber is situated on Highway 169S, Grand Rapids MN55744, and is the town's premier stockist of all woods and specialises in importation of MDF. L&M Supply 1200E Highway 169 Grand Rapids MN55744 discount department store, 13 departments 42,000 items at a deal everyday.'

I snapped out of my waking coma to see her still rattling on. Without trying to be ignorant we left her chattering to a point in the far distance while we attempted to find ourselves a campsite passing a middle-aged couple in the doorway who entered carrying a portable multi-barrelled rocket launcher.

We found a camping spot at the Itasca County fairground, with no fair, just a large paddock area presumably designed specifically for the fair and, I hoped, rodeos.

The concept of some baccy-spitting cowboy trying to hold on for dear life to a bull or horse with a serious attitude problem in the name of sport had always intrigued me. I'd love to have a go, and would even wear their terribly bad clothes. For me it is the ultimate test between man and beast and would be the best bootneck challenge ever, especially after a few *Jagermeisters*.

The campsite was a welcome setting, the owner eager to help us in our quest and wouldn't hear of us paying for our spot. He would even hook us up to an electrical point. For the first time we'd have air conditioning in our living area and electricity for our microwave. After our first shower in five days, we had the confidence to step back into the real world, no longer afraid of what affect our armpits would have on the general public. We shut the windows, put on our thermal underwear and blasted ourselves with arctic air and feasted upon microwave cheese on toast. If heaven was half as good as this, I would stop going ashore dressed as 'Karate Jesus' and start attending church religiously.

'It's cool to go places working people are happy.'

~ Neil Young, singer

Grand Rapids was how I'd imagined small town USA. If the stereotypical view of a northern English town was soot covered back to back terraces below chimneys puffing toxic gases into a dour sky, here was my idea of urban USA - a horizon of cables spanning a busy road, cables from which hung road signs and adverts, cables from which hung traffic lights, and cables just going from A to B with questionable purpose. It was a scene that I'd loved since watching '70's American TV. On a practical note, instead of digging up half the road 3 times a year to repair or install a new underground cable like us stupid Britons do, they just get a crane and crack on - easy peasy lemon squeezy.

Similar to Bemidji, the commercial area of town was a collection of unattractive cuboid buildings. The Vacation Guide I carried did mention the Central School - a classic Richardson Romanesque building that was the landmark of the town. It was indeed grander than its surroundings but far from memorable as was publicised in the guide. So unmemorable in fact that as I am writing this I have forgotten what I was writing about. The Vacation Guide I carried did mention the Central School - a classic Richardson Romanesque building that was the landmark of the town. It was indeed grander than its surroundings but far from memorable as publicised in the guide. One thing that I did like about the guide, now I had the freedom of reading it of my own accord, was the vacation planner that listed resorts, campgrounds, and B&B's all with their own strap line to entice potential guests. I looked for ludicrous ones that I could ridicule but found most were quite sane, some even inventive. "A place to make friends with your brain", I especially liked, a man sat peacefully on a pontoon talking about the previous night's ball game to a jar containing formaldehyde suspending grey matter - tremendous. 'Blue Moon Resort' needed a new marketing campaign to attract its potential visitors. Its attention grabbing crowd puller was "Also have a newer motel with porch overlooking Hill Lake", suggesting that anyone in need of a win-dowed room and modern amenities such as a porch should seek alternative accommodation.

Vacation Guide rolled tightly and pushed firmly in-to back pocket looking like a 1980s football hooligan, we headed to that most American of institutions - the mall. Unfortunately, on this occasion it was more UK than US similar to walking into a small town shopping arcade in, say, Shrewsbury.

Fitz saw a travel agent shop, immediately entering it to look at the prices to fly to Belize. Worried he was suddenly doing a runner, he reminded me that his sister was working in a hotel in Belize City and was thinking of meeting us when in New Orleans. 'Fuck me', said Fitz in an overly loud voice.

It brought a unilateral silence of stares from the customers and staff alike. Trying not to implode with embarrassment, Fitz politely said that he'd just seen his sister in a brochure. While it may not seem a big deal to a layperson, when miles away from home with nothing to remind one of family, it's rather comforting to see a sibling in a brochure in a back street shopping arcade of a backwater town, most of whose inhabitants would struggle to pinpoint Belize on a map. It was the only contact Fitz had made so far with his folks and so walked out with the brochure as a keepsake. His sister was rather attractive, so I was happy for him to keep the magazine that I would often read in my 'private time'.

Looking further afield in the arcade if it was possible to look far, it was a mush of faceless franchises. With time to kill, we took a peek into a sports shop. Three shop assistants converged as if we were the first to cross the threshold. It was apparent that we were the first Britons to have entered as we received the obligatory furrowed brow when communicating through our strange accents. It was another example of global marketing where in such a backwater there wasn't anything for sale, save baseball boots, that we couldn't buy in any sports shop in any small town. Considering I knew nothing of baseball, my imagination was gagged, Fitz; however, had recently developed a weird obsession for rollerblades, confirming he would buy a pair and to hell with the consequences. The footwear section was striking in gleaming brass encased in polished tongue and groove and displayed an impressive range of rollerblades from the inexpensive to the ridiculously expensive. He would never resort to wearing beginner's equipment, watching a roller disco allowed him a degree of experience, so plumped for an expensive pair. The assistant fitted the various straps while spouting off a complicated nomenclature that went in one ear and out the other. Fitz nodded insanely, agreeing that they were the perfect choice. He rose unsteadily to his feet as if rising from a long-term coma. The shop assistant left Fitz to try them for comfort and to make a decision in private. Holding onto me with a vice like grasp his confidence soon turned to cockiness. Standing was easier than expected, so within no time he could stand and shuffle. He turned, not in a sweeping arc but a series of short shunts with his left leg pivoting on his long gangly right. It was a turn all the same. He was ready to conquer Norfolk upon his return. He'd initially doubted the wisdom of purchasing of a pair. He thought his blading silently through Attleborough onto the A11 towards Wymondhem would cause shock and consternation to the elders of the village and ridicule from his contemporaries as he glided, legs pushing, arms in over extending circles.

'Oh God look at Fitz,' he expected them to cry. 'Three months in the States and look at him, thinks he's a bloody extra in Baywatch.'

But now as he stood in the mirror he thought '*sod them*.' 'Good way to keep fit,' he pronounced.

'And a good way to break your neck,' replied I.

'No chance,' he stated, holding on to the brass rail like an apprentice ballerina.

He pushed himself away again and tried this time to execute a spin that didn't have the turning circle of an oil tanker. Bad mistake.

In the world of cartoons, one of the most often used methods of catching criminals is to lead them into a slick of marbles. The legs would rotate sending the feet into painted swirls before crashing down on the floor dislodging a rubber mask that would uncover the face of Mr Jefferson the Hardware store owner.

Shaggy and Scooby had just caught Fitz. His legs thrust forward, his body not doing the same. His arms flailed wildly catching the rack of T-shirts. The polished floor prevented his catastrophic attempts to gain permanent footing and sent him accelerating into a rack of pool cues via fifteen pairs of trainers. He sat there silently for a second, shocked at events. I couldn't breathe as I cried with laughter. Pulling a T-shirt from his ear, pushing a cue from his shoulder, he looked up at the shocked shop assistant who had rushed in as the crashes started and burst into hysterical laughter. With the last of Fitz's dreams of being a rollerblading champion shattered we asked the guy clearing up the mess where the best bars in town were. He admitted he never went to bars. This concept was totally alien to us, we could only assume he spent his crazy nights watching a slightly loud TV playing a whole series of 'Frasier' eating Low fat crisps and diet cordial.

The racket had attracted the supervisor from a curtain at the back of the shop. She'd actually been out of doors past 6:35pm and informed us that the best place to go tonight would be 'Cap'n' Hook's' a pub with more apostrophes than anywhere except the famous 'Tin't In 'Tin' pub in Barnsley.

'It's really popular,' she explained. 'Tonight is croquet night. People from all over come for the croquet.'

Surprised this most quintessential of English lawn games was played in this neck on the woods, I couldn't believe that people would flock from afar to watch floodlit croquet. Although I never donned a striped blazer and cricket whites to play croquet at school, preferring to dodge dog shit and broken glass on council run football and rugby fields, I loved any sport. While I was never proficient enough to play in the upper echelons of military sports teams, I'd once excelled at 'bootneck cricket' the game where the fastest bowlers would bowl bouncers on a concrete gym floor from 18 yards at a batter sufficiently protected by one glove, one leg pad and an old size 4 cricket bat, until unconsciousness, missing teeth or a broken gym window ended the game. So while I had no urge to knock balls through garden hoops with similar minded pillocks, we thought it a good way to spend a surreal evening. We traipsed back to the RV passing a convoy of tanks on the way. A helmeted soldier had his head out of the cupola of the lead tank and seemed to be saying into his microphone, 'Tourist Information Office three blocks, set cannons to Uranium tip, that'll shut the bitch up.'

Upon arrival at the bar it seemed our recognition of North Minnesotan accents had gone awry. It wasn't croquet, it was something far worse - karaoke.

My ears first bled to the banging of foam skinned drums, strumming of fake guitars, hammering of fake piano keys, singing of fake sincerity watching Top of the Pops back in '74, with Slade strutting their glitter in front of perms and basin cuts. My first experience of the real thing was sixteen years later in 'Cats Meow' - a highly popular haunt for the younger generation on New Orleans's Bourbon Street. In my innocent youth I actually thought I was witnessing a great form of entertainment, right up there with electronic trivia machines, bar skittles and Californian soap operas. However, after enduring an hour of 'I Want To Break Free' and 'Unchained Melody', I realised that although I could make a decent crust from this should I actually bring this back to the UK; it was highly likely that I would need to fork out a larger sum in medical and dental bills to try and mend my body broken from numerous kickings I would receive from importing this invention that was slightly worse than the hydrogen bomb.

'Cap'n' Hook's' was situated on the road out of Grand Rapids perfectly positioned for passing traffic. If this place pulled in folk from all around then it must have been from towns with a population of two or three at most. The place was deserted other than a check-shirted girl pitifully singing her heart out to two guys so dirty they appeared to have just climbed from a mineshaft. I thought I saw a tear as she cried out the chorus to 'A Wind Beneath My Wings'. I cried also, in pain. Her tuneless screeching suggested she had glue ear and a voice box full of sharp glass and helium. For effort I'd give her 9 out of 10, for attainment I'd give her 1, with no double entendre implied.

After a tuneless rendition of 'Heart Of Glass', we couldn't take much more and the final straw came when one of the filthy miners got up and belted out at the top of his voice 'I love Rock 'n' Roll' and apparently hideous clothes. It was a strange sound, one that I'd only ever heard on a wildlife documentary showing the guttural grunts of an amorous silverback gorilla.

As we left, we passed the girl from the sport shop who seemed surprised we were leaving so soon. Realising that we didn't really find the concept of karaoke appealing, she recommended the 'Rendezvous Bar' downtown that maybe more our cup of tea. It certainly was, a neon lit sleaze pit where a respirator was needed just to prevent instant lung cancer. The jukebox music played staple 70's and 80's rock to a room full of males dressed in stereotypical manliness - baseball cap, vest, and dirty jeans. Everyone drank from bottles and everyone talked about manly things, even the women. This was no place for the squeamish. A whole baseball team straight from practise spat baccy in unison and tormented a young man with his girlfriend at the dartboard. The sport shop girl seemingly was stalking us, but rather being scared we talked for a while. Her name was Billie-Jo. I asked her if she liked rodeo, stalling after such a straight question she eventually answered 'yes' Fitz and I exchanging a 'thought so'. As we guessed, it wasn't long before she wandered over to the baseball team. She readily admitted many girls in these parts were not only rodeo lovers but baseball groupies. Standing next to the pool table we were challenged to a game by a hulk of a man whose awesome appearance was somewhat ruined by the fact he wore pink National health type glasses, once worn by incontinent schoolgirls all across the UK. His myopia clearly made him the world's worst player so we accepted the challenge and immediately regretted it. I forget his name, I forget everything apart from the fact he was an Alaskan salmon farmer. I remember this as it was the only thing he talked about, repeatedly over and over again, Fitz laughed as I struggled to turn the conversation away from spawning cycles and hatchery licences. My game thankfully suffered as a consequence and was able to lose quite heavily allowing me to make a feeble excuse of the RV having Rubella and I'd have to leave forthwith.

The next morning we awoke to air strikes on the Tourist Information Office. Comms allowed us to speak to the paddlers and a rendezvous was organised for around 3pm, enough time to get a hearty breakfast and a few hours of aimless wandering. We sought out and found a side street diner that looked and smelled just how we expected such an eatery to. We fought our way to the red PVC swivel stools around the counter just to appear well-versed in these surroundings. Happy that we received free refills of coffee we intentionally mulled over the menu while we drank copious amounts of free refills, before deciding on the 'Sack Rat' a speciality breakfast of Hash browns, eggs, sausage and toast, just like in a McDonalds. The difference here was it was delicious and filling. The thought of eating sweet maple syrup in the morning was one part of an American breakfast I couldn't stomach. But in this place even the pancakes were delectable, so we pigged out slowly on a pile of pancakes so high that I had to stand on my tip toes to take off the top one. Eventually our hostess stopped serving our bottomless cups as we'd spent nearly two hours in there, so with a hearty tip, amounting to considerably more than the cost of the coffee we'd drunk, we set off in search of action. It was a choice between the two attractions Grand Rapids hoped would pull in the masses. One was the Birthplace of Judy Garland.

Visiting the birthplace or home of a celebrity has always baffled me. I suppose I don't posses the voyeuristic curiosity of some or maybe I'm not star-struck by legends of stage and screen; they piss and shit like the rest of us. Yet the main reason for not committing myself was that I refused to visit a place advertised as being 'Toto'lly 'Oz'some'. Cringing at the advert we realised from the picture and the carriage on the front lawn that we'd passed it on the way to 'Cap'n' Hook's. So rather than spending money to go inside I could at least explain to my son, while watching the 'Wizard of Oz', that I'd seen the carriage carrying Dorothy et al to the doors of the Emerald City, and that it had previously been owned by President Abraham Lincoln during the American Civil War. I'd tell him this prior to bedtime to lapse him into a deep coma, instead of the usual routine of having to run round the house chasing after an hysterical 3 year old Olympic athlete, pyjamas round ankles, with a trail of used bog roll hanging between his clenched buttocks thinking I was trying to chop off his 'tail'.

The alternative to Judy Garland's birthplace was Grand Rapids Museum of Paper Manufacturing. I could envisage indigenous tribes in the Congo organising savings clubs for a bus trip to Minnesota, just to see the Grand Rapids Museum of Paper Manufacturing or a mafia godfather on his deathbed asking his first born to honour his father in death by taking photographs to make a panoramic collage of the entrance to the Grand Rapids Museum of Paper Manufacturing so that he could be buried with it to forever cherish within his coffin.

We were stumped. With nothing better to do, we reconnoitred possible landing points for the lads. Potogama Park was ideal but didn't have overnight storage so we had to use a small fisherman's landing point near Pokogama Dam in a small housing area. There wasn't storage available here either but we gambled on some kind-hearted neighbour securing the kayak for the evening.

As we'd planned on getting some aerial photography and video we headed for the small airfield. 'Big enough to cope small enough to care' could have been the airfield's motto. With doe eyes again we promoted our venture and after a Jedi mind trick with the airfield rep, managed to get a free 1/2 hour flight in a Cessna piloted by a guy named Chad Beer. We were bowled over by such a marvellous name that neither of us could take our eyes off his name badge to continue conversation.

The flight was 'interesting' to say the least. Thermals buffeted us into cold pressure, rolling the plane like a boat on rough water. The variety in throttle speed was distinctly disturbing, often so decelerated I could see the propeller spinning. To try and take my mind off our instability and the engine coughing like a phlegm-filled pensioner, I marvelled at the scene beneath. In the distance, lakes dotted the woodland landscape like puddles in moss. The true course of the Mississippi's water ran dark below the wider expanse of water that made up the modern river, turning within the expanse of woods that blanketed the area up until it reached the suburbs. The white flash of the kayakers' paddle blades distracted our gaze and even though the river was still in its infancy it was amazing how irrelevant they were on the expanse of rippled glass.

We thanked our lucky stars that we hadn't gone to the Museum of Paper Manufacturing. The ugly cereal box of the paper mill churned out steam next to its candy striped chimneys that blew smoke like a chain-smoking hag. It could have been even nicer if they had dug a toxic waste dump next to the river and knocked down a few trees to make a multi-storey car park.

Flight finished, we met Rob and Sean at the park directing them to the mud bank that pretended to be a boat landing a mile further upstream. This didn't exactly impress them. There is little worse than thinking you've reached the end of a long slog when dead on your feet, only to be told that you aren't at the finish, but a mile short. Can you imagine finishing the London Marathon only to be told that someone had miscalculated the distance and the finish line was another ten minutes away? You'd be peeved I'm sure, so we didn't take it to heart when they eventually finished in a sour mood.

They'd paddled a marathon distance during the day. Indeed, they'd paddled a marathon distance each day for the past week. If this wasn't bad enough they would be paddling at least a marathon distance everyday for the next 13 weeks so that last mile; that in some quarters may have been labelled 'character building', was actually soul destroying. My sympathy faded when bombarded with complaints that there wasn't anywhere to secure the Klepper overnight.

'We can ask the locals if we can store it in their garden or shed,' I suggested.

It went down like a lead balloon. 'We can't impose on people like that.'

Being a bit of an idealist, I was of the opinion that the locals who, so far, had drenched us with the milk of human kindness could spare a bit more. 'You're paddling the length of the Mississippi, busting a gut for charity, all you want is a bit of garage space to keep the kayak. If someone does turn us down, fuck 'em, there'll be more of the kind-hearted souls we've seen so far.'

Sean agreed, realising they deserved help from any quarter, plucked up the courage to knock at the door of a kind lady who, as it happened, was delighted to help.

At his success, Sean's mood lifted, Rob's didn't; he still seemed down. He was with the wrong people for sympathy, and didn't get much change from any of us when he complained that the RV was too far away, still too big etc etc. We tried to explain that the river wasn't purposely built for our expedition and unless we'd come out here for a month checking every landing site on the river there were bound to be check-points that weren't ideal, and no matter how much he grumbled the RV wouldn't shrink-to-fit. Unfortunately, this didn't satisfy him and continued to grumble quietly to himself. Fitz confided in me that he thought Rob was having some sort of crisis. After taking stock, I felt for Rob. I'd never known him to be like this and after considerable consideration of everything that had gone on in the past few weeks I came to the unequivocal conclusion that Rob was in a foul mood because he realised I was going to win our wager of who could grow the longest hair. His strenuous exertion in the humidity of the Minnesotan sun obviously caused profuse sweating and the last thing he needed was a head of hair that would fill two mattresses. Besides, his head is amongst the largest in the entire kingdom and realised that if his mop became too bulbous it could cause the kayak to become top heavy and tip over. I, on the other hand needed to keep my locks flowing to insulate my bonce from the deep freeze of the RV.

Hair growth competitions aside, the cinema was our entertainment until we trudged as a foursome back to The Rendezvous Bar as we'd heard on the grapevine that a live band would be playing 80's rock music that Sean has a perverse penchant for.

The band played all the usual stuff a struggling rock outfit plays - badly. This was a band in the loosest possible term, a four-piece outfit that regurgitated rock anthems from a bygone age. Loud renditions of everything from Bon Jovi to ZZ top with out-of tune guitars led by the wailing lead singer deluded in thinking that wearing a black zip up mini dress, black fishnet stockings over furry thigh high 'fuck-me boots' made her look sexy. Upon reaching our table we looked at anything but her, hoping our embarrassment would discourage her to stay any longer than necessary. Fitz accidentally made eye contact and regretfully gained her attention. Placing her size 9 spiked heel in between his legs, she screamed 'I hate myself for loving you' into his face. He mouthed silently to us, 'She has breath that smells of chutney.'

Whether it was mango or lime he didn't specify but conceded that it had left him hankering for poppadums.

With the chad factor reaching unprecedented heights, it was a case of getting out before we got irretrievably drawn into this world of bad dancing, condiment-breathing songstresses, and salmon farming pool sharks.

The following day was one of those days that does not recognise the man-made concept of time. With no agenda, we just plodded through the morning twiddling thumbs and strumming fingers until Sean and Rob decided that it was time to leave. It wasn't until this point that for the first time Judy Garland was mentioned. Rob's ears pricked up like a lurcher's. Judy Garland? Totolly Ozsome? House?

'Well, if you've been, I want to go.'

We lied and told him that it wasn't worth going to see. It didn't matter. He couldn't miss out.

It's Judy Garland's birthplace for Christ's sake.

Trying to lead him back into the Klepper like a bewildered sanatorium patient, he struggled from our grasp and bolted to the RV. He wasn't going without visiting Judy's house. To our chagrin, we relented and gave him his wish, so while the paddlers went dead star spotting, Fitz and I sat by the riverbank discussing names for them. This wasn't in anyway churlish. Childish maybe, but certainly not churlish, as in a supermarket the previous day we had decided on alternative names for ourselves as we'd become bored with our own. Naming Fitz 'Bacos' after the bacon bit topping, he named me 'Tartare' after the fish sauce emphasising the second syllable to give it a rather camp pronunciation. For Rob we decided on Rubydoo as a mate of Fitz's had called Rob it one day. Rob afterwards needed to know the origins of the name unsatisfied that it was just silliness without any real meaning; perhaps he was trying to reassure himself that it wasn't anything derogatory but he would often hound Fitz about it. Sean in commemoration of a character in 'Dumb and Dumber' was called Sea Bass, although we bastardized it to C. Bass and therefore named him Carl Bass.

They returned despondent. Judy Garland's house wasn't open, bizarre as it was a Saturday, so Fitz teased Rob further going into detail how wonderful the place was and how he felt his time in Grand Rapids had been so fulfilling because of the trip there. Rob swallowed it hook, line and sinker and paddled off as he'd paddled in, under a self-generated cloud. We'd also told them of how they would be introduced from now on. Sean wasn't impressed. He didn't like his. It wasn't the fact that he was being named after a homicidal homosexual, it was because he didn't like to be introduced as Carl, which when you look at it, was a fair one.

Our parting shot to Grand Rapids was sticking 'I've met the Marines' stickers all over the statue of the local paper industry founder. We gave him a pat on the shoulder and bid farewell to this town of exceptionally friendly people but shit singers.

'I decided not to park there.'

~ Carl Showalter, Fargo

'Fargo' is one of my favourite films. It is set in and around Brainerd, our next stop. Anyone who has seen the film would suppose it is a rather depressing place to live, yet we drove towards it with high hopes.

Hunting down the Chamber of Commerce - a strange white castellated tower that doubled up as a water tower, we found it closed. In our desperation we decided that a nearby *Burger King* would be the best substitute. It was. A smiling assistant was immensely knowledgeable, so knowledgeable, in fact, that his gregarious helpfulness was tempered by the warning that Brainerd was only second bottom to Statesville Penitentiary in the league table of great nightlife.

It didn't bode well. As we headed to the police station to find a safe parking spot, we were; to say the least, worried to be wasting a Saturday night here. Yet as cheerfulness over adversity is a quality ingrained in Royal Marines, we saw optimism even when surrounded by police asphalt and mullets. After a lengthy talk to a more than helpful Sheriff, we were in better sorts, and heeding his advice headed to the 'Blue Ox'.

It was like stepping into a scene from the film 'Roadhouse'. I can only imagine the Sherriff recommending it as a place to start a fight. Ill-lit wall-to-wall bikers strutted their beards to another painfully loud rock band, while the heavily tattooed barmaid shoved bottles into the grizzled hands of heavily tattooed customers. It was interesting to observe the dance floor where a group of four girls danced around not handbags but their bottles of Budweiser - these girls were obviously wise to bootneck minesweeping.

The band were having a rest so patrons danced to more placid tunes of George Michael, then a collection of more upbeat country songs, before the band returned to belt out thrash metal. Throughout these songs, whether a ballad, lilting country jingle or the scream of blood curdling devil worshippers, not once did their dancing change. Not in the slightest. Not in style, in speed, or in rhythm. It was as mono-rhythmic as one could be on a dance floor, as if they were dancing to a tune from an invisible Walkman and not what everyone else could hear.

A girl overhearing our accents asked me to dance. I gracefully declined on the grounds of it being impossible to dance to 'Bohemian Rhapsody' without looking a tit. This theory was proven as she sweated and toiled in all manner of strange erratic movements, concentration etched on her face while trying to co-ordinate the movements of a newly born piglet to the words 'Galileo Galileo'.

As we talked, a young bloke sat next to us, politely interrupting our conversation. He was on his own, which immediately put us on guard. People who drank on their own were either a serial killer, an anorak that were so boring that no-one would go out with them, or federal fire fighters flying around the States to report on potential fire hot spots. Fortunately, he was the latter. We soon struck up a rapport so great that we all decided that this place wasn't exactly for us. His name was Phil and he recommended that we head for 'Tropical Nights', a UK style disco that once inside, felt like a club in a holiday camp complete with plastic palm trees, second rate lighting and lonely singletons in desperate need of botox and a shag.

We did our usual bit, taking the piss out of all and sundry much to the amusement of Phil, until yet another rather sweaty woman asked me to dance. I kindly refused on the grounds that I had a serious case of lumbago, discouraging her enough to find a less discernible quarry.

'Do I look like Rudolph fucking Nureyev?' I asked Fitz, unsure of my tmesis being an accurate middle name.

'Stop wearing tights with a sock down the front then.'

It was a fair point, but what else does one wear when it's too hot for jeans?

A waitress, tickled at my discomfort, took it as an opportunity to get me a drink.

'No I'm not Australian.' I pre-empted.

'I know, we have English students working with us at the hotel where I work during the day,' she said, introducing herself as Trish.

It transpired they were a dozen or so English students on work experience. Being so far from home, a few students were homesick.

'Why don't you come over tomorrow and offer some moral support?'

'Meet a load of lonely female students?' It'd be rude not to.

A rather pyro-centric night ended in a 'Perkins' diner at 4am with Phil offering us a King's feast on his fire department account card. Relenting at his insistence, we treated ourselves to 16oz T-bone steaks, which isn't as good as it sounds at 4:40am, especially with a complimentary side order of pancakes.

Having our body clocks totally out of synch, we didn't arise until 2pm. With steak still weighing us down, trying our new breakfast pancake mix probably wasn't our best idea. Since the start of the trip, pancakes had been thrown at us whether we'd asked for them or not, so it was only reasonable for us to buy some from the supermarket along with an array of sauces: maple, strawberry, and cinnamon in a splendid '3 for 2' offer. Having the culinary skill of the Muppet chef, it wasn't long before the RV was covered in pancake mix, milk, and water. I tried my best, but the end product was completely inedible. Pancakes in the US are far thicker than our paper doily crepes but even the thickest of Perkins' doormats were positively anorexic compared to the cushions I managed to produce in the frying pan. Eating these bloated corpses of dough, was a conundrum of whether to burrow in or just hack it to death with a blunt knife. No matter how much sauce we piled on the leaning pancakes of Brainerd, they still tasted of low grade cardboard. Finally beaten, we heaved three quarters into the bushes to probably choke a gaze of ravenous racoons and renamed it gruel mix, never again to see the light of an open cupboard door unless we needed it for a spoof forfeit.

Bellies still rumbling, we hoped our meeting would at least result in free food. Taking the rough guide written on the back of a paper tissue to Madden's Hotel we got lost twice, ended up at the ends of dirt tracks, and nearly gave it up as a bad job. It was pure coincidence when we saw a small sign directing us to the 'Madden's Resort'. Surely this wasn't it. When Trish said 'hotel' I'd expected a 'Days Inn' type affair located on a gravel patch just off the main road. But as we passed a small private airfield adjacent to the entrance, we realised it was substantially more upmarket than first thought. The driveway cut through an immaculately preserved golf course on the way to a complex of impressive wooden buildings that reeked of opulence. Trying to put on our most English of accents, we entered the imposing Madden Inn passing wealthy middle aged wrinklies smoking cigars the size of their golf bags that some underweight and underpaid hotel porter was struggling to carry behind. As Trish was working until 4pm, we spent an hour orientating ourselves. Minute by minute we realised we had dropped on a motherload of luck. Not ones to look a gift horse in the mouth, we tried to think of a way to spend the next week here while waiting for the paddlers. Wandering around the inn, we peered into a grand wood panelled conference room, an olde worlde bar, a high-tech gymnasium, an inviting indoor pool with adjoining whirlpool, all facilities that we had little need for, but would be nice to use all the same.

***

The air conditioning of the concourse hit him like a jet of dry ice. After seven hours stuck in the hot and sticky Mexican Airports of Cancun and Guadalajara separated by having the privilege of sitting on a Mexicana plane next to a fat man with the world's most active sweat glands, it was a welcome, if not body shocking, relief. It was getting late. The hold up in Guadalajara had meant the plane landing at 10:30pm - not a good time to arrive in a strange city without an intended address.

It'd been an impulse buy getting the ticket in Cancun. He'd spent a week indulging in unspeakable debauchery, but now he'd done it, seen it and got a cheap T-shirt, while trying to take his mind off the permanent shits from endless beers and dodgy tortillas, he'd purchased a ticket from a back street travel agent. With itchy feet and a ravaged ringpiece his thoughts only gathered once seated in departures. The girl in San Francisco he'd been writing to wouldn't know he was coming to visit her. He couldn't notify her, her phone number was back in Belize somewhere in the devastation of his locker. He couldn't even get international enquiries to help him, her address was on the same piece of paper in the same locker in the same country that he wasn't currently in. Shit.

Unperturbed, he looked at the large-scale map of San Francisco and Oakland scanning for the Millbrae area. He at least had remembered Millbrae and that she resided on Tioga Drive. Fortunately, it wasn't too far from the airport so he should arrive there before it got too late. Like a small child confused in a supermarket without the comfort of a mother's hand he looked around for the exits to the City.

Wearing a cheap stained T-Shirt, Guatemalan shorts and flip flops carrying a stretched polythene shopping bulging with semi clean clothes, he felt rather conspicuous. He looked rather gypsy-like but hey, the bag had got him from Belize to here without tearing. It had even withstood the cage of chickens he'd shared a bus seat with between Belize City and Chetumal on the Mexican-Belize border that had seemingly mistook crusty socks for feed and had steadily pecked holes around the rim of the bag. Loyalty was a rare thing indeed and if the bag was a dog, he'd be it's master.

He tightened his grip protectively around the stretched handles and walked into the warm air, smelling the smell unique to each individual country. Spotlights lit up the concourse where taxis left the kerb in quick succession. He waved unnecessarily at the yellow cab that had already stopped.

'Alright mate, Tioga Drive Millbrae, please.' He jumped into the back seat excitedly.

'Hnh?' His mouth was a derelict cemetery of teeth, crooked yellowed pegs that had long since been forgotten.

'Millbrae please.' Of all the cabs, in all the world, he had to walk into this one.

The driver had an East African appearance with a wrinkled face that had weathered too many winds.

'I not understand.'

'What don't you understand, Millbrae or please?'

'Millbrae?'

'It's a place in San Francisco.' Sarcasm, despite being the lowest form, sometimes feels so right.

'Where is it?'

'What, San Francisco?'

'No, Millbrae. We are in San Francisco you not know?' Touché.

He realised that the conversation was quickly spiralling into nonsense. Getting to Millbrae was the priority, so he removed his sarcastic head and inserted a cassette labelled 'how to help fuckwit taxi drivers.'

'So, Millbrae you know it?'

'No, I tell you already, where is it?' The driver gesticulated his hands in desperation.

'You're the taxi driver, I had this stupid notion you may know the way.' The cassette had got stuck.

'I only be here two weeks. I live Ethiopia.'

'Brilliant.' Well at least he'd met an Ethiopian; you don't meet one everyday. Pity it was today, at this hour, in this taxi.

'You got a street map?' He didn't like asking the obvious but with this geezer it might not be as stupid as expected.

'Yes, yes, yes,' he returned. 'Do you think I'm an idiot?'

Over his shoulder, the driver threw him an A-Z guide. As he flicked through, it was more of an H-G past X through to L. It had been so used in the past two weeks that half the pages were torn out and replaced haphazardly with no semblance of order. Finally he found Millbrae, and orientating himself by somehow struggling to hold six pages together with his teeth, feet, knees, and anything else on his body with a double 'ee' in it, dictated to the driver where he should be going. Unfortunately trying to peer through the punch holes while being in a strange town in a strange car with a very strange driver proved too much and within a matter of miles they were completely lost. Pulling into a gas station, a police car stood at the entrance, both officers tucking into chilli dogs.

'I know,' he thought. 'I'm lost, I'll ask a policeman'. He jumped expectantly from the taxi and, carrying jumbled pages of crumpled cartography, walked to the black and white car. A police woman jumped hurriedly from the passenger side and menacingly wielding a baton ordered, 'Step on the sidewalk buddy.'

'I'm a bit lost, could you please tell me how to get to Millbrae?'

She came closer. He looked around to see if he could see a 'wanted' poster displaying a criminal with similar characteristics. 'Get back in the car.

'I only want directions to Millbrae.'

'I don't know. Now I've told you once, get back in the car.' Her robotic orders weren't worth replying to. It was obvious that she was in the remedial 'community policing' class and he really couldn't see why he should help her raise her grades. What sort of place was this anyway, where taxi drivers and the police didn't know how to navigate around their city? At this moment he wished he was back in Cancun.

Once they finally found Millbrae, Tioga Drive was, in fact, pretty easy to locate. He couldn't remember the number but it had an 8 and a 5 in it. No problem, it could only be 58 or 85, Tioga Drive couldn't be that long being a 'Drive'. His Aunt Lil lived in Arncliffe Drive in Ferrybridge and the numbers there only went up to about 120.

They turned up the hill and through the orange street lighting he scanned the doorways for numbers… 2034, 2036, 2038. Bollocks, bollocks, bollocks. It certainly wasn't Arncliffe Drive.

He could only laugh at his pathetic predicament that he'd put himself in. He wished now he had her number, her address, and a dollop of sense. He then remembered he'd left his wardrobe door open in his drunken rush to leave for adventure training three weeks before. No doubt when he returned, all that remained would be a half eaten chicken that had been paying rent in his wardrobe for the past six weeks and a 1983 SHOOT! Annual he'd amazingly found at a Benque stall on the Belize-Guatemalan border.

He opted for a house numbered 2085. Knocking on the outer door he waited nervously hoping she'd be happy to see him. Unless she'd aged 56 years and developed a hunchback and memory loss it wasn't her. From behind the mesh she asked defensively who he was. When asked if his friend was there she took it as a prefix to a break-in and hurriedly slammed the door in his face. It was now just short of midnight and to try and find her now was pointless. With his navigationally challenged taxi driver still in tow clicking up the meter, he resigned himself to defeat and the only sensible option available was to find a bed for the night.

A 'Comfort' Inn was conveniently situated only a few blocks away, so without hesitation they pulled into its layby. His body by now was so emphatically tired he could hear the hotel's duvets cooing his name. The layby was obviously next to a large window as the receptionist had clearly seen him coming.

'You have a room just for the night?'

'Only the Honeymooners Suite is available, Sir,' she replied glibly.

It wasn't time to question what romantics would spend their honeymoon in a suburban Comfort Inn. Of more concern were the numerous keys on hooks in reception, indicating that nearly all the occupants were out or the receptionist was telling a big fat porky through her pearly white teeth. Options were low, so he chose the latter and begrudgingly handed over the $85 - two days pay to him. To rub salt into his seeping wounds, the receptionist said, 'we have an early party arriving tomorrow so can you kindly vacate by 8am.'

Wearily he trudged to the elevator doors. He realised he had only 7 hours 54 minutes before he left the room that he hadn't yet occupied, so with a spurt of faltering steam he strode less than smartly to the room. Inside he was impressed with the set up. An enormous TV the size of a box designed to hold a flat pack wardrobe cut into the shape of an enormous TV dominated the corner of the room. He switched it on by the massive on/off knob that could have been made from a small tube of Pritt-Stick carefully stuck into the cardboard. It was the first TV he'd seen in about five months and so watched like a time traveller from 1765 in awe and wonderment at the moving pictures in front of him. Conveniently numbered 69 the remote, easily copied by a six pack of Kit Kat's with the back strengthened by cardboard cut from the base of a frozen pizza, got stuck on the porn channel. Two scantily clad blondes stepped into a jacuzzi to join a rather hairy and naked stud. Feeling a rush of blood to his nether regions he stepped into the bathroom and by coincidence was faced with a similar looking jacuzzi with a bottle of complimentary champagne cooled in a bucket of melted ice.

He could take the advice of his body clock and get his head straight down and therefore take no advantage of the amenities available, or he could position the TV so that he could lay in the Jacuzzi, watch porn on the bathroom mirror and drink complimentary champagne until his genitals blistered. Sometimes, decisions in life are rather easy.

***

If you hadn't guessed already the 'him' in this short story was me. It was just to illustrate my only ever brush with American opulence and now in Madden's I was surrounded by such splendour that we felt like Princes William and Harry, but I had to be the ginger one.

Outside we admired the view across Gull Lake, a shimmering glass surface cut by the zip of speedboats and the ungainly grace of pedaloes. An island stood quietly in the middle, looking wild and untamed; a couple of wooden jetties sticking out into the lake the only reminder that it had ever seen man. We took a walk along the adjacent beach and lay on the sun loungers devising a way to stay here without forking out a penny. The water lapped against the sand in wavelets made by the passing craft and lulled us into a restful contentment that was broken by a jet skier beaching his machine with a gravel skid 10 feet away. We'd have to learn to do that before the week's end.

Trish greeted us warmly and introduced us to two English girls wearing kitsch French maid outfits. We thought we'd better err on the side of caution, so asked Trish to seek the manager's permission for us to park our RV in the car park for the week - ignoring the golden bootneck rule of never asking an unnecessary question such as, 'Do we have to wear helmets?'

Trish sounded quite encouraging as we gave her our promotional literature saying that it would be good PR for the hotel if we stayed, so we were slightly miffed and mystified as to why the duty manager said no. With our penchant for ignoring the rules of management, we were determined to stay but didn't want to compromise Trish by parking our RV next to the staff accommodation. To try to look as inconspicuous as possible, we camouflaged our dazzling white 27ft RV in amongst other family size automobiles - right outside the manager's window. I attempted false bravado in front of the girls, saying, 'If he's got a problem he knows where to find us.' However, reality told us that we could have done with being in another car park out of the way.

That night, we met the twelve students all here for three months work placement as part of their BA (Hons) Hospitality and Tourism Management syllabus. As a teenager who'd never furthered their education to college/university level, I'd lazily stereotyped students as gothic layabouts that pissed up in bars serving diluted beers, induced all manner of substances from dope to Jif, from E to anchovy paste, then emerged from four years dossing straight into overpaid jobs where for the first five years of their careers they would be resented by anyone who'd been in the company more than three months, before realising that they'd have to do a day's work if they were to get that executive job that Uncle David had promised them over a lunch in the director's box of some shitty rugby club. But my attitude had changed somewhat over the years, probably as I was now one of them, labelling myself as an 'immature' student of English. With no financial incentive but a big tick on their CV as reward for their graft, these guys played hard in between working their tits off for a hard bed and breakfast scraps. As we talked, characters emerged, trying to pull fast ones over a management stratum that continually hung the sword of Damocles over their heads, threatening course failure should they empty the slops bin in an unprofessional manner.

Fitz and I seemed to be a novelty and they were rather pleased to meet some fellow countrymen in this backwater. A minority of the girls hated Brainerd, the resort, the USA and anything with more than two syllables. But the majority exuded positivity and had accepted the Americans into their bosom, so it was natural to try and stick with these guys. Trish admitted she hadn't yet understood the British use of irony and sarcasm so she sat laughing on cue with a slight perplexion when anyone quipped a line that brought a chorus of chuckling, and looked horrified as Fitz and I laid into each other, not realising the words 'wanker', 'cock sucker' and 'bell end' could be thrown with tongue firmly in cheek.

Our necessity to stay was strengthened even more as we awoke the next morning to a knock on the door. Fearing it was the management bringing along a troop of suited heavies to evict us from our prime spot we gingerly rose. Fitz peered from within the folds of the blinds to see three of the students carrying an array of fruit and pastries. To be in the company of such fine female forms was a pleasure in itself but to be waited upon hand and foot by the same was, well, it would take more than a troop of heavies to shift us now. Even if we got an emergency call from the lads on the river I imagine we'd have had to finish our grapes and manicure before being hauled to our feet from the chaise long by some mistress swathed in satin. They'd even proffered some guest passes to give us a free reign of the resort's amenities. Politely we accepted. After our free breakfast we took a guided tour around the resort noting all facilities that would take up our time and, more importantly, had a fee that we wouldn't have to pay. I'm sure if there had been a crochet workshop charging $40 we'd have attended just because we could get it for nothing. To our horror we were told the complimentary guest passes were not valid to be used on 'The Classic' a golf course used on the PGA circuit and the premier course in Minnesota. Before going to bend the resort manager's ear to give him a good old British tongue wagging, we remembered we were squatting illegally in his car park, eating gratis food and generally kicking the arse out of his unbeknown hospitality.

Instead of wasting our time, we set up a daily schedule:

9:30am: Wake to English students dressed in French maid's outfits bearing gifts of fruit, pastries and bacon.

10:00am: Swim to unwind, before partaking in casual conversation around the pool with attractive people steering clear of those who seemed working class.

Noon: Leisurely staff discounted lunch of pizza pie.

1:30pm: Into plus fours (or cut off jeans), polo shirt (or scabby t-shirt) and flat cap (or silly hat) to play a one-sided game of golf on the social 9 assisted by educated caddies whose knowledge doesn't extend to understanding the bootneck word 'hoofing'.

4:00pm: Tea and tiffin in the RV before an early afternoon pedalo session around Gull Lake to soak up the waning sunrays.

5:45pm: Sundowners of Gin &Tonic, and comms check with the paddlers.

6:00pm: Sit around the periphery of the nightly barbecues, talking over loudly, so British accent lovers would invite us to share their delicious meals.

8:00pm: Shit, shower, and shave and frequent the local bars to find fault in everyone, including ourselves, but especially men who's arses seemed too high for their underwear.

O/C: Retire to our beds, content in the fact that we'd yet again found happiness from A-list scrounging.

We justified our rather ostentatious routine by convincing ourselves that Madden's was an ideal control point to co-ordinate the expedition. The paddlers knew of our location so moving to an alternative site would only confuse matters…

I decided our scheduled sunset radio conversations would omit where *exactly* we were and what *exactly* we were doing. They hadn't seen a soul in two days and conversation between them had nearly all but dried up, unlike their blisters. I suppose there is only so much you can talk about with nothing to stimulate you other than scenery that, after a while, no matter how spectacular or beautiful, can become repetitive. I sympathised with Rob so, careful not to spill my melting ice cream, told him to keep his chin up as we'd surprise them on their arrival.

We dragged ourselves away from the pool for a couple of hours every day to liaise with the local community to promote our venture. The local US Marine Corps Recruitment Officer, a more than helpful chap called Staff Sergeant Michael Jones, managed to jack up an impromptu radio appearance as he had scheduled personal advertisements for the USMC.

Upon arrival, the radio station kindly informed us that we would be doing a full blown twenty minute interview.

'What, now?'

'Oh ya,' smiled the producer.

Not having the benefit of any media training we set about our task like any bootnecks in our situation would - by cuffing it.

The radio station was called 1380 KLIZ 'the Power Loon', a local station with a Loon as its symbol, a heron type bird that indeed looked like a lunatic. This station had a 'Power Loon' a mythical bird holding magical powers to broadcast classic rock to northern Minnesota. Inhabitants of the area scared to question such a beast's musical taste, as incurring its wrath would only lead to it playing nonstop Toto medleys.

The DJ herself was amiable and welcomed us with a sprightly handshake before putting us into position, introducing us to the unseeing audience.

Any talk show host or interviewer worth his or her salt should know that a fundamental part of questioning is to actually ask questions. Her one question was, 'So tell us about Mississippi Madness expedition.'

From then on she just smiled like a simpleton, nodded and repeated active listening prompts like 'Ya,' 'aha,' 'interesting,' 'really,' 'really?' without actually ever asking anything.

It started slowly, me trying to explain the reasoning behind the expedition, attempting to nurture improvised stories to make it interesting. Fitz would occasionally put his oar in and correct me but after my initial fumbling I switched onto chat show autopilot. I was going blue but I didn't care, breathing could wait. I had things to say and lots of it, no life necessitating action was going to quell my moment of glory. The interviewer was getting scared, she saw the devil in my eyes cranking a lever that was winding up my jaw muscles. My molars were pulling seven g's from the speed of the lift of my jowls. Sweat poured from my brow as my cardiac rate heightened to a speed comparable with taking an E and amphetamine cocktail to quench the thirst of an extreme aerobics workout. Unfortunately, it all had to end, but it was going to be on my terms. There wasn't a chance of her cutting across to the newsroom before I was finished, so cutting her off repeatedly I received the old 'cut' signal from not only her, but also the producer in the adjoining room. Finally with the importance of 'breaking news' I was democratically booted off the air 26 minutes after first inhaling. The interviewer looked relieved as the newsreader started a headline about some farmer that had lost his arm in a bailing machine, the 3rd to do so that week.

We felt good, our first brush with the media had gone better than planned, even Staff Sergeant Michael Jones, (he pronounced his rank every time as if he'd been born with it) admitted we were naturals. So it was with great expectations that we depressed the play button on our tape deck to listen to the recording of the interview. After 30 seconds we had to turn it off.

My teeth nearly shattered from cringing harder than I'd ever cringed before. We pressed the button again, and again had to turn it off after a minute or so. We could only listen in short shifts. We now knew how a film star would feel looking back on his first screen appearance playing a saxophone in a chicken outfit.

We were bad. It was evident that I'd kept cutting off the interviewer mid sentence. She'd actually tried to ask questions but it was I who just ranted on regardless in a torrent of verbal diarrhoea. 'Canoeing in a klepper is errm harder than doing it in a errm modern equivalent.'

'Really?' she had at least managed to crowbar a one word interjection.

'You could errm drive from New York to LA in your car, but errm the equivalent for the paddlers would be errm riding on a unicycle errm wearing roller-blades.'

We wept with embarrassed laughter in the cab. I was just a total tit. Fitz, on the off chance he got a word in, sounded camper than a row of tents.

We nearly threw out the tape but decided to keep it for posterity with the promise that it would never be played in a public domain unless we wanted to embarrass our kids.

Thankful that we'd kept our anonymity we found the only way to forget the past hour was to partake in some free water skiing - for free with our Madden's guest passes.

As it happened, the interview, for some strange reason, had been a bit of a success. It wasn't long before we received a phone call from the other local radio station. They'd heard our interview in their ongoing attempt at industrial espionage, and invited us to give a more up to the minute update for their listeners. Learning from our past endeavours, I asked Fitz to take the lead, as I didn't want to take up the rest of the day. However, this DJ was considerably better. He'd obviously undergone formal radio host training from a reputable radio host university - enrolling from a spam email list headed 'Bang Her With Your Love Truncheon'.

Not wanting a repeat of our last interview he prevented me going onto Duracell mode by frequently asking questions to each of us that could only be answered in short sharp bursts. It was a far better interview, so we were fairly disappointed when no recording had been made. Now no one would know that I could stop talking for more than three seconds.

A timely interview with the local paper and a photo feature on the arrival of the paddlers, our PR for Brainerd would make the week complete. To give Brainerd a chance we took a few hours in between strutting around like media whores to see what the town had to offer instead of lazing by the pool, playing golf and wrinkling in thrush-infested jacuzzis.

The town's attraction was its locality. Like most towns in the area amidst the forests, lakes, and wildlife, it was the natural beauty that brought families from afar to wonder at the abundance of natural treasures. Brainerd itself didn't really do itself credit. Typical as flat pack town, the area was dissected by a highway lined with gas stations, fast food takeaways, and mini-malls. Streets and avenues cross hatched the tree lined suburbs, a separate business district that wasn't exactly Wall Street, a couple of parks, named in memory of some long dead hero, and a high school that boasted stadia only equalled in the UK by professional sports teams completed this cloned town.

Unique to Brainerd was the Paul Bunyan Amusement Center that just seemed to be an excuse for fat kids to bounce like pin balls of lard between hot dog stands, burger stalls, ice cream parlours and cotton candy sellers. Disappointed at not witnessing a teenage coronary, we looked for other sources of amusement to fill our day.

Brainerd sported its own International Raceway - motor racing circuit to you and I - that immediately brought a flicker of excitement to Fitz's eyes. Unfortunately we visited just as a meet had ended, so Fitz had to settle with looking forlornly at the departing convoy of trucks painted in metallic ego, featuring the occasional lightning or skull and cross bones or scantily clad lady on some petrol head's cab.

The day of the paddlers' arrival at Kiwanis Park went smoothly. A reporter took a couple of snaps and interviewed Sean and Rob, amazed that they had arrived exactly to the minute we had said - not realising they'd stopped short to await her arrival.

After Fitz and I secured their Klepper in another friendly neighbourhood, we set off, Rob especially eager to discover what surprise that we had in store.

He then noticed. 'What you done to your hand?'

We were on a kayaking expedition. Rob and Sean had just completed the tremendous feat of paddling 347 miles in twelve days. They had struggled along reed bedded streams, skirmished through mosquito-infested swamps; shot precariously over deadly dams before toiling across life-taking lakes. They had laboured around impenetrable beaver dams trying not to run aground or get sliced open by the sharpness of submerged branches, slept on ant nests, next to hornet nests and eaten their dried rations in the company of venomous snakes. They had whetted their parched lips only occasionally to prevent running out of water and battled on through 100% humidity and shadeless sun to finally reach us unscathed and fighting fit.

I, on the other hand, having tried to get too much lift on a 7 iron on the 7th hole on the social 9 had subsequently pulled a ligament in my hand. It hurt like a bastard. I felt thoroughly ashamed.

So, after calling me a soft twat, they wanted to know where I'd been playing golf.

'All good things come to those who wait.'

We turned the corner past the private airfield and into Madden's. The lads' eyes lit up as we cruised through the shade of pine and splendour. It was similar to the feeling of watching children watch the postman walk up the driveway on their birthday.

Too tired to really make the most of the facilities, they were more than happy with the basic necessities of a steaming hot shower and wholesome food that hadn't begun as tasteless dehydrated granules in a bag before being mixed with boiling water, expanding into tasteless moist granules in a bag.

After a few hours kip, they managed to summon up the energy to get out for a beer. We took them to the 'Blue Ox' so Sean could get his fill of rock music, before heading off to 'Tropical Nights' where we could get cheap drinks courtesy of Trish and ogle dancing cellulite.

Resting in the grandeur of Madden's did Sean and Rob the world of good. They were fresh, rested, and were raring to take on another 2000 miles. In the mood they were in, it wouldn't take them long. It was Sunday morning and a breakfast at Perkins was on the agenda.

In the US, eating out for Sunday breakfast is an institution. The whole family, Gramma and Grandpa included, get in their station wagon and drive down to the local diner to feast on eggs, bacon, pancakes, and syrup all on one plate. I couldn't fathom how it was accepted to pile all your hot savouries and cold sweets onto a single piece of crockery. In the UK such a combination is commonly called 'swill' and no matter how many times I witnessed it I couldn't prevent myself from asking for pancakes on a separate plate that would bring curious looks from gum chewing waitresses.

A queue swirled outside the building and over countless Sundays this same line of hungry diners had worn a bald patch a foot wide along the carpet from the doorway to the maitre d's lectern. Despite its length and the hive of activity in the restaurant it shortened surprisingly quickly. Our mouths watered at the smell of 1000 breakfasts, and it made it doubly annoying as Fitz and I, because we were so skint, settled with the pancakes that were Trish's side order.

We browsed through the Brainerd Daily Dispatch Sunday edition and found a smaller article than we'd hoped for with an under exposed photograph of Sean and Rob pulling into a bank. At least it was our first bit of exposure. Now wiser to these sort of things we would, in future, seek verbose journalists who knew about shutter speeds and aperture settings.

Everyone full of swill apart from Fitz and I who were hankering for lunch, we returned to Kiwanis Park. A couple of the girls from Madden's came down to video Rob and Sean and to wish them luck. More pre-embarkation administration followed, before the paddlers left. The next time we'd see them would be the city of Minneapolis.

There seemed to be no reason to leave with them. We were in radio contact for reporting lines, we all had charts. We knew where they were, and they knew we'd been invited to a barbecue. We'd also volunteered to give one English student's visiting boyfriend a lift back to Minneapolis on the Tuesday morning.

This may seem an awful generalisation, but for some reason, many American men find it hard to consume the weakest of alcohol without becoming total bell ends. So it was with no great surprise that after the aforementioned barbecue, a few of these under age drinkers decided it would be hilarious to smash bottles around the car park of which we were the only occupants. The morning light showed us that fortunately they hadn't damaged the vehicle but had brought us to the attention of security. All fingers pointed to us, which naturally got my back up. Fitz, a more placid character, defused the situation but the outcome was the same. We were being forcibly kicked off the resort. Not wanting to drag the girls who'd illegally smuggled us here into the unpleasantness, we begrudgingly agreed to leave, hoping our tyres would negotiate a safe passage out.

Realising what a good thing we'd had, we returned to the Sheriff's car park and sulked all day in the heat and humidity of the un-air-conditioned RV. It would have been preferable to continue on, but had promised that geezer a lift the next day and couldn't let him down.

A phone call from Trish cheered us up. Wanting to give us a proper send off, she'd organised a free room but as thanks wanted to tape our music as she'd now become a real Anglo music fan.

While she taped, she told us about her life. We were shocked how naïve a 21-year-old could be, as she was reviled with shock when Fitz and I both admitted to having had a one-night stand - not with each other may I add. God knows what she would have done if we'd reminisced about our experiences at that age - watching helplessly as victims of genocide watched each other die, drinking fermented diesel in the Central American jungle, getting punched after trying to insert a 500 baht note into the grisly false vagina of a Bangkok ladyboy nicknamed 'John', or just living in 40 Commando's grots that were havens for naked cider parties and vomit stains.

Trish showed us her library of photos. It was going to be a long night. I looked through her graduation album, a keepsake to remind all Americans just how stupid they looked with inch thick train-track braces. All her classmates each had a pen picture with a short profile and a moment that they considered being the highlight of their year. Jocks boasted of winning certain football games, and most girls seemed to find a wet 'n' wild fund raising day the most memorable. All these paled in comparison to my favourite, one boy had felt that 'getting new spectacles to read an interesting book while on a train journey' had been the highlight of his year. I commended him on his dry sense of humour. Trish was adamant he was serious. I then felt slightly sad for him.

We felt humbled by the crowd that turned up at the pizza parlour to say goodbye. We'd only been there a week but our presence seemed to have had a positive effect, probably as neither of us had tried it on with the many gorgeous girls amongst them. I had a partner, Fitz was just rats.

Before sleeping in our free deluxe room, we made sure we had a trampoline contest on the expensive bed. I narrowly won, executing a daredevil back somersault with half twist landing half on the bed and half on the emptied mini bar. The guests below must have thought they were below the honeymooner's suite.

Promising to keep in touch, which invariably means never keeping in touch, we gave them all signed photos of the team, not because they asked, or that we were pretentious pricks, but because, as yet, we'd only managed to shift 4 of the 500 we held.

We'd enjoyed their company and thanked them for their hospitality, especially Trish, despite her insistence that the bifocal trainspotter was serious about reading a nice book.

'I'm not interested in a huge audience because it brings headaches'

~ Nick Lowe, music producer

Our journey down Highway 10 was far more interesting now we'd taken up the most interesting game a number plate spotter could think of. With each US State having its own unique licence plate showing where it originates, our challenge was to spot a plate from every State. A fellow spotter told us it would be nigh on impossible to see one from Alaska or Hawaii plate due to location, or from Rhode Island due to its size, plus the people were all flat heads who thought they needed passports to cross a State line. This naysaying only made our quest even more attractive - and geeky.

There was no way we could now finish the trip without seeing all 50 State plates even if it lowered us to the level of the local anorak. Highway 10 was a spotter's delight, as we picked off number plates at will, Minnesota obviously, Wisconsin and Iowa were plentiful as neighbouring States. The Dakotas were everywhere as well as Missouri and Illinois, two States we were to travel through. The bloke who we were taking to Minneapolis must have been sat in the back thinking we were the Sad brothers watching 'Love Story' in Sadsville. Nevertheless, it kept us happy as we got sucked onto I94 into the city.

Big City = Big trouble, so after dropping off our bored passenger we followed Staff Sergeant Michael Jones's directions to the nearest USMC establishment to get local advice on where to stay.

Minneapolis had a sizeable USMC detachment, in this case a police detachment. This didn't bode well. Military police are renowned for being no-mates with chips (or in this case fries) on their shoulders. Going through main gate security we must have looked a pair of utter morons jumping up and down with euphoria in the cab the barracks as we noticed an Alaskan plate.

Our cautious entrance was needless. As soon as we introduced ourselves, expedition paraphernalia at hand like muscle bound Jehovah's Witnesses; a bespectacled man, dressed sharp as a pin, warmly welcomed us. He introduced himself as Captain Jim Zagrzebski, the officer commanding the detachment.

Before giving us the free reign of the barracks and a hook up to the RV, he warned us of the pitfalls of wandering around Minneapolis city centre.

Minneapolis and its Siamese twin Saint Paul are known aptly as the Twin Cities. Minneapolis' population neared 400,000 making it similar to Leeds and its relationship with Bradford. High skylines give US cities a bigger feel, and Minneapolis, like many cities was just the central part of a metropolis, making the 400,000 inhabitants just a fraction of the urban sprawl within Hennepin County. The county administered the seat of Minneapolis plus 45 other municipalities making the population a total of 1,100,000. Virtually every highway displayed signposts indicating you were entering yet another city limit. Jim suggested we take it easy the first night and go to the nearby Mall of America in Bloomington. Thanking him, we made use of their gym and did repetitions of press ups, pull ups, sit ups and Jim's surname.

From the outside, the Mall of America didn't look particularly impressive. Thinking back to the super malls that were sprouting up around the UK, all seemed to be sprawling affairs with a glass edifice as the hub of shopping annexes - architecturally similar to Victorian prisons where convicts of consumerisms voluntarily incarcerated themselves into unmanageable debt. This just looked like a massive concrete warehouse. Once inside, we became immediately lost. It suddenly became the size of Renfrewshire and I half expected to cross paths with a Sherpa and his yak. It is the mother of all malls, but unlike mothers, it wouldn't shrink with age. Looking at the store map it had more symbols than the O/S map sheet of Greater London. One third larger than anything in Europe, the central atrium holds a fun fair, complete with a roller coaster, on par with any theme park. It is rather surreal peering through a third storey shop window reflecting a car whizzing by at 70 mph. With a few boxes of plaster of Paris you could sculpt 258 full sized Statues of Liberty to fit inside. If you were a true masochist and browsed for ten minutes in each shop it would take three and a half days before leaving. People actually go on vacation here. To accommodate such shopaholics, there are over 7000 nearby hotel rooms. I doubted my wife would be overly excited should I cancel the forthcoming Orlando holiday in favour of the local Arndale Centre and I'm not sure the folks back home would be as impressed with a postcard that read:

'Had a lovely morning walking around Marks & Sparks, the sights in Poundland are amazing! Storage boxes cheaper than home! Kids loved riding on the escalator and spinning in the revolving doors. Wish you were here xxx'

It somewhat curtailed my hunter gatherer approach to shopping, instead adopting the alien concept of 'browsing' that I surprisingly enjoyed citing my new surroundings as a commercial landscape to appreciate. We wandered aimlessly with local gang members who came here for their down time away from drive-by shootings, car-jackings, and drug dealing; after all, the carriage of guns and the wearing of bullet proof vests were strictly prohibited while browsing tat. Security was high profile, violent crime virtually obsolete. After my brush with death way back in 1990, I found comfort amongst relaxed consumers whose only threatening behaviour would be during a sale.

The top level looked like any entertainment plaza in Europe, just without the smell of stale piss. Bars and clubs lined the way, so it took little navigational skill to fall into a bar I think was called 'Club Pretentious'. We promised an early return to the USMC base as it was absolutely vital that the following morning's drive required clear heads that could decipher WWII code if we were to avoid entering some run down ghetto and attracting unwanted attention in a vehicle worth more than the average home. We left at 4am with Fitz's teeth fearing dissolution due to a surfeit of soda, and I fed up of hearing about upcoming promotions.

'You're not allowed to park here,' said a security guard as we opened the RV doors. In his hand he held a pad of yellow carbon paper. His intent was clear.

With sobriety brings enterprise. 'Hexi bloc?' Fitz said to me.

'Wi cana rappa titzin,' I replied.

Fitz turned to the security guard and slowly said, 'Sorry... I is bad English, holiday now. We is Luxembourg gays.'

The security guard eyed us up. His knowledge of Luxembourg and homosexuality, we hoped, was poor.

'I... am... writing... you... a traffic... violation... citation,' he said, as if saying traffic violation citation - the grandest ever name for a parking ticket - could be made more understandable by latent phonetics.

'Megawaz wet' laughed Fitz, offering a hand to shake.

The guard ignored it. 'You have any ID?'

Fitz again laughed, and got into the cab. I followed.

The guard instructed us to wait.

'Thanking please!' Fitz said, winding down the window. Like a latter day Thelma and Louise we sped off, not over a cliff, just a speed bump, regaling in our gay Luxembourgian criminality.

After another breakfast gratis, we took off with a downtown map to hand and confidently headed towards the seven prominent skyscrapers that dominate the skyline of Minneapolis. Our previous attempts at contacting the Minneapolis Rowing club had been unsuccessful over the phone, so we thought a personal visit would verify our intentions. Being a large city with an even bigger river it made sense that the Minneapolis Rowing Club would be a well-heeled circle. Hopefully full of pro-military toffs that had spent a time at Annapolis or West Point Academies, they would be more than happy to take in a quartet of commandos for the week donating food, beer, and comfort in the process.

In my world, to tell people that I am a commando is quite embarrassing. I know not of any mate in the same situation confessing their true profession unless, of course, it was to court favour with a policeman after some routine law infringement. To tell people in the UK that you are a commando is to me, and many others I know, a hanging offence. Macho ego trips are not my forte and I'd much rather tell people that I gouged out cats eyes for the roads or that I sold Stanna stairlifts in Belgian bungalows. It is the usual that wherever Royal Marines go, their occupation is anything other than what it actually is. In the towns where marines are based, the women are wise to our guile, although when away on trips, a gullible prey can be found.

I 'trapped' a girl on the pretence that I was a dolphin trainer - an old classic that never withers with age. Sceptical at first, she was won over after I'd explained that my recently acquired suntan was from a fortnight's exchange with Sea World in San Diego to pass my final dolphin training exams. The last module of the 'Diploma in Dolphin Studies' was the riding phase, and it was the part that had the highest failure rate. She was surprised to learn that young dolphins had to be broken in, in a similar fashion to horses. A neoprene saddle would be worn on the animal for a while to let it get used to the feel of weight on its back, and a bit placed in its mouth. Once settled, a rider would then ride the dolphin, usually rodeo style with the frightened dolphin bucking its body up and out of the water in sheer panic. Having no control as yet, the rider would wear breathing apparatus as the dolphin often finds tranquillity in deep water. Only because of this method, cruel as it looked, could the dolphin learn to have humans on its back. An inexperienced rider and trainer would then have to pass numerous practical exams. This would include riding a saddled dolphin in waterborne three-day eventing. This consisted of show jumping, where the rider and dolphin would have to negotiate a series of hoops and fences both below and above the water line. Aquatic dressage required finesse, control and style before the third discipline - the infamous 'Cross-Water', an endurance event of four nautical miles across open water. The animal and rider would have to jump, leap, dive over, through and under natural and man-made obstacles including the dreaded 'land jump' where fearful dolphins could stop dead on the land or simply refuse to jump, throwing their mount with hilarious consequences. Only after successful completion of the three-day event could he then progress onto attempting to ride without a saddle. These were the final riding exams that gave the applicant a license to ride any dolphin anywhere in the world, excluding China as they didn't conform to the rules set by the International Dolphin Federation. These were the exams I'd just passed and now I was just about to depart for a season to ride Blackpool's famous comedy dolphins 'Flippy and Floppy'. She admitted having never heard of this pair of underwater tricksters but was suitably impressed to take me back to her flat for 'coffee' - which has to be the worse aperitif to sex ever. Coffee breath? No thanks.

So it often paid not to say your true occupation, unless of course you *are* a dolphin trainer or you are in the US where their pro-military stance was in stark contrast to the British society of the 90's. Here in the US we obviously had to say we were Royal Marines as it was a charity expedition approved by the Royal Marines. But if we added the word commando, however much we may cringe, it could get us that little extra which could be the difference between a rump and a rib-eye steak.

Our expectations were high as we drove downtown. We were ready to use the 'C' word to any Harvard gimp that was straightening his cravat while ordering some under class to hurry up finish waxing his oars in the boathouse. However, the boathouse was extremely difficult to find. It was signified on the Minnesota DNR River Charts as an approved boat landing, but its geological topography gave nothing in the way of urban pointers. This made it rather hard to correlate with the downtown street map that had somehow negated to show the Rowing Club's position. We knew we were near, as rowing is usually the pastime of the rich and the houses in the area were large and expensive. Double, triple and quadruple fronted mansions hid behind thick conifer along impeccably maintained roads. Designer clad joggers plodded under the shade of trees away from the early morning sidewalk heat. We pulled the RV over to park adjacent to an MRC sign and took off on foot down the steep lane to find the boathouse. The lane was anything but well maintained, a bad feeling crept over us as if we were approaching the execution spot of a slasher movie; weeds overgrew the chain link fencing, seeds had doggedly taken root and forced fissure cracks in the concrete. We turned on the U bend and saw a large wooden building that had seen better days. Could M.R.C. possibly stand for Minneapolis Rat Crèche? Paint peeled from the uprights and the apex of the roof. It was definitely a boathouse; empty boat racks were fixed, rusting to the building wall. The only reference to it currently being used for anything other than a squat was a curled piece of paper notifying any interested parties that the M.R.C was contactable on such-and-such number. Although we were disappointed that we weren't to be pampered by the rich of the city at least we could make contact, the number was the same as the one in my diary. As had happened before there was no answer. We now had a problem. There was nowhere to safely stow the kayak. *Fuck.*

In our planning we had designated spots along the river that could be possible storage points; the rowing club being one of the ones we thought we could guarantee. In the small towns it hadn't been a problem as most were tourist traps they had made provision for boat storage. Here in a large industrial city, overgrown waste ground, steep slopes and large factories hand railed the river - hardly ideal. Finding convenient kayak storage is not as easy as one would think given that Minneapolis was built on the industries of the river.

The mid 19th century brought great wealth for the traders who saw the Mississippi River as the main artery between north and south. It is therefore unsurprising that the river at this point is hardly picturesque. It did indeed remind me somewhat of home and the rundown industries banking along the flowing sludge that masqueraded as the canals and rivers of urban West Yorkshire. I could see memories of a yesteryear city that once throbbed with the daily grind of a bustling waterway. Today it was still noisy but now it was the background noise of the more road-reliant industries of modern commerce. We successfully managed to get caught up in the morning traffic that carried us away from our destination on a commuter rip tide that was impossible to drive away from. Eventually taking a 13 mile detour we found downtown. Glass fronted office blocks reflecting an identical glass fronted office block gave a strange mirrored feel to the road. We passed under the futuristic skywalks - glass walkways that at five floors above the raging vehicular river connected sixty two blocks of downtown's most profitable organisations. To find your way around downtown Minneapolis prepare yourself with a flask, sandwiches and a bottle of tolerance pills. It isn't exceptionally large, just very compact and busy, which made it all the more confusing. If Washington DC was the city of trees; Minneapolis was the city of confusing one-way streets and swearing. The map I had wasn't exactly small scale - I may as well have used an antique globe drinks cabinet to try and navigate our way round - at least I could have had a wee dram to calm my nerves.

We were in a concrete maze where we found streets that changed name half way down, avenues that ended suddenly, and roads that were shown as having priority on our side yet in reality gave no one priority unless you had balls of steel. Fitz's were distinctly that as we became emboldened in our 27ft monster truck smothered in the maelstrom of swirling traffic that hooted, braked, sped, and honked the wrong way down one way streets diverted due to ongoing roadworks. At the point where we hit our 23rd bollard passing what I'm sure was a sign that said 'Welcome to East Sussex', I put down the map and finished the sandwiches much to the annoyance of Fitz as they were his. Picking the crumbs from my shirt I turned the map the right way round and somehow managed to escape the whirlpool emerging like Indiana Jones from the concrete jungle and with a rush of relief found the lost office of tourist information.

We found the office on the east bank in the Riverplace - a redevelopment of shops and restaurants. A lady with an Irish surname greeted us merrily with a soft Minnesotan lilt. Once we told her of our British military origins her facial expression changed from having a shit-eating grin to pursing her lips so tight she looked like she had a cat's anus for a mouth. Abruptly she passed us onto a confused young helper before scurrying into the back probably to ring up some local Noraid representative to bring some burly males 'of Irish origin' down to the office to stick red hot needles in our eyes. Our apathy for her obvious nationalistic ethics were put aside, yet were more annoyed that she'd passed us on to a young lad that seemed bewildered by his job.

'Are you aware of anywhere we can store a kayak?' We thought this may be a tricky one, I'm sure his training hadn't yet brought up the problem of two foreigners on an expedition wanting to secure stores.

'What's a kayak?'

It was clear it was going to be a drawn out exercise.

'Are there any parks along the river?'

'Umm.'

'Police stations or Fire Stations along the river?'

'Err.' He clearly hadn't reached the part in tourist information office training where he was supposed to help tourists - with information - in an office.

'How do we get to here and here?'

'Well…'

'Why is the butter in the galley so hard?'

'Sorry?'

'What city are we in?' He jumped with excitement at the chance to answer that one but then it was lost on him.

We turned our attention to another guide who'd just finished with an old couple. I couldn't be sure but I think I overheard them asking for help to locate craft fairs and specialist retail outlets for slippers and other soft shoes. The guide, who'd been attending their needs with loud monosyllable words, turned her attention to us and we were impressed that she actually seemed to know her job. She readily helped us, indicating that the Army Corps of Engineers at the Lock & Dam would possibly be able to help us. As it was just over the river we decided to walk, taking the bridge at Central Avenue that looked over to an old stone arch bridge. Ingeniously referred to by the locals as the Old Stone Arch Bridge, it's a city landmark that stands old, stoney, archy and most of all proud amongst the rust and crumbling masonry of the newer structures. We stood where it had all started.

The city grew around St Anthony's Falls, which we were now walking over. For the fur trapper, the soldier and the settler, the river provided the transportation that the new settlement of St Anthony depended on. Named by Father Louis Hennepin, the settlement grew on the east side of the river where the falls powered the mill wheels to grind the flour and powered the saws to cut the lumber. St Anthony, which grew into Minneapolis, soon flourished and became the nation's epicentre for these two industries. To aid the increase in water traffic, both in number and tonnage that the early part of the 20th century witnessed, the US Army Corps of Engineers built a series of twenty lock and dams on the Upper Mississippi to create a series of 'steps'. This meant that vessels could either ascend or descend the 420ft difference in sea level between St Anthony Falls and Granite City 669 miles away in Illinois. These locks are not to be thought of as similar to the hand operated locks of Britain where people on boating holidays safely negotiate their pleasure craft through small pools of water supervised by a Lock Master short on conversation but long on drags of his pipe. The ones on the Mississippi are huge. Lock and Dam Number 1 at St Anthony falls has a chamber that requires an amazing six million gallons of water to fill for each locking procedure. This eight minute transfer of water is equal to about a $1/10^{th}$ of the average daily output of the whole of the City of Minneapolis. Each locking procedure takes around twenty minutes; that is the time for a vessel to enter the lock, fill or empty the chamber, then leave the lock. The vessels that utilise this chamber are no pleasure cruisers either. Although private traffic is allowed through the systems, priority is given to the commercial vessels that still ply the routes. A modern scene of the Mississippi will often encapsulate it wind-

151

ing its way through the landscape with a tow and barge on its water. A barge itself is a floating compartment 195ft long and 35ft wide. They interlock to create an awesome craft pushed by the tug, itself only 65ft long and 18ft wide, but has a strength to size ratio that would put powerlifting champion of the XIII Ant Olympiad to shame. While not the industry of old, these gargantuan craft still dominate the river, necessitating the upgrade of the River lock and dam system to withstand the 150,000,000 tons of traffic that they project will chug its way through by 2015.

Vessels commonly consist of fifteen barges coupled together, making 1000ft pontoons piloted with such skill that they manoeuvred like a rowing boat on a mill pond. Not wanting to look like a covert reconnaissance team of some fundamentalist death squad, we went straight to the visitor's viewing gallery and questioned a man who looked official. Welcomed immediately, within a tick we were in the control room drinking coffee with the Army Corps of Engineers Lock Masters. Amiable with crude banter, Fitz and I at once felt at ease and by the end of our visit had arranged the kayak to be secured in their compound shared with the River Sheriff's boat. Satisfied we had completed that task with aplomb, the newspapers would now be our next port of call. Unfortunately, we yet again got caught in the Minneapolis maelstrom and managed to arrive there nonplussed at having to spend a small fortune to park on a patch of waste ground that because of its locality was someone's license to print money by hand writing a sign saying 'car park' and pretending it was a car park. We were also rather deflated ten minutes later as we left feeling that the relevant journalist wasn't particularly interested in doing a piece about us. Maybe as we weren't a 'if it bleeds it reads' type story, I suggested Fitz punch me on the nose to see if that spiked his interest. Unfortunately he was more interested in a serial killer who had a penchant for killing men called Andrew than a heartwarming feature on two extraordinary lads paddling 'Old Man River for a good cause. He'd even said, 'Don't call me, I'll call you,' as we bid farewell. Hoping his name was Andrew, we returned to the RV. Our timing was, as usual, perfect. The highway madness meant it took us even less time to get lost. Finally, some significant time later, relief washed over us when we saw the required exit to get to the USMC base. It was totally irrelevant that we'd taken the long way round the city's Orbital Highway. Go to Paris from London via Budapest and Delhi and you get the idea.

The paddlers were rather laissez fair at the turn of events. Another extra mile or two the next day was accepted as the new variable of the trip, although a complaint about the security of the kayak, in a fenced police berth in an army compound, did make me exasperate. If only I'd hired a section of Special Agents with the few dollars I had.

At the USMC base they showered and refreshed themselves with proper food. It's amazing what character metamorphosis food and a wash can bring to people recently bereft of such luxuries. Once fed and watered they were ready to take on the world. They both chirpily regaled their last five days on the river. They'd been through some of the most picturesque scenery so far, many others before them had obviously agreed as the riverbanks were interrupted every so often by vast houses, mostly new, all expensive. Some were traditionally clad in wood, others were futuristic - a dome shaped house had caught their eye and the owners were kind enough to allow the paddlers to camp in their garden with the offer of dinner, which was especially generous considering they must have looked like The Wild Man of Borneo and his scruffier brother, Gregory, first thing in the morning.

To the Mall Of America we headed. Fitz and I tried to adopt the pose of informed tour hosts but our disguises were soon rumbled when on entering the Mall, we escorted them straight to the cleaners' rest room. Despite their strenuous activities over the past few days, both Rob and Sean shopped like New Year sales veterans, Sean especially fervid in his window shopping. Nearly anything that had a Stars and Stripes on it, and let's face it that's quite a lot, he would coo as if at a newborn baby. I could see his credit card sweating, knowing it was to be mangled through countless machines. Before he surpassed his credit limit we passed 'Golf Mountain'. Knowing him as the competitive type who couldn't resist a challenge, we dragged him away from financial ruin and into a game. At last, no more looking at ceramic eaglets, water coloured presidential seals and wrapping paper embossed with Maine lighthouses.

Rob decided he needed a bit of time to himself and so declined the challenge in favour of some shopping of his own choice and, as it turned out, a secret haircut which, by definition once seen, cannot be classed as secret.

Being a Friday night, the paddlers decided that a night on the town was in order. Taking our advice not to go and tempt fate by being a clueless drunkard at the mercy of unscrupulous downtown gang members and more frighteningly, taxi drivers; we decided on another night at the Mall Of America.

Having multiple bite wounds from the odd dodgy cabby I tended to shy away from using taxis in the big cities, especially when my knowledge of an area was similar to that of the average American teenager's familiarity of global geography.

Once, when trying to get from the southern end of Central Park to the Jetty for a spotter's tour of the Statue of Liberty, I naïvely put my trust in a taxi driver. Not quite having a local accent I was easy prey to this smiling thief who escorted me past streets that were getting numerically higher. On looking at my 'Stupid Tourist's NYC Guidebook', I realised I was going north - the wrong way. On querying his choice of route he pacified me with the old 'it's a short cut' ploy. Not believing that going north could ever shorten a distance to go south, he eventually lost patience. He pulled over.

'Well buddy, if you wanna get out here you sure can.'

I looked through the window at the rundown, decrepit streets of beggars and drunken layabouts drinking from brown paper bags.

'Where are we?' I asked, my change of tone indicating that I'd just shit my pants.

'These are the bad streets.' He made sure I heard the pronounced *bad*.

Not wanting to waste another dollar on unnecessary waiting or unnecessarily being murdered, I agreed that it would be wise to continue in the comfort of his lovely cab and not by foot as my feet needed a rest anyhow. It went without saying that at the journey's end, after a distance similar to the Paris-Dakar rally, his only tip was never to visit Taunton unless he loved violent retribution. I stormed off to see the statue with a hole in my pocket big enough to pass through a grapefruit with a haematoma.

I digress. Back in Minneapolis, we took to the same clubs that we'd experienced the previous evening.

The night proceeded splendidly. Neck oil flowed aplenty and Rob seemed more at ease than I'd yet seen him. At 2am we stumbled out into the car park, hoping to see our friendly security guard, but only succeeding in inadvertently following a group of women shrieking and screaming. Hearing our accents, they immediately seized the opportunity to introduce themselves. They were on a Batcherlorette party and invited us all for drinks at their room at the Sheraton. We declined the offer, for reasons unbeknown to me, and returned to the admin vortex of the RV.

Within five minutes of entering the infestation of the grime ridden RV that again looked like a Manila council tip; we were outside of the Sheraton, except Sean who had a severe weary on and opted to get his head down amongst the sand and silt of his bed. Getting into the Sheraton without a room in a state of grievous drunkenness should be quite taxing; security in this sort of place is usually quite high. So with a plan best utilising our commando guile, sharpened by the ravages of combat, honed by continual adversity, unhindered by alcoholic toxins, we walked to the rear of the building and straight through an open fire exit. Finding the room we found a party that played Andy Williams to a pair of dancing geriatrics. Checking the door to make sure it didn't notify the corridor of the Minneapolis Rotary Club meeting we entered and were welcomed with a glass of Mountain Dew and a bowl of pretzels. Looking around it was a mixture of the old and the new, the ages ranging from around 14 to around 84. Despite the 70 year age difference within the group it was a happy bunch that feasted on snacks and sodas. Amongst the crowd sat the bride to be. Obvious not because she looked ridiculous in a mock wedding dress covered in condoms, nor was she trying to escape to the toilets with some bronzed Adonis to 'rub his belly better'; but for the fact she was being presented with small gifts from the many around her. She looked as though she should be tucked up in bed with an Enid Blyton novel in large print. Not wanting to upset the apple cart by asking her if it was legal to get married before puberty I sat beside her and wished her well. I was surprised to find she was 19.

'That's quite young isn't it? Your man must be a real catch.'

'Not really,' was her mystifying answer.

'Then why are you getting married?'

'Because I don't want to catch HIV or any other sort of shit like that.'

Was this the saddest indictment of young America? Where a young girl felt compelled into getting married to any old Tom, Dick, or Harry, just to avoid dying slowly from an STD?

Totally bemused I turned my attentions back to the pretzels. At least they didn't confuse things. Seeing Rob chatting to a bearded lady, I looked around for Fitz. Rob answered my quizzical look by informing me that he'd just left with a woman to get some ice. Ten minutes later he returned, with the woman who looked comically flustered; her ruffled dress so tight, she looked like she wore a chef's icing bag.

'Long way to the ice machine is it, Royal?' I asked him.

He smiled knowingly.

Pressing him further to tell me if and where he'd engaged in certain activities, he denied anything had gone on in the vending machine alcove in between the snacks and the cold drinks machine. Only then when the woman sat down did he admit that things had become pretty heated and dirty romance had blossomed in the reflection of a vending machine window. Trying to get more info, I got another drink.

'I wouldn't use that ice if I was you,' he said. 'I had no option but to use it as an improvised hand wash.'

Taking his advice, I looked across to the woman he'd just ejaculated over. She was already fast asleep.

'God, you must have been really good,' I said before offering ice to a grateful old woman sat next to me.

We awoke surprisingly early and stayed the morning in the Mall car park getting the RV into a reasonable state before setting off on foot to collect the first set of photographs. Having been designated expedition photographer, I'd blagged my way onto an intelligence photography course run by Dizzy, an old Naval photographer friend. This course was to equip me with the skills needed to complete a pictorial diary of the trip. However, I couldn't get hold of a similar camera to the one used on the course, so bought a second hand SLR that had definitely seen better days. Without a user manual for the trip, I wasn't at all confident that the film taken so far would get into the final stages of any competition. On collecting them I knew they wouldn't even get into the 1st round of an under 11's photography competition at the local carnival. Out of 24 exposures on the 1st film, six were so out of focus it looked as though I'd taken the pictures through a handkerchief. The iconic photograph of us four stood at the Headwaters next to the Mississippi trunk marker turned out as an odd shaped silhouette and a couple of others looked like it had been 3:30am not 3:30pm. The second film was hardly better, my shot of a bald eagle looked like indiscernible fluff on an unfocussed sky. Needless to say I was highly embarrassed and before showing the pictures tried to play down the excitement of Sean and Rob. Sean had specifically wanted to see the photos from the air in Grand Rapids. I finally plucked up the courage and managed to show him plenty of photographs of a far off river running through far away forests. There was a good shot of Grand Rapids paper mill and an excellent one of the back of the pilot's head. However, the closest I got to capturing the essence of the paddlers' tribulations was a processing blemish that I convinced Sean was a shot of their synchronised blading. Their disappointment was palpable. These photographs were for post-expedition lectures, to forever chronicle our once in a lifetime trip, and for our great grand children to show us on our deathbeds, dribbling into our cocoa to remind us of what we had achieved in our younger days.

I felt terrible. I'd let them down. I tried to look on the bright side and took solace from the fact that some of the photographs had come out OK. Thankfully, the paddlers took the same view and after giving me well-deserved grief they got bored and waited for their own pictures at the while-u-wait counter. Thankfully, their pictures were excellent. What struck me straight away was the difference in our trips. Fitz and I had, amongst the chopped heads, pictures of drinking by the pool. Sean had him drinking coffee out of a metal mug in a mosquito-infested swamp of a campsite. We had photos of us in shorts, sun bathing until we blistered. Rob had pictures of him dressed up to the hilt in nylons and a hat to prevent the insects from eating his brain. It was so clear to see we were on two different expedi-tions; commonality only being our friendship and start point. We wouldn't even be finishing together. Looking through their pictures I had to admit that Rob had taken some great shots, one a fantastic picture of the Bald Eagle that we'd heard so much about especially as it had been taken with a cheapo disposable camera. The downside was that it rekindled the laborious stories of their encounter only now it had the added titbit of how the picture summed up the experience.

In my humility of being a totally useless photographer I took the others' advice and opted to use the SLR in only certain circumstances i.e when my point and shoot camera developed a contagious disease. Just when it seemed Rob would never shut up about his Bald Eagle, heaven sent a message in the guise of a phone call. Obviously it wasn't God congratulating the guys for their excellent progress so far, or to tell Rob he was the best photographer in the team, or indeed to tell me to enrol in a remedial photography course, but a local radio station tipped off by the British Consulate that we were in town. After an initial introduction it turned out that we were to have a live phone interview and who better than Rob to give it. He did make a remarkably good start considering we'd stitched him up and put him straight on the spot. However, his flying start flapped into a bit of a fledgling dive. He went off on a tangent, burbling on about something to do with his hometown Hull and its white phone boxes. He was brought slightly back on track by the interviewer who asked about the canoe.

'For starters, it's not a canoe. It's a kayak.' That told her. 'And it has a lot of stigmata attached to it.'

We all looked at each other totally confused. 'Stigmata?' we mouthed silently before smothering our laughter into cupped hands. In the time we'd been out here not once had we seen blood emerge from any part of the kayak. We had, however, seen sun cream ooze out of Sean's sweating pores, if that counted. We promised to check on our return to the compound whether it had developed a bleeding crown of thorns - or not.

Still giggling we made our way to the house of Lee and Sandy, the couple we'd met at Lake Itasca having earlier arranged to meet the jovial psychopath at his home.

They were certainly in a nice neighbourhood. 'Southfork' was a purpose built community with every convenience at hand for even the laziest, TV addicted, pizza eating couch potato. We pulled up outside Lee's house to a warm welcome. He invited us all in and my first thought was, *Where's the furniture?* The only item that could be considered as such was the patio furniture utilised as a dining room set. Above the plastic table the kids had made a banner welcoming us, which made us all feel quite special. Lee admitted times were hard. They were only living there because Sandy was the estate warden and so got the house rent free.

Despite their obvious poverty, Lee plied us with beer and Sandy made a beef roast that would have Delia drooling. It was without one of the most humbling experiences of my life. This man who looked as though he didn't have two dimes to rub together had offered us his sincere hospitality putting himself out of an already empty pocket. We had earlier slated him for his incessant bullshitting. He was still a habitual storyteller, but his generosity could not be held in question. He offered his phone for us to phone home not taking no for an answer, gave us copious amounts of beer, and a meal fit for a king's wedding reception. While eating, it came to our attention that the family didn't take a thing. All noticing this, we offered for them to join us. Neither Sandy nor Lee would hear of it and forced us to eat more beef, more mashed potato, more fruit salad. I felt grapes piling up in my oesophagus; my sides were coming apart at the seams stretched by an ever-swelling stomach, and ever increasing guilt.

161

After the usual after dinner chit-chat we settled down on the floor with the kids to watch a film. They were so poor they didn't even have cable, which I presumed was a basic right of every American citizen as stated in the Fifth Amendment. Full of good food and embraced within the cossetting of human benevolence, it wasn't long before my eyelids were the weight of lead slates and for me, the film lasted about twelve minutes.

I was woken by one of Lee's brood eyeing me up from about an inch away. Lee was getting ready for a solo crusade to the lakes. We packed our belongings with slightly heavy hearts, we'd miss this weird family and no amount of gratitude would be enough for Lee and his clan that gave so much with so little.

***

Sean, at last, was able to proudly hoist the Welsh flag alongside the White Ensign. Happier now than ever, he and Rob entered the lock chamber with another small pleasure craft together with a commercial paddle steamer that dwarfed them both. Thinking this was possibly dangerous I asked the lock keeper who assured me all was well. He was a quiet, articulate man, bespectacled with the look of an accountant more than a lock keeper. More surprising was the photograph of him and his brother in their Navy SEAL days in his wallet. To top the surprise-o-meter his brother was no less than former professional wrestler and film star Jesse 'The body' Ventura.

Jesse Ventura, for all you not familiar with American shoot-em up blockbusters, was Arnold Schwarzenegger's sidekick in 'Predator'. When told that after a gun battle that he was bleeding, he replied the immortal line, 'I ain't got time to bleed,' while sucking a golf ball of tobacco in his bottom lip - what a man. His brother told us that Jesse was now in politics and had been voted in as Governor of Minnesota to the abject horror of his opposition. So surprising in wider circles; one reporter stated that people in Washington could not be more surprised if Fidel Castro came loping across the Midwestern prairie on the back of a Hippopotamus.

Described as a 'great big honking bullet headed shovel faced mutha who talks in a steroid growl and doesn't stop', Jesse won over the voters with his caustic humour and such statements as 'To put a bullet in the same hole from 25 metres, now that's gun control' and 'If everyone were to go by these old hunting and fishing treaties, why can't they (the Native Americans) go out in birch bark canoes instead of 200 horsepower Yamaha engines and fish finders?

They say a population deserves its leaders…

As the lock water lowered, it became apparent just how vast the basin was. Only by comparing it to a human being could we gauge its size, the paddlers now so tiny and insignificant within the chamber it literally made me swear. They were being swallowed in an ever increasing enclosed compartment yet ever decreasing in size until just as we thought they would disappear, the sluice gates opened and they paddled off along the next stretch of the river, which only happened to be about 200 yards before they had to repeat the process at lock number 2.

Having washed my mouth out we bid our farewells to the lockkeepers thanking them for their hospitality and once again set off to pastures new.

'I know I have an awful lot to learn from the people of Minnesota'

~ Al Franken, comedian

Thinking I'd finally unravelled the spaghetti of the Minneapolis road system I managed to get us lost for one final time, venturing unwittingly through St Paul. Deciding not to stop in Minnesota's capital city, as we needed clean air to breath, we headed over the St Croix River into Wisconsin on I94 towards Eau Claire, a town we'd already passed through on our epic journey to Bemidji.

Not wanting to drift too far away from the river, we turned south, intersecting Highway 35 back into Minnesota at the lads' next anticipated stop in Red Wing. Having planned to meet them in Winona further down river, and because it was a beautiful balmy evening, we decided to press on.

The scenery was as changing as my receding hairline; only far more welcome. Further into Wisconsin, a molehill gets labelled with a spot height but here, as we drove along the river's edge, vertical sand coloured bluffs rose like Neptune and his bodyguards either side of the shimmering water, shading us from the early evening sun.

We seemed to be driving through the middle of a half eaten fossilised Victoria sandwich cake, boulders for crumbs resting at the roadside released from their height after years of precariously clinging to the cliff edge that had been their home for the last 300,000,000 years. Schoolchildren marvelled in their geography lessons at the age of these formations, created by the ebb and rise of ancient oceans.

Formed from torrents of glacial melt water, we were now in the breathtaking Mississippi Valley. This section was locally known as Hiawatha Valley, its many landmarks associated with Native American folklore. The river had widened so far that we saw the other side as a broken horizon. We were passing a stretch of the river that bulged like an egg in the belly of a snake and was here, in 1922, where Ralph W Samuelson invented water-skiing. An early extreme sportsman/screwball he decided it would be fun dragging a man stood on a plank of wood behind a seaplane.

Framed by wood covered bluffs, Lake Pepin was created by a natural dam at the confluence with the Chippewa River. At over 5 miles wide it not only accentuated the river's appearance but also acted as a natural filter, with the pollution accumulated from the cities settling in the 30 miles of the lake, preventing the scum of Minneapolis industry and the effluent of Jesse Ventura's mouth from flowing further downstream.

We stopped at an eatery on the Lake City bypass and took a protracted look at the river. It would be easy to see the river as just another stretch of water and many who lived and worked here probably never even gave it a second glance. But by just sitting and enjoying the view, even from our lousy position behind a totally unnecessarily large bin by the side of the road, its immense beauty offered an aura of calm, yet for those in the not too distant past, the opposite bank of the Mississippi was the New World's limit of exploitation - where we now sat a mysterious land only walked by the natives. It was easy to see why it held back all but the most intrepid explorers.

It was time to continue. If we were to meet the lads in Winona, we felt it wouldn't harm if we stayed a night in a couple of towns in between. But we made the

165

assumption that most people make - that no nearby town was worth stopping for. Unless you are specifically heading for them, it is easy to drive past these lost towns of the USA. The highways bypass their heart, instead sucking you along the road built specifically to house mandatory fast food joints, mini malls, faceless motels, and gas stations before spewing you back out again onto the highway without once really seeing the America of real people. It was a case of déjà vu all along our journey; a recurring nightmare of concrete and neon, deceiving you into thinking the place you were now detouring around would have no character. This modern day road system may help traffic congestion in the towns themselves but over the years create social oxbows, cut off from the outside world, steadily becoming small enclaves of self-sufficient individuality, that ironically give these places their beauty. Winona was such a place, visually encased in an era where Grandpa would wave off the family as they went into town to buy the weekly provisions. On first impression though, we saw ubiquitous uniformity, where an outer cordon of corporate USA retail outlets ensured everyone who passed through felt the urge to buy pet grooming gloves, washable lint remover and battery farm chicken.

Shadows became swallowed by the darkening car park as we pulled into the downtown police station. The night watch was obviously on duty, as it took an eternity for someone to drag their arse away from the TV to answer our intercom message. Puzzled why on earth anyone would want to spend a night in their car park, the couch potato took us to see the duty sergeant. He welcomed us with open arms and couldn't do enough for us. Within fifteen minutes we were hooked up through a cell window and gladly breathing cold air.

Within twenty we were in their changing room reading their pornography and enjoying steaming hot showers typically containing empty shampoo bottles (I knew they were empty as I'd been trying to scrounge some) and used sticking plasters fallen from some wart ridden athlete's foot.

Ensconced within the confines of the RV, checking the local nightlife was becoming our post drive pastime, one that was challenging our meagre budget.

As I didn't think as a 27yr old man I'd have to produce ID, I was refused a drink for the first time since I was 15 trying to act 18 looking 13 when I was kicked out of the 'Precinct' a pre match watering hole for Leeds United fans in the 80's. We took to playing a game that I hadn't played since I was about 9 years old, ironically around the age where I started regularly imbibing home brew beer. Fitz had only played it because his schoolmate made him play it when visiting his house. It was here that we embarked on a slippery path to table football addiction. Known in the US as 'Foosball' for some reason it gripped us. Not satisfied with just a couple of games, the night was a toil of wrist flicks, shoulder twitches, reflex pulls, instinctive pushes, and general foul language, as we became embroiled in a titanic struggle to be crowned the nightly foosball champion. I can't recall who actually won as by the time we'd finished we were mentally exhausted, but I know the next day my wrists felt as though they'd been stamped on by a large man wearing studded diving boots carrying various weighted objects around his person. Fitz felt the same and we looked like a pair of nursing home coffin dodgers spilling cereal all down our fronts struggling to feed ourselves.

With four days and an officious bartender to kill, we set about acquainting ourselves with Winona.

167

Needing to stock up on provisions, we drove to the mall we'd passed on our drive the previous night. Having the luxury of air con all night, upon opening the door, we were hit with temperatures hotter than a bowl of mouse shit chillies and the humidity felt we had walked into the kitchen of Mrs Moist, busy steaming a pudding for the forthcoming pre monsoon jamboree.

Other men we saw wore the tell-tale 'w' under the chest, suggesting moobs were hidden under cheap material. Previously acclimatised to the jungles of Central America and South East Asia, Fitz only having recently returned from the jungles of Brunei, neither of us could remember being mugged so badly by the moist swaddling cloth of humidity. Sweat patches and prickly heat sprung from pores that we didn't know we had, and taking the only option for survival, we ran into the supermarket. Bunkered from the heat, our shop was more leisurely than usual. We couldn't face a walk round town in this heat, so shop hopped between uninteresting chain stores. We even spent two whole hours in a discount superstore, a pastime usually unique to those who seem to think it's OK to show a sunburnt cleft the size of the grand canyon within the confines of an ill-fitting off-white vest and to talk to their unwashed offspring with language that would make a soldier blush. Trying to fill the day exploring aisles displaying a super-cheap range of anything one could buy for no apparent reason was easier than expected and getting carried away we marvelled at the execrable kitchenware. We pondered on whether the chinchilla range, including the impressive pot stand and chic oven hob covers, exuded more class than the 'fowl' range of decorative ceramic wall ducks and a wonderful rug that displayed the regal grandeur of a honking goose through 100% woven polypropylene.

Showing the resistance of special forces operators under interrogation, we steered clear of purchasing the plethora of tacky bargains and purchased a brace of no sweat deckchairs. Once bought, we sweated and toiled back to the RV trying not to melt.

Despite the interesting aesthetics, we couldn't muster the energy to walk into the midday heat of Winona's inviting streets so did what most Britons do when it gets over 18°C. We slept.

Named after the beautiful Sioux Indian Princess Wenonah, daughter of Chief Wah-pah-sha, Winona began as so many other towns along the river did here in Minnesota, in the sawmill and logging days of the 1800's. Some folk say very little has changed downtown, which I could well believe as we strolled in the now bearable heat through the quiet streets lined with buildings dating back to the 1850s. We were headed for the local newspaper office to do our PR bit and got strange looks when we asked an old man, with ear hair as thick as cotton wool, tending his immaculate garden, if we were near the office.

'It's a hell of a way from here,' he pointed, leaning an elbow on his hoe.

'How far you reckon?'

'Well it's about 15 blocks that way. It's close on a mile,' he motioned still pointing a quivering finger.

'Thanks very much,' Fitz replied.

'You guys not got a vehicle?' he shouted from behind his white picket fence.

'Yes, why?'

'You not gonna drive?'

Trying not to sound facetious as he'd been all too helpful, I said 'Normally we would but we need the exercise. Thanks again.'

Whistling through pursed lips with an exaggerated turn of the head he said, 'Well good luck,' as though we were embarking on an Antarctic expedition.

Walking back from the newspaper offices down the shaded sidewalks bordered with manicured grass, we thought ourselves in typical American suburbia - wood panelled houses, grey, white, pinks even yellows gave the buildings a gay character, in the 60's sense of the word. Double-seated swings swayed in the breeze upon the wooden porches littered with blooming flowers. Birds sang heartily just to tell us they were happy here, and it was no surprise. To turn the tables on American tourists, I would describe the place as 'quaint'. Everything was neat to near perfection, everything respected, nothing neglected. This was the sort of place I would choose if I had to live in the US. Before we came out here I'd watched the film 'Grumpy Old Men' with Jack Lemmon and Walther Matthau and I commented to Fitz that it looked just like the place where it was filmed.

To my surprise, I wasn't too far out, as the film was shot in Wabasha, Minnesota's oldest city just up the road. Fitz has never forgiven me for researching that.

Walking along this living postcard we came to the conclusion that it was preferable to stay in small town America. There was plenty to do in Minneapolis but money wasn't exactly flowing like Roman wine. There were too many distractions in such a big place, too much administration to organise across city limits, too much nausea in the choking cloak of buildings. We were algae floating in a savage ocean of people. No one knew us; I don't suppose anyone particularly cared. Not that the people we met weren't friendly, nearly all we had so far met were far from unpleasant. It was just that here in the small towns we didn't feel lost and insignificant.

Also a great insignificance was my bank balance. I was totally skint.

We'd been given around $1500 each by pusser in the form of CILOR - cash in lieu of rations - to subsidise our survival while on adventure training. The outcome of my fervent extravagance was that I was down to my last $50. It was time to start budgeting. I had no alternative but to sit in bars sipping water like a teenage druggy. We spent time playing free foosball and pool in a bar we considered our local, enjoying light-hearted competitiveness until we were challenged by the bar owner. Her name was Leslie, an Amazonian Goddess standing well over 6' tall in her sandals. Detectably intimidated, I mistakenly agreed, foolishly wagering a paltry stake. Agreeing, I realised she must be quite good or else she'd have refused. I wish she had, she leathered me all over the table. If I'd lost in a similar fashion on the RM Poole guardroom pool table I'd have had to run naked down the main drag. Fortunately here, the wager was financial and appreciated her spending her winnings on us.

Quizzical as to what two Brits were doing in little ol' Winona, she was impressed by our tale. She was meeting up with friends at closing time, so invited us over to Wisconsin for a drink.

Wisconsin, we didn't realise, had a closing time of 4am, two hours later than puritanical Minnesota; therefore, at 2am a cavalcade of drunken motorists take their nightly trip over the Mississippi River and State line to add insult to their already injured livers. 2am in a Minnesota bar is like walking out of a morgue; 2am in a Wisconsin bar is like walking into a party animal's birthday party. Just to add further irresponsibility to the festivities you could also buy fireworks in Wisconsin.

In a party of eight, we were introduced to various couples. Most were intoxicated to the degree where their cognition reduced to acting like teenage lovers. Some may say that people in their mid 40's snogging and fondling at a pub table is a public show of affection. I say they should be shot like rabid pigs. A couple, Mike in his late 40's and his girlfriend Jade, in her early 20's, were so engrossed with each other's bodies that a cortege of student doctors turned up to learn anatomy. It was a voyeur's wet dream watching these two mauling each other like lion cubs; Jade's left knocker at one point in full view where I hoped it wouldn't sag into the ashtray on the table.

Why I don't know but again we were asked to dance to un-danceable music. This time they could suffer the consequences. Using my shirt, I managed to slide gracefully on my back over the wooden dance floor as if on air using it as an improvised 'Shroud of Kathmandu', the famed dancing aid to confuse all but Fitz who knew its true power. Leslie, who grew taller with every beer, and Jade found it quaintly peculiar that both of us were now half-naked sliding across the smooth dancefloor on our knees like kids at a wedding. With a little encouragement they joined in. It obviously hadn't been a popular move as Mike became enraged with jealousy, deciding that feeling Jade's genitals in public was passé and was more fashionable to conduct a bizarre argument about the 'Shroud of Kathmandu'. It peaked with her storming out - I should say 'peeked' as her tit was still visible out of her over massaged bra. Mike returned to his seat looking exasperated. It was clear he'd underestimated the shroud's power.

Refusing a lift due to her intoxication, we watched Leslie drive away in her brand new Corvette. Drunken logic deduced that with the roads being so straight, she wasn't going to take a plunge into the Mississippi after swerving from the bridge. If she died, at least it would be in a decent car.

The wind blowing in our faces while sitting in Garvin Heights Park was the perfect way to see in a new day. We admired the vista to the Wisconsin bluffs, high on the landscape to the north, near to where Princess Wenonah, a Native American version of Shakespeare's 'Juliet' made her legendary suicide leap from Maiden Rock for the love of the brave she could not marry. High to our right sat Sugarloaf Mountain - an 85ft high column of rock cut by quarry workers to commemorate the original height of the bluffs, a nice gesture in between demolishing the area. Mark Twain described this area as the 'Thousand islands' and as we looked over, the river was dotted haphazardly with islets breaking up the water into a series of meandering channels surrounding the small copses of land that we now could just make out hosted the occasional small boat moored at their edge. The view was magnificent, the air clear. We could see for miles both up to where in the distance we could see Eagle Bluff, the highest point along the Mississippi, and down the river towards La Crosse, our next port of call.

The 'Arts & Rivers Festival' added brightness to the already pretty streets with bunting fluttering errati-cally above our heads. Small stalls of original paintings, prints and ornate frames, Native American artefacts, and modern day statuettes lined the pedestrian walkway in between small areas where children danced to the old time music that took our ears on a trip back to the 19th century. Tempting as it was to buy many of the impressive pictures that were going for half of nothing, not having a bean between us was rather problematic so looked regrettably at the steals that we could have purchased for posterity. In 20 years time I would not be able to remember the $40 of beer I'd consumed, but would have longed to look at the wall adorned by a fantastic watercolour painted by a long gone artist bought on my travels down the Mississippi. From that moment, I decided that I'd starve myself of beer and try and keep my money for things that wouldn't end up in the bilge tanks of the RV within 24 hours.

A school band was announced on the tannoy and the sparse crowd swayed over to the tent where sat about 25 teenagers playing what I think was Sousa but in all honesty sounded like a crowded TV room in a rest home for the over-flatulent. The brass section was so out of tune I wondered if I was the only one laughing. I was. It seemed I was the only recipient of Grade 6 on the flugelhorn. It was remarkably bad, as if the festival organiser had the previous evening taken aside the local music teacher and asked him to put on a band.

'Sure, no problem,' said the teacher, agreeing without hesitation. 'Shit!' he then exclaimed, realising he didn't actually have a band to put on.

So with the lure of free candy, he coaxed 25 kids from their beds and shoved an odd looking instrument into their hands and just said 'blow,' which especially confused the girl on the keyboards who was now tinkering on the keys in a fashion to suggest she was thinking, *I wonder what this one does?*

Ears ringing as if being smacked with boxing gloves we departed, feeling slightly sorry for the red-faced kids.

Needing to schedule our meeting spot the following day, after confirming we could secure the kayak at the marina, we spent the afternoon on the adjacent beach. It was one of those places where the locals came to hang out and look good. Unlike the majority, we failed miserably. We parked next to a gleaming pickup truck that pumped out music so loud that people miles away at the Arts and River Festival were thankful that it drowned out the music of the blubber lip band.

He was all of 19 with hair greased back so tight we could see the veins in his skull. He sat on the bonnet, glistening in factor 2 oil, shades on, looking out the corner of his eye to see if anyone was looking at his shiny biceps that, looking at the veins and the redness, had just been subjected to a pre-beach workout. We sat staring, not in envy, but in curiosity. I'm sure some women would find his statuesque appearance attractive, yet I was flummoxed why any female could possibly find chewing tobacco sexy. The ball of baccy he pulled from his tin would have filled a kangaroo's pouch, before stretching his bottom lip to cram in as much green tinted baccy as humanly possible.

I'm a vehement anti-smoker. I've done enough childhood passive smoking to give a bull elephant emphysema, but the after effects of chewing baccy I find even more repulsive. The residue of chewing baccy is pure and simply - spit. OK, so there is no repugnant smoke smell and I dread to think of a way to get passive spitting, but the lad sat on his pickup bonnet was now bent forward dribbling a rat's tail of brown spit slowly onto the floor. After a quick spit that projected gunge 5ft to his, and our, front, he then built up the big one. Sucking until he was blue in the face, he summoned up a gargantuan ball of phlegm and tobacco that was wholesome, full, and probably chewy, like the ones you have first thing in the morning if your suffering from a bad chest (and secretly have a quick nibble on before disposing of it). Squeezing it through clenched lips, the phlegm ball dropped heavily forming concentric ripples in the sand.

Within thirty seconds he'd been joined by an attractive young lady, who seemed far less irritated by this habit more suited to hospice camels. Not ones to forgo current trends, we lathered our bodies in pusser's mosquito repellent and medical iodine that, as I'd found out while deployed in Iraq, when mixed together wasn't an approved sun tan lotion but stained us a lovely bronze. Despite the warnings of its danger it never did me any harm, in fact it did the opposite - I grew an extra testicle. We returned from the RV bathroom to bask in our no sweat deck chairs looking like a pair of heliotropic Wham! throwbacks, our bottom lips stuffed with toilet paper trying to look cool, spitting bits of pink look roll into the sand.

Rob and Sean were in high spirits. They'd been overwhelmed by hospitality in Red Wing and Wabasha. Minnesotans had definitely squirmed into my cynical heart. I just wondered how many British would have invited in a pair of stinking Americans paddling down the Thames and treated them to dinner and free reign of their house.

Within twenty minutes of returning to the police station they too were reading porn and partaking in particularly hot showers. It was good to see the Rob and Sean we loved. I just laid back and enjoyed their company.

'You said it was two locks,' said Sean.

'No I didn't, I said one,' replied Rob.

'No, two.'

'No, one.'

'Two.'

'One.'

'I'm telling you, you said two. How many did he say Fitz?'

'I'm not getting involved.'

'I said two.'

'Ah see, you said two.'

'No, I mean one…'

…And so it continued. They'd been wonderful company for the last 24 hours, but here in the marina as they were about to set off again, we were glad they were leaving. Initially we thought it trivial to argue over the number of locks and dams to negotiate, but if each took two or three hours to pass through it skewed the planning for their evening stops. At Sean's behest we gladly left them to argue in peace, allowing us to sit at the river's edge to plan our next move.

'Sorry, I couldn't help overhearing you guys. Australians?'

'Britons,' replied Fitz through gritted teeth to the androgynous individual so ridiculously clothed he made Liberace look downright bland. To add further comedy to his appearance he had teeth so protruding it would have been possible for him to eat an apple through a tennis racket.

'That's even better, you guys must like a bit of culture.'

'Too right, I've got an ELO album,' I returned.

'You guys want to be in a film?'

Having visions of us being whisked away to an ill-lit garage, where waited two insatiable super vixens covered in Angel Delight, our interest perked.

'What film's this?'

'Well, I'm from the Illinois School of Dance and I'm doing a short film entitled "The Dance of the River".'

Not quite understanding the context of the film, we agreed and discussed what we'd do with our first million dollars when we became the next pair of Hollywood stars.

It seemed simple enough: sit on an ornate bench and just look into the far distance across the river. We did as asked, both noting that this acting lark was easy, god knows why people got awards for it. From our rear, the click of a tape recorder was the introduction to the classical music that flowed on the river breeze. Our stares no longer were transfixed on some distant imaginary object but of five whirling girls dressed in flowing multi-coloured taffeta circling us in what, I assume, people in the arts world would consider 'contemporary dance'.

'Stop!' shouted the director in a moderately aggressive squeal. 'Guys, you need to stop ogling the girls and just fix those stares across the river. Surely that can't be hard?'

How hard is it for two bootnecks not to look at a quintet of hot chicks, waving their silky arms in some sort of druid trance, doing knicker-showing high kicks, arses swaying 6" from dribbling faces? Fucking hard, I can tell you.

'OK guys, I need extra. Can you look enigmatic?'

'How the fuck do you look enigmatic?' whispered Fitz. Mona Lisa was the only enigmatic thing we knew and she just looked miserable.

So, we sat there looking 'enigmatic'. To a third party I looked vexed and Fitz just looked constipated. Trying again to ignore such a surreal predicament, we sat and stared like the two enigmatic mute idiots that he wanted us to be. Flinching with every near-miss wave, all we could do was to promise we'd never talk of this again. If the lads found out, they would automatically laugh, call us names, and kill us with stones.

Minnesota had treated us well. The people were incredibly friendly, extremely helpful, and always willing to learn new information such as the UK was near France (no joke). Their northern charm cloaked their inbred desire to shoot, spear, maim, or kill anything that had no choice but to be covered in fur or feathers. And so it was with appreciable sadness that we crossed the Mississippi over into Wisconsin, possibly never to bounce back into the State that offered glass lakes with endless shores, immense woodlands that carpeted spectacular wildlife, and a people that were never meant to work in an office. It had a beauty that could only be appreciated once you had left.

*'Men worry more about the things they can't see
than the things they can'*

~ *Julius Caesar, Emperor*

As pioneers of 'police station vacations' we headed straight to La Crosse Police HQ. They hooked us up and were extremely informative on the local attractions. However, a less friendly officer ordered us to move the RV to the next bay as we'd parked in his. So we moved. The good cop from the good cop bad cop duo asked us to move the RV again as we were now in his spot. This was fine, he was clearly embarrassed about his colleague's directness and the arsing about they had caused. Fitz reversed the RV round again. Whether it was in his impatience to get the RV parked as soon as possible or whether he was deliberately aiming for the bad cop's car wasn't clear. What was clear was the smashed indicator light of the bad cop's nice shiny motor, in full view of the good cop. Grimacing like he'd just sucked a lemon, Fitz looked forlornly at the gobsmacked police officer with a 'you won't tell him, will you?' expression. He looked a little sheepish himself, after all, it was he who asked us to park next to the bad cop's car, admittedly he said 'next to' not ' 'in to', but that was a mere technicality. He could play it a number of ways, but to his eternal credit, after the shock of seeing us trash the car, he himself started chuckling. His joy became rather falsely infectious as we imitated his chuckle, offered when pride is exchanged for sycophancy. It appeared they were the best of enemies and as our RV had no mark, he would cover for us. He unfortunately declined to cover our request to screech around the car park, leaving a rainbow of burning tyre marks, as we smashed the hell out of the whole motor pool as if in an episode of Starsky & Hutch (with me wearing Starsky's knobbly buttoned cardigan).

Once voted the best small city in the US, it felt quite bohemian and reminded me somewhat of Greenwich Village in New York. Here though, we didn't have the pleasure of overtly camp transvestites with 6 o'clock shadow dressed in purple velour catsuits and 6" heels elevating them to 7ft tall. The downtown shopping district looked authentic film set America - streets of flat-roof chocolate-bricked buildings sporting faded signs rounded corners to identical avenues where square windows upon high were dirty from storeroom neglect. Despite the skyline being long since forgotten, at foot level things were more energetic.

The humid evening was lively to the scene of people, young and old, milling around the streets browsing expensive antique furniture shops windows, small art galleries and bric-a-brac stores selling 'exclusive' wares that looked strikingly similar to ones sold in Bemidji, but with La Crosse being a stop off for the paddle steamer tourists the prices were slightly inflated.

We followed a concentration of people towards the river. Dixie music then hit us as we turned onto Third Street from where we saw the wedding cake tiers of the Mississippi Queen, the middle steamboat from the trio that ply their trade up and down Mark Twain's America. It certainly looked grand, a 382ft long floating palace, it ferried the middle and upper classes up and down the river in unbound self-indulgence. I can confidently say that it ferried people in these social classes as a week in a class 'F' (standing for 'frigging tiny') with the luxury of bunk beds but without the luxury of a view cost over a $1000. If you could afford a window, a fortnight in a superior veranda suite would set you back a nice $9170. That said, they are vessels of immense beauty, both inside and out, and I'd be very surprised if many passengers actually complained at the standard of their hospitality. Around the 'Queen' today was the occasional meathead dressed overtly as a Secret Service agent, which is sort of counterproductive. Feeling brave, one voyeur questioned the man, asking him why their high presence, not quite in a Travis Bickle way, more in a nosey tourist fashion.

'We have on board an ex-president, Sir.' He replied sternly. He'd obviously used 'Taxi Driver' as a training film.

The man's eyebrows raised. 'Which President?'

'I can't tell you that Sir, it's classified information.'

Which rather contradicted his initial statement unless, of course, he revelled in curiosity brinkmanship, teasing enough information to reinforce his important and not-so secretive job. However, I'm sure the local Assassination Squad would take any opportunity to crack a Presidential steamboat slaying, irrelevant of personality.

With the evening bright, we ambled to the Riverside Park and walked happily along the walkways bordered by immaculately manicured flowerbeds inhaling the easiness of life along the river. I felt I was walking through a sixties scene, swaying red white and blue bunting lining the way along where smartly dressed children with slide rule partings wiped ice cream from their freckled faces giggling below fluttering star spangled banners. There seemed to be an unhealthy amount of grease in fathers' hair and Mothers clutching frilled white hankies seemed too preoccupied with little Johnny's dripping ice cream to enjoy the festivities. We passed a bronze statue, a pair of Native Americans playing a game similar to La Crosse, from which the first French fur trappers gave it the name Prairie La Crosse.

A strange young man called Nathan Myrick left West Port in New York and at the age of 19 decided to park his backside on the banks of the Mississippi to settle here without obvious aforethought why the hell he was doing it. He cleverly realised he was not only in a beautiful spot amongst the bluffs and forests of the river but at a strategic point between 2 of the main lumber ports in the area. And so eight years later when he got itchy feet again and took himself off to St Paul, he left behind a prosperous village.

I tell you this because we were interrupted, as we read the inscription on the statue, by a leather clad biker. Short, squat and bald headed, Kurt sported a goatee beard and earrings making him look the least likely history teacher in actual history, whether he knew that, I don't know, but him being a history teacher I hoped so.

He kindly gave us a quick, but detailed, resume of the beginnings of La Crosse and equally as importantly the league table of local bars. He was from intra state but was here for a biker rally that would be taking place the following day. The word 'bike' again pricked up Fitz's ears and so we gratefully accepted his invitation to join him the following morning for a couple of sociable ones at the campsite where he was staying across the river in La Crescent. It would be an ideal way to spend the morning, as the campsite was conveniently next to the marina where we'd scheduled to meet the lads.

Feeling the usual excitement of waking in a new place, we pigged out on our usual healthy morning breakfast of melted processed cheese and beans on toast and chocolate milk. Normally it's a breakfast for spoilt brats that threaten parents with an hour of blood curdling screaming if they can't have chocolate first thing in the day. However, we had both developed a sweet tooth. I for one can't stomach more than 2 chunks of chocolate in usual circumstances, but on the trip many things had confused my taste buds. The things that make up the foundation of a daily diet weren't like the things back home. The milk was sweet, the bread, although lasted an eternity before going stale, was sweet; baked beans were sweet, even the cheese was sweet and far less enjoyable than a vintage cheddar so sharp that it could cut the gums. So at breakfast, instead of a British style fry up, we could eat similar ingredients with the feeling we were consuming a deep fried chocolate gateaux sandwich. Over the first month, our rations had permutated from a healthy, savoury based shopping list to one that Augustus Gloop would have written prior to his visit to Willy Wonka's chocolate factory. Whether it was my mind playing tricks on me, but I was sure I was developing love handles, and when I was needing a sugar fix I swear that in the half light Fitz had the profile of a cherry topped choux bun.

We crossed back over into Minnesota to meet Kurt. We entered the campsite and realised immediately we were hunting a leather-clad needle in a haystack of chrome, tattoos and bald heads. This was obviously where the majority on the rally were staying, and an impressive sight it was. We thought ourselves rather regal in our California Flyer. In the trip's early stages we'd pull up in a Mall car park and display on a bit of card in the windscreen, 'YES WE'RE RICH', before talking overly loud to no one on the mobile phone about the recent development of our shares on the Dow Jones. But here we were small fry. RV's that were the size of buses, RV's the size of buses that hydraulically extended widthways. RV's the size of buses that hydraulically extended widthways pulling trailers that were the size of buses. These weren't just homes on wheels, but mansions on wheels. Too big to even fit legally on British roads these were pure and simply the Kings and Queens of the American Highways. After a couple of laps of the site we had the feeling we wouldn't find Kurt. As the tell tale sulphurous methane smell had started emanating through the plugholes from the bilge tanks, it was a fine opportunity to empty them. Speaking to a middle-aged gent in the queue for the dump, (which on this occasion we couldn't get for free) we admitted our envy for his monster of a mobile home. Gleaming chrome reflected starlets of light around the edges of his ultra luxurious machine. He allowed us to take a look inside through the door that opened like a normal bus (but a lot quieter and with no dried school boy bogeys). The driving seat was basically a vibrating, massaging, leather recliner, with an armrest full of buttons that looked equipped to give out 'Jim'll Fix It' badges. The dashboard surrounded him like Jean-Michel Jarre's keyboards with buttons and digital displays more suited to a Space Shuttle flight deck. Behind, was a huge luxurious dining and lounge area that was bigger than our RV. With a fridge the size of a double wardrobe, the kitchenette sporting every gadget that people with or without gravity could ever want, and a bedroom in the rear that would have been more becoming in a Sheikh's palace, we could only coo like an old women at a Tom Jones concert. This envy only made us realise that we now felt like were driving the Trotter's 3-wheeler of the RV world. Asking if the man was on vacation he told us he was permanently on holiday. Retiring early, he'd decided a life of tending his garden and tinkering about in his garage wasn't for him so he and his wife sold the house and bought this monster and just cruise for the rest of their lives, usually up north in the summer and down south in the winter. What a life. If I'd worn a hat I'd have doffed it in his honour. His weather beaten face showed he was living the outdoor life and he admitted the only thing he missed was being able to have a crap without knowing he would have to smell it a few days later, and RV shit did tend to smell somewhat. Out of everything on this trip the 'honourable dumping of the shit' duty was the worst. Fitz seemed to have a double-sided coin as I again lost the toss for the privilege of doing the job. It was to get even worse.

We were now at the front of the shit queue. If it wasn't bad enough standing on a concrete slab that showered away any putrefied turds that had slipped, I had an audience of fellow dumpers ready to critique my dumping technique (and believe me, there is one). As I opened the tap to allow out the waste of the past week, I had the sensation that my chest and neck was getting wet. Realisation soon dawned on me as my nostrils flared due to that unmistakeable smell of raw shit. I looked down. I was being finely sprayed with liquidized shit and piss. Looking in blind panic trying not to get an eyeful it appeared that the hose had perished in a few places and was spraying bits of all sorts (but not sweetcorn) into the air and more worryingly, all over me. Holding the hose at arm's length, I looked to the sky hoping I wasn't missing the dump hole or I'd then have to sweep the lot in, without a brush. I clamped my mouth shut and tried to breath through my nose but something of an unknown nature leapt into my right nostril. I snorted out a shitty snot rocket and instinctively opened the corner of my mouth to able me to breath easier but suffer the ignominy of looking like a poopy Popeye. To say Fitz was laughing heartily was an understatement. I wasn't. Although too preoccupied with being spattered in liquid faeces, I could hear the stifled sniggers of the queue as they witnessed the stupid Englishman with poor dumping technique getting spray tanned by effluent. Upon finishing, Fitz threw me my wash bag that I tried to catch without it touching any of the lumpy brown bits of sullied water that I was smothered in. In the shower, where I didn't find globules of shitty piss, I found pissy shit. I tried to just scrub initially but all it did was push bits of gut wrenching grit under my nails so my strokes became softer finding the softer nuggets of poo in my hair, in my body hair, even inside my ears. Extremely unpleasant was pulling a tiny bit of pink toilet paper stuck in the Velcro of my moustache stubble. A tad lower and I'd have puked myself inside out.

Come the next dumping, instead of tossing a coin we'd have to fight it out, probably to the death. I added a trident and net to my shopping list.

Having last seen Sean and Rob arguing over lock, dams, and the ternary numeral system, they admitted ignoring each other for the first seven hours after leaving Winona. Like burgeoning humidity, their ill feeling had burst into a storm of arguing that had cleared the air with a new freshness. Agreeing they'd both been equally obtuse, they realised dam counting was irrelevant when compared to their friendship. They now seemed even closer and definitely had more verve and energy than before. Whether they were now acclimatised or their bodies conditioned to the rigours of 30 miles a day paddling, I wasn't sure, but they talked with busy tongues, walked with springing bounds and shopped like it was the last day of sales which to be honest, was normal for Sean.

Earlier, they'd even trekked to the top of the 570ft high Grandad bluff at the end of Main Street. An extreme adventure to some, it was just a warm-down from a full day's paddling for these two. They also wanted to go on the Heileman's brewery tour where they could see the world's largest six-pack - huge tanks dressed as cans; but we unfortunately had missed that day's tour.

Fitz and I tried to be more like the locals. When travelling I often try to avoid looking like a tourist by carrying things only the locals would, such as a baton loaf, car battery or a sword that, on occasion, has got me into trouble. We tried one of the many coffee shops around Caledonia Street. There aren't many places where I've been able to pick a Daphne Du Maurier book from the shelf and sip coffee. It was a treasure trove of old dog-eared books, their previous owners possibly with tales more interesting than the contents themselves. I looked for a number of my favourite reads 'Nha Trang and his Carrot Called Benny', in the murder section I searched for 'Dial 'D' for Dermatitis', and in the mystery section I couldn't locate any of the Diazepam Baby mysteries ('The hunt for the Mengicoc-cal Twins' is my favourite of the series). Being in such surroundings I wanted something delightfully more decadent than instant coffee. Looking at the list of a 1000 ways to serve coffee, I decided on a Café Frappe Latte, which I'd heard was fashionable in these parts. Like buying tank tops and flares, I instantly regretted trying to be chic. The Café Frappe Latte was basically sweet cold milk poured onto undissolved coffee at the bottom of a glass. She could have saved on washing up and spooned coffee granules into my mouth where I could have washed them down swigging from a milk carton. It somewhat spoiled our time in there but not

188

wanting to make a fuss endured it by cocking my head at the woman behind the counter lifting the glass smiling 'mmmm' with a ridiculous milky brown moustache. At least it didn't contain pink toilet paper.

Later, we ate well. Fortunately, a most attractive waitress served us. She gave us each a sultry look that unfortunately encouraged us all to give her a bigger tip than necessary. She was good. We then hit the bars at Rob and Sean's insistence. They both got hammered and since the start it was without doubt the best night out we'd had so far. We even had drinks bought by a mysterious woman, who on asking if we recognised her turned out to be the foxy waitress who'd served us earlier, a rare example of someone looking better in work clothes than in their glad rags. Despite getting a freebie, my penny-pinching plan had fallen flat at the first hurdle. I concluded that this ill-fated scheme should be knocked on the head as a bad job relying on the next few towns not to have bars that would unfairly suck money from my pockets.

We were genuinely sad to see Sean and Rob leave as they paddled off into the afternoon heat to meet us in Prairie Du Chien. With a pocket of time to kill, we spent an afternoon on Barren Island, hardly an apt name for a place so full of joyful people. We toddled to the sand by the water's edge in Pettibone Park, an ideal place for people to relax, play beach volleyball, and picnic. For a few of the males it also seemed an excellent place to spit tobacco.

The scenery along Highway 35 maintained the beauty that had begun further north. The road either dipped its toe into the river or maintained an arm's length. From wherever the road led, we could occasionally see small hazes of insects swarming from the water's edge. Some swarms were pretty unremarkable.

Some were frightening, massive black waves that bubbled like bingo balls amongst the reeds. We passed through one that battered the windshield like torrential hail leaving a thick smear of splattered pus. Oncoming traffic wiped their wipers on this boiling sunny day wiping away similar gunk to our own. It wasn't a good time to run out of windscreen wash.

***

Never in my life of raffles, lotteries, betting, had I won anything. Not even a bottle of Pomagne that you would always have a 1 in 3 chance of winning at the straw tombola stall at the local carnival. That all changed once we entered Prairie Du Chien.

As per usual we made a B line to the tourist office situated just off Highway 18 crossing into Iowa. Both ladies were enthralled by our stories of bravery in the RV, surviving in only 180sqft of air-conditioned mobility. Being a promotional week we were each offered the chance to win a mystery prize in a lucky dip. Excited beyond belief, I didn't hesitate to dip in eagerly awaiting what prize my number had won.

'Number 12!' I proclaimed, dreaming of a holiday in the Bahamas or maybe a Chevy pick-up that I wouldn't be able to afford to send back home.

'12 Nancy 12!' repeated the woman, holding the bucket trying to peek at the winning list as expectantly as I.

'12, 12, 12,' hummed Nancy, trailing her finger down the list accentuating the pause for added effect.

I was getting impatient, Nancy had my future in her hands. I was tempted to jump over the counter to snatch away the list of glittering prizes. Fortunately, Nancy drew breath to announce the big news.

'Oh my, number 12, you've won!'

My heart skipped a beat. I steadied myself against the counter, remembering the location of my passport and suntan lotion. I inhaled deeply. What glory was I to behold?

'12…' Nancy said, her tone heightening in expectant celebration. '12… is a Wisconsin drinks cup and pencil!' she exclaimed rather more wildly than necessary considering she was handing me a plastic soda cup saying "Wisconsin, Go to it".

'Fucking get in!' I exclaimed, clenching my fist. 'Oh, sorry, terrible language.'

'It's OK hunny, we all get a lil' excited time to time.' replied Nancy.

I showed off my pencil (a HB if you are interested) to an envious Fitz.

This was reciprocated when Fitz won a 'Great River Road' lapel badge that he promptly wore, asking for Nancy's mirror to check how magnificent it looked.

This did, however, cause arguments afterwards. We could never agree on who'd won the best prize.

Once the realisation had set in that our lives would never be the same, we queried the entomological phenomena we had witnessed just half an hour earlier.

Also known as the Fishfly, or Dayfly; the Mayfly, a misnomer as it appears mid June to the end of July, is one of nature's more bizarre creations. From the insect family Ephemeroptera meaning 'living for one day' the Mayfly naiads live together underwater for up to four years. Upon reaching adulthood, they metamorphose into a chinook of winged beasts launching from the water solely to breed before withering and dying within a day. We had to pick that day in Prairie Du Chien.

We were told there was no way of escaping it as the Mississippi was a handrail for the insects' 24 hour fuck frenzy… if you only had 24 hours to live what would you do? Having no developed mouth the Mayfly is hardly a pest to crop farmers and indeed their short existence is of infinite importance to the river's ecology becoming a short but necessary gorging for the river animals bereft of such abundant protein.

Wisconsin's second oldest town, Prairie Du Chien or as we ignorantly called it 'Dog field', was historical for the fact that it hosted the only battle of the 1812 war in the Mid West. Rather than return it to the Americans, the British as per usual, destroyed the first fort on the Upper Mississippi, probably turning it into a multi-storey car park. It developed as a fur traders' settlement and still maintains a rather strong French contingent and everywhere names reek of Gallic influence. None more so than Villa Louis - a tourist attraction on the Mississippi's largest sandbar, St Feriole Island. Low as low could be, any slight raise in the river's height had significant impact on the once thriving district. Devastated by the floods of 1965, the community was moved onto the higher ground on the mainland, some refusing to move, instead building their homes on stilts until the island was turned into a tourist park and the residents, probably fed up with tourists' camera flashes, moved on. This is where we rested, walking around the marina and taking a leisurely stroll around the silted grounds of the park.

As well as weird flying fuckers, my mind was taken by the intense itching around my legs. Presumably from wading through long grass away from tourist tracks, I had more ticks on me than a primary school register. With ticks, the trick is to remove them without leaving their head embedded in your skin, which can lead to all manner of nasty, potentially fatal, diseases. Although now frowned upon (like religion and four star petrol) one of the many tried and trusted ways of getting rid of these critters is to singe their arses. In doing so you'd then pinch them from your body once they'd lifted their head out of your skin to see who was burning their arse. My legs are like Chewbacca's, so when I tried to singe the first little bleeder, I neglected to check the lighter wasn't on 'flame thrower' setting and scorched a path of burnt hair from my ankle to my calf. How funny Fitz found it.

How painful, thought I. It wouldn't be the last occasion of singeing on the trip.

The Mayflies were again storming sporadically around the water's edge and many pleasure craft owners in the marina were covering up in readiness for tonight's orgy of flying fornication. Their disturbing appearance had freaked us out somewhat, and as the night drew in we were frighteningly in awe at the continuous sight of millions of these Mayflies swarming around anything and everything that lit up or buzzed. Drawn by the males using the light as beacons, the females would breed giving the poor male his one and only bit of nookie before he would jump off, smoke a fag (through his nose one would presume given his lack of mouth) then die a happy Mayfly, leaving street lights feet deep in piles of dead insects. The golden rule when in a Mayfly storm is to never use or be near anything that buzzes or lights up, I take it Ann Summers cancels her parties around this time of year.

Stories have been told of men leaving their convertible cars under street lighting unaware of the impending hordes, then returning to find the inside of their car knee deep in rotting carnage. People have nearly choked to death, caught with their torches lit full beam trapped within the maelstrom unable to breathe without inhaling something winged and crunchy.

This wasn't our only problem. Stuck inside the RV, the windows popping like popcorn kernels, the sound of desperate Mayflies trying to use our interior light as their mating ground, we found Sean and Rob running late, way late. If that wasn't bad enough, our mobile phone wasn't working. Correction, it was working but not in our area. Not happy, since the whole idea was to have 'roam' capability, we were told by an albeit helpful operator that the codes needed to speak in this part of the world wouldn't be accessible until the following morning - this in the land of 24hr pet shops and all night estate agents. I could do nothing until the following day. Sean and Rob could be floating upside down for all I knew in which case the mobile wouldn't have been much use unless equipped with a lifeguards recovery hoop which as I recall wasn't one of the facilities featured. We braved the tornado of Mayflies and asked the marina attendant hiding behind his mesh whether he'd seen the lads.

'Ain't seen nothing but these pesky little bastards,' was his droll reply.

Hitting the local police station knowing they would have the phone number of L&D9, we spoke to the lockkeepers. They had seen them pass a good few hours previously, which was initially good news; we could map their position. The problem was that we mapped their position to have reached us a couple of hours ago.

'Maybe they've just overshot the marina?' suggested the police officer.

This was rather optimistic. Both were superb navigators and would have been able to stop at a buffet size sausage roll had it been marked on the map. Not wanting to alarm ourselves we chilled out in the fact that they were both big boys and adept at overcoming the odd disaster. They'd probably been caught in a Mayfly storm and rested it out until they'd run out of light and bedded down. Not having communications, ironically, was a slight relief. We couldn't get in touch with them, they'd be encountering similar hurdles, so we'd all be swearing in equal volumes wondering where each other were, but confident in the fact everyone was safe. Our separated procedure was such that if we didn't meet our radio contacts within 24 hours then local authorities would be notified. Our time frame was such this would be necessary by noon the following day. Keeping calm we waited in the marina car park and settled in the bar to a couple of beers with the romance of mayflies still ringing in our ears.

'Being different isn't being weird.
The problem is mainstream thinks you are.
That's what herd fear does.'

~ Dom Mee, Maritime adventurer

The morning of the first snow is always a special one. As I now looked out of the window the ground was not white with virgin snow but brown with Mayflies that had fucked themselves to death. Concentrated mainly around the now extinguished lighting many had spread leaving a carpet of nauseating remains. I could now smell why they were also called the Fishfly. The acrid mustiness was all I could smell as I stood on the RV entrance. Even Fitz's faulty nose was offended by the odour and decided that fish was off the menu for the foreseeable future.

There was still the underlying problem of not seeing the paddlers. Getting our phone sorted was one thing. Rob sorting his was another thing entirely. Somehow I wasn't too confident and my pessimism was unfortunately proved right - his number was unreachable. We guessed they wouldn't move from their position if they hadn't made contact, as was the plan. We set off in search of the small orange and blue dome tent they called home.

We'd exhausted scouring the Wisconsin river bank, so took a trip along the Iowa side. We hadn't expected to enter our fourth river State under these circumstances.

'Yeah Iowa looked quite nice from the river but the first thing we saw was Rob and Sean washed up dead in a small eddy.'

As we passed over the river we scanned the bank northwards, but as it was likely they hadn't arrived yet it was more of a cursory appreciation of the scenery. Looking south we saw our first river casino, the 'Miss Marquette Riverboat Casino' looking probably less glitzy than it did at night. Still it raised interest in the RV as Fitz was considering a career as a croupier on leaving the Corps, and the idea of being bankrupted by casino owners somehow seemed more romantic if it was on the river.

Taking the more obvious south route, we looked into Marquette Harbour and as if our eyes had in-built kayak radars saw the black blob of the Klepper. Out from under the shade of the café patio we found both waving frantically as if buffing invisible windows. Not wanting to look too worried by kissing them after a 4 year hostage release, we sauntered lazily over. As soon as we were in talking distance we all asked simultaneously, 'Where have you been?'

Sean reckoned that we'd planned to meet in Marquette and not Prairie Du Chien over the bridge. I couldn't agree but later, upon reflection, something inside told me that we had indeed plumped for Marquette. God knows how we'd gone to PDC instead.

As bootnecks, they'd fallen on their feet and stayed at the marina owner's house and had been fed and watered quite splendidly. Bizarrely Iowa had escaped the Mayfly invasion and having travelled down the western edge of the river they had rarely come into contact with the swarms. Our tales of fighting them off with sticks running around with coats over our heads were met with disbelieving looks, both probably thinking, *'Anything to take the blame away from fucking up.'*

It was 10am on a Sunday. Already the sun had heated the pontoon's wooden decks enough to burn the paddlers' bare feet and our naked torsos. Sean had put a thermometer in the seat of the Klepper. It showed a scorching 110°F. They were already sweating profusely, Rob especially; his fairer skin meant he covered up more than Sean and considering they wore life jackets over clothing, it was going to be an extremely uncomfortable eight hours on the river. Just like every other day. Not wanting to receive a karate chop I withheld the fact that we sometimes had to turn down the RV aircon.

Iowa's bluffs continued their lofty way presenting this part of the Mississippi Valley as wonderfully green. The road, still named Highway 364 took us higher above the river than we'd ever been. The designated viewpoints we stopped at gave us a breathtaking of the river's immensity below. The crystal blue skies carried a soothing breeze that rustled the leaves around our heads as we stood on the wall avoiding vertigo by not looking at the 100ft drop below. River traffic was busy. We watched as two gigantic barges passed safely within inches of each other. It was the first time we'd been able to look up or down the River rather than along it. Showing the jagged V shape of the channel that its geological forefathers had cut over aeons down to the glass plain of the water, it seemed even more majestic as it carried the insignificance of man's most awesome inland water vessels - it showed that the river is America, and man is just a visitor. When we have decided to blow ourselves up leaving the cockroaches and rats to rule the planet, the 'Big Muddy' will still stroll on by, totally unconcerned.

Pressing on, it was as if we'd woken from a dream and were now driving the roads of rural England, the only difference being the centre line was to our left. The landscape painted a Wordsworth colour wash. Rolling hills, sloping down into dells, shaded the fringes of the open fields that swept across the lowland. The meadows wore the familiar black and white polka dots of Friesian cows grazing themselves to an early death. We passed the odd smallholding struggling to keep their heads above water. They all seemed to think that their problems against the multi-national farming conglomerates churning out conveyor belt meat would be solved by keeping piles of rusting junk from past generations in their yards.

The sky had now clouded over. Within ten minutes of leaving the cyan skies of the overlook we now felt the patter of rain on the windscreen. Within twenty minutes it was as if in a car wash, crawling at 10mph through the downpour that drummed a deafening bass on the roof of the cab. Within half an hour the wind had picked up so quickly that we thought the paint would be stripped from the cab. Headlights were on full beam not to see but to warn others of our presence. This was futile. They'd have the same view as us, which happened to be nothing but the torrent of water raging against the glass. We were totally and utterly blind to what was in front. Rain turned to hail that crackled on the glass like chips in a frying pan. Our view suddenly turned for the better as the rain abruptly stopped as if in apology. The air was slate grey, the sky even darker. From the beautiful colours of the Mississippi Valley we were now in a monochrome storm only coloured by the yellow sparks of lightening from clouds so low we felt we could touch them. The thunder growled, annoyed that we dare drive through its domain. We braved its warnings, both sitting bolt upright as more lightening strikes shocked our hearts. Fitz drove with an alertness to suggest he was driving 90mph around a rally circuit and not inching along a straight highway looking for other drivers abnormal enough to drive in these conditions. All the vehicles that beamed their lights had pulled over deciding to weather the weather from the comfort and relative safety of the verges. Not us - I donned the deerstalker hat and tweed cloak of Sir Cuthbert Shittington - turn-of-the-century storm chaser, accompanied by his basque, stockings and feather boa wearing assistant Fifi L'Amour - transsexual dance reject, played by Fitz, and punched the core of the storm.

Feeling like Chitty Chitty Bang Bang on the aptly named Great River Road, as at this present moment the road was indeed a river, we took the main road into Dubuque. Vehicles' right wheels, hidden in the extra depth of the road's camber, churned the arch-high water like mill wheels. The cars going more than 3mph turned the water into a sheet of spray drenching the stream of the sidewalk. This was definitely not a day to walk to an interview in your new cream dress - or drive looking like you'd just finished a shift at the Moulin Rouge, so Fitz left behind Fifi L'Amour and returned to normal wear. We aquaplaned to a stop in the suburban side roads of town. Totally disorientated, we looked for anybody we could ask for directions. Not the easiest thing to do in a country where to see a pedestrian walking the streets is like a wildlife safari, especially in these conditions. Amazingly, we saw a woman standing on her wooden porch shaded by the colonnade above. Fitz shot over, hastened not to miss the chance. He trotted, shoulders hunched under the shade of an umbrella. It made me wonder, '*Where the hell did he get that?*'

I've never in my entire life possessed an umbrella. Fitz, I'm sure, didn't. You need to be a certain type of man to own an umbrella, surely? And Fitz didn't fit into any of the pigeonholes that I put male umbrella owners in - city workers, golfers, fishermen, wankers.

The topaz coloured 'Pippins' looked like a typical townhouse and advertised that it served 'just good food'. Tempted, as a solitary cuppa had been breakfast, I realised as I turned out my pockets, that I had 49c, enough to get me perhaps one strawberry shoelace. Fitz seemed happy chatting with the bespectacled lady on the porch. From within the house first came a similarly aged man, most probably her husband, then an older man, and then another woman. From next door came a young woman carrying her baby. Whether Fitz had begun an impromptu comedy act or singing turn, I wasn't sure, but there now stood a crowd that bowed the wooden flooring. Hoping they all weren't going to end up in the cellar below, I decided to join the party.

The talk was of the weather, and all were interested in the UK's varied climate that differs about 3 degrees in a year causing drought in the summer and gridlock in the winter. This storm we were now in the middle of didn't stop their son; however, as he came from the house, mountain bike hooked on his shoulder to meet his radical friends who had equally expensive looking bikes inverted on the car roof.

'Perfect,' he said looking at the skies.

He was going mud biking down the nearby hills where they would scramble down the slopes of the forests skidding through the mud slides avoiding rock fall, trees and the odd felled cyclist. It sounded fantastic, and Fitz asked if the runs would accommodate the RV. I wouldn't have put it past him to go if they could.

With directions to the police station, we thanked all for the hot tea and promised we'd call in if we had time.

The downtown area had a slightly downbeat feel to it which, in all fairness, was probably due to the down-beat weather still trying to spread unhappiness with damp winds and dank drizzle. The police were helpful but, despite the size of the station, the outside car park was unbelievably small. They had their own multi-storey affair that had a height restriction preventing RV access. They offered us a parking space in a police zone on the main road and a police sticker to put in the window. One may assume there'd be a number of jealous, anti-social vandals out there who'd see a recreational vehicle as a legitimate target. After all, if we could afford an RV we could easily afford to respray the paintwork ruined by car keys and replace the aerial, hubcaps and windscreen wipers. To put a sticker in the window telling all and sundry that we were with the police was a red rag to a criminal bull. Should our $40,000 of radio equipment go missing, David Wilson back at the British Embassy who had signed them out, would be notably distressed if he had to explain that one. So, although thankful, we declined his gracious offer.

The nearest other station to the river was 'out east' over the bridge into Illinois and East Dubuque, a small scruffy urchin clinging to the coat tails of its healthier brother. To find the street was easy, to find the station on the street wasn't.

Sinsinawa Avenue crossed under the Dubuque Bridge, and seemed as though all the scum and lowlife had thrown itself over the edge into the road we were now on. The western end of Bourbon Street in New Orleans gets intoxicatingly seedy: the strip bars more frequent, the drinking holes more delinquent. Sinsinawa Avenue looked like the poor end of the western end of Bourbon Street. All places designed for night enjoy-ment look drearily hung-over during the day, but here it hadn't got out of bed refusing to reach for its morning cigarette. The afternoon greyness did nothing to enhance this insalubrious strip of flaking masonry and dusty windows from which hung shorting neon signage that hung lamely like butchered cattle. Deciding to try and find the station on foot we parked in a gas station forecourt and plodded right past the police station. Fitz first noticed it only because he'd turned to see someone walking out onto the sidewalk from within a peeled blue steel side door. Hung above the door was a small winking neon light; its bland incandescence said 'Police'. We checked again the signs bedecked over each doorway: 'Go Go girls', 'Bud-Lite', 'My Brother's Place', 'Going East', 'Peep Show', 'Police'.

In the UK I've often heard of shops having to change their livery to keep in with the traditionalist nature of the market square, but this police station was taking it way too far. We entered into what could only be described as the front room of a squat. It was seedier than a watermelon wearing a dirty raincoat. On the front counter newspapers were left discarded next to full ashtrays. A stain-ridden armchair sat in the corner adjacent to an ancient TV that fuzzed its way through some low budget soap. A sole officer came to our aid politely asking us our business, hypnotising us into eye contact while slowly trying to clear the newspapers without us noticing. He too couldn't help us; it was only a satellite station and didn't have many facilities, a mop and bucket being obvious ones.

Stumped, and with the night drawing in, we took a chance and went to the boat landing behind Sinsinawa Avenue. Its only resemblance to a boat landing was that there was a ramp into the water, other than that you would have been mistaken into thinking it was a council tip. Amazingly, there were another couple of RVs. We expected them to be the American version of our travellers, moved from one piece of waste ground to another. They were fishermen travelling upstate. They were staying the night as they refused to pay extortionate trailer park fees. Happy that we were amongst the tightest people currently in Illinois, we felt comfortable when they offered to look after the RV for us while we went for a couple of jars down in Sinsinawa Avenue.

Things hadn't picked up since we'd left a couple of hours earlier. We bar hopped until we reached a strip joint, not for sexual titillation but morbid voyeurism of life forms that would frequent such a place. A black curtained alcove was the gateway to blackness. The first sense activated was the smell - a delinquent miasma of forgotten damp mixed with sickly sweet perfumes. Solely visible was a neon strip around the bar and the raised platform in the middle of the room that provided us with a sight for sore eyes. It was apparent that this was a place where pound shop prostitutes and dancers came to make their final buck from those without the ethics to seek more productive pastimes. Older than God's dog, she spun slowly to wiggle her pendulous boobs that hung forlornly to her belly like two spaniels ears. Her fluorescent thong looked as though it was cheesewire cutting through a ball of cellulite ridden edam. She smiled a smile that screamed 'velveteen rub' that did nothing to encourage us to roll dollars into her knicker elastic. As the only patrons we stuck out like racing dog's bollocks and felt wholly uncomfortable having to endure her gyrations that weren't taught at the Royal Ballet. We made small talk with the friendly barmaid, drinking the beers quicker than normal. I wanted to leave, Fitz wanted us to leave, and probably they wanted the two blokes hiding their faces not paying a cent for the entertainment to leave. We left scurrying like naughty school children from the stickiness of degradation into the fresh but not quite clean air of the outside world.

One night in East Dubuque was quite enough. Other bars had been entertaining enough, the people friendly and welcoming, but all in all, it wasn't a place you could spend your life in unless you were of no fixed abode and drank paint thinners.

Boasting that it was Iowa's newest and largest welcome centre, we found the 'Port of Dubuque Iowa Welcome Center' a minefield of reference on the river. The staff assistants were more than helpful and contacted the local paper the Telegraph Herald to inform them of the kayakers' impending arrival, which saved us a job. Now out of Wisconsin, our map charts were coming to an end. The Minnesota Directorate of Natural Resources (DNR) had supplied the expedition with handy flip charts. Wisconsin had done the same. Iowa had sent us plenty of directives and bye-laws but nothing to navigate with. Illinois hadn't sent us anything, so as soon as we reached Illinois we were blind. The US Army Corps of Engineers had sent us the charts for the lower Mississippi but had forgotten somehow to send us the Upper charts. So as a bridge we knew we had to cross, now was that time to go trip trapping. Although the Welcome Center library contained such literary gems as 'From Limestone to Concrete ~ The History of the American Boat Ramp' and 'The A to Z of Mississippi shoes', there was nothing to give the guys direction on their next leg. The tourism office directed us off in search of the biggest hunting and fishing shop in the world. I think we actually found it.

I said the Wal Mart in Bemidji had an array of weapons that would make the armoury in a commando unit look inadequate. The shop we now stood in had a counter of weapons longer than my garden. It was absolutely crammed with handguns, knives, and other hand held weapons of singular destruction. Behind the counter a weapon rack boasted shotguns, semi-automatic rifles, machine guns, and grenade launchers where uranium tips were optional. A box of cluster bombs sat next to a separate stand promoting multi barrelled rocket launchers under the ceiling-hung 'Moose Buster' nuclear warhead. In the fridge next to the ice lollies, glass phials of nerve agent rested along-side the test tubes bunged with anthrax cultures that were on special offer. Admittedly my imagination got the better of me at the latter end of this list…

I've been around weapons all my adult life, but never had I seen such unadulterated display of weapon mania. If people want to hunt, fine, but what purpose, other than to kill things repeatedly, is there to own a US Army issue M16 Assault rifle? It's 5.56mm bullet would be hard pushed to kill a gerbil unless from point blank range, even then he'd probably just stare and carry on gnawing your tax return.

There is a fine line between love and hate and we'd been informed that such a relationship existed between Iowan's and animals. This fine line was evident as we looked through the counter's glass casing at the high quality hunting tools sparkling with usefulness or menace depending on your intent. Maybe I just didn't understand the ways of the hunter, but I wondered what use a fisherman or hunter would have with a knuckle duster with an 12" axe blade attached. I was shocked at what we could buy here and it was greatly unnerving to see the weaponry available on the open market. God knows what you could get underground.

The ethical argument of US gun laws is a book in itself and not wanting to show prejudicial views I will hit you (in a non-violent way of course) with a profound fact to ponder on.

Between 1963-1973, 47,424 US Servicemen tragically lost their lives in combat. Back home in the good old USA, during the same period, firearms killed 84,633.

Ask any British layperson which UK city they regarded as the most dangerous and I'd wager many would say London. As a bit of research prior to the trip I'd discovered London had a murder rate of 2.1 murders to every 100,000 inhabitants. The FBI has a big city murder rate league table taking in all cities with over a population of 100,000. According to the preliminary figures of a report done in the same year, it showed that London would have been 188th in the league of 213, positively Regional Counties Sunday Division III. Amongst the top 30 were six of the cities on the expedition trail. Minneapolis was the 'safest' at no. 30 with 'only' 23 murders per 100,000. Both Memphis and Baton Rouge were also outside the top 10. St Louis was the 7th most murderous city, with New Orleans 3rd, and Washington DC 2nd with murder rates of 71.9 and 73.1 murders per 100,000 respectively. If you fancy being murdered, visit the city of Gary, Indiana. Although having a population of only 116,000, around the same number as Exeter, Devon, 104 people were murdered there that year, at a horrific ratio of 89.6 per 100,000.

We found the necessary maps but they only took us to Lock and Dam 13 at Clinton, Iowa but at least they could get there without blindfolds. With a bit of time to kill (no pun intended) we couldn't think of a better place than here to browse. A veritable Aladdin's cave for anyone with bloodlust it sold, apart from the weaponry of a neutral country, accessories that made us both giggle silently like schoolboys reading Playboy in a library. Behind racks of dried rations, we found camouflaged masks that would have not looked out of place in some dominatrix dungeon, windproof Wellington boots (surely waterproof would have been better?), and more disturbingly deer musk and scent of stag piss for those who really wanted to get close to nature. We tried unsuccessfully to play 'When The Saints Go Marching In' on the duck callers that were basically expensive camouflaged kazoos that majorettes had probably discarded once promoted to xylophone player.

The video shelf then took our attention. The two main categories of video were split between 'Instructional' and 'Pleasure'. The 'pleasure' category was for those who preferred to sip beer and laugh merrily in their over-worn armchair and watch the merciless bludgeoning of docile woodland creatures in such classics as 'Elk Madness' and 'World of the Wild Turkey II ~ *Super Slam*'. The instructional videos were for novice hunters who wanted to learn additional ways to injure, maim, and crucify vermin that were obstacles in the food chain such as elk, moose and black bear. Amongst these titles were the 'How to hunt' series ranging from Wild Boar to, believe it or not, sheep. What sort of one eye would want to hunt a sheep? It's hardly the biggest ego boost to tell of such tall stories down the local hunting lodge.

Rob and Sean stayed overnight to recharge their batteries. Not wanting to sample the delights of East Dubuque, we had a couple of quiet beers in the Dubuque Marina club and played pool with a man too drunk to ascertain the right end of a cue. It would have been easy to accept his wagers, we'd have walked away millionaires, but felt it exploitative to deprive him of his savings, rather we humoured him when receiving abuse that we weren't real men for not wanting to risk $5 a game.

Two news reporters from the Telegraph Herald met us on the marina jetty. As they wanted to get some good snaps of the lads on the river, they'd commandeered a boat. Only this wasn't an ordinary boat, this was a luxury cruiser that would take us a mile or two up and down the river. It was one of those boats that lithe women would sprawl over at boat shows and would entice in people with no hope of affording one, just as long as they removed their shoes as they looked on with envy.

More surprising than the boat was her skipper. It was the drunken pool player from the night before. It was one-way recognition. He swore he'd never seen us before. He wasn't lying, the state he'd been in.

It was the first time Fitz and I had really been on the river. We'd paddled for about 100 metres back in Brainerd but that was just punting clumsily along the bank. Here we were on the Big Muddy, and on it the Ol' Man felt even bigger.

The 'American Queen' berthed in town was a perfect backdrop, its 60ft high stacks reaching for the sky. The reporter Mike Krapfl, in his article wrote, 'Mark Time, a corporal in the Royal Marines Commandoes (sic), jumped from his seat on the cruiser and aimed his camera. It would make a good shot for the expedition scrapbook.'

It wouldn't. It'd likely be a tiny dot in the background partly obscured by a blurred bridge. My photography was getting progressively worse to a standard of 'god awful', yet Sean and Rob wanted photographs that would win Kraszna-Krausz awards. Not only did they want shots showing beads of sweat glinting from their foreheads while droplets of water were caught falling from the synchronicity of their paddling, but also wanted them to include a backdrop that took in 2 miles of riverbank and anything that was uniquely American i.e. paddlesteamer, Stars & Stripes, or a memorial for a road sweeper's commitment to duty. It couldn't be done with the camera I had. I'm not a bad workman blaming my tools. I am just a bad workman, but there also is a saying the right tools for the right job, and my lens was OK in the right hands to take normal photographs from normal distances.

Neither were particularly happy with the photograph in the newspaper. I thought it was good. The paddlers were focussed sharp as pins, the softened paddle steamer as the backdrop, but to them the shot didn't show them close enough. Despite having a lens costing $8000 the photographer still couldn't satisfy their need to have their blackheads plastered all over the new. It actually made me feel better.

Lock and Dam 13 was in between our present position and our next rendezvous point, the Quad Cities, so it was imperative we sought charts to cover this leg. Clinton, we were told, didn't have a DNR office so the only hope was Savanna, a small town on the Illinois side of the River.

Another picture postcard town, Savanna's day lazily strolled by, people actually walked here, giving it a fifties feel and their clothing added to the authenticity.

The brilliant white Post Office and Visitors Center staff gave us directions to the DNR offices and gave us a plethora of flyers and handouts to attract us to their home. It was quite unnecessary, we found the place highly attractive, but we were on a mission and didn't have time to wander aimlessly around the streets of white picket fences, bowling green lawns, and antique shops.

Finding the DNR offices wasn't easy. We expected to find, as we had before, a modern building, well sign posted and standing in grounds that received attention. We passed it a couple of times before realising that the littered farmyard with a garage was our intended destination. On entering, any hopes of the inside looking less like a PLO hideout were soon dashed. An old fan's blades circulated the heat with the speed of a geriatric hamster's wheel. The reception office was the study of an eccentric professor, paperwork strewn everywhere on the tables, some that didn't look as though anyone had sat at them since the river was formed.

Shouting for attention we were greeted by a young lady. She immediately sat at her desk, a small bureau that was the steady platform for unsteady piles of paper.

'Is the manager here please?'

She looked around uncertainly before answering, 'I'm the manager.'

Not sure whether or not her actions were to make sure no one heard her lie, we gave her the benefit of the doubt. We were also unsure whether she suffered from stigmata as she bled from strategic points on her face. After Rob's radio debut it would have been ironic if she did. As she talked to us, eyes wide like an engrossed toddler, she scratched off scabs that were like freckles on her face. She then picked a mole until blood trickled down her neck.

'We're from the UK and...'

'Where?'

'The UK.'

'Never heard of it.'

Thinking she'd misheard me say Ukraine I approached a different angle. 'Great Britain, we're British.'

'Oh OK, Great British. I think I've heard of you.'

Now she was well informed as to our origins, we took things to the next level. We asked if she had maps. Not so plentiful here, the river was no longer the recreational passage it was back in Minnesota, more of a trade route that was intermittently interrupted by the few speedboats that used it as their playground.

'We only have about ten left.'

'That's OK, we only need two,' checking that we hadn't suddenly cloned five-fold.

Thinking I was being flippant telling her that Lock and Dam 13 was in the opposite direction to where she was pointing, she looked confused. Her confusion made us confused. Surely she knew which way the river flowed, it was at the bottom of the yard. She then insisted her pointing was in the right direction.

'South is definitely the way the river flows and south is left as we look to the river,' said Fitz pointing.

'Oh wow, I never realised.'

I was scared to ask any further questions in case her brain caught fire.

As I took a closer look at the charts confirming their suitability, Fitz nudged me. With her back to us our surreal host was writing lines like a naughty school-girl.

'I must not take animals to bed'

'I must not take animals to bed'

'I must not take animals to bed'

I was totally beguiled by this woman who was seemingly a Dali painting mixed with 5 pints of muppet stock, poured into a human shaped mould, refrigerated for 21 years, then released into the community under the guise of 'underpaid worker'.

Hastily bidding farewell, like a comedy duo leaving the Munster's house, we bumped into a uniformed gentleman.

'You guys OK?' he asked, obviously witnessing our meeting with Miss Spandacon (we later named her this for no other reason that we liked the name).

He was the manager, but we didn't tell him of her self-imposed field promotion, after all she'd helped us get what we came for, and bewilderingly more.

'Determination is power'

~ Charles Simmons, author

Dropping off the charts at Lock and Dam 13 for the lockkeepers to give to the lads, we set off to the Quad Cities.

A metropolis of, yes you guessed it - four cities, the 'Quads' is a conglomerate of Davenport, and Bettendorf on the west bank of Iowa; and Moline, and Rock Island in Illinois. The Mississippi River separates them and here runs east to west, so Davenport and Bettendorf are counted as the northern pair.

We knew there was a military camp on Rock Island but as it was in the middle of the river we expected it to be of restricted access so took the easy option and headed for the first police station in Moline.

We didn't like the look of Moline's suburbs as we drove through. They were bitterly run down and neglected. Upturned garbage bins spewing stinking rubbish into the overgrown gardens of broken down cars and bug-infested settees.

At the police station things didn't improve. Jaded from a life with miscreants, the police Desk Sergeant had a vulgar ardour for distrust and gruffly questioned our presence. Skirting round his uncivil nature we passed him our expedition portfolio to give credence in our wish to use their car park.

'You ain't a Marine,' he grumbled, pointing at me.

'Why do you say that?' knowing exactly why.

'Marines don't have long hair.'

'This one does.' I smiled trying not to sound facetious.

'Military can't be like when I was in…'

…If I'd heard this once…

'Here's my ID card to prove it. I hope it clarifies matters.'

He scrutinised it, checking that the elongated jaundiced head on the card's computer image was the same person as the long-haired lout that stood before him.

He bluntly threw it back, prickling up the hairs on the back of my neck.

'What's your name again?' he asked, as he turned a new page in his notebook.

Without wanting to suggest he had the memory of a goldfish and if he did, he should have noted my name while holding the card, I replied, 'Time, Mark Time,' just like Bond would.

I watched as he wrote 'Ty McCharm' in his book. Fitz started to laugh.

'Something funny?' he sneered.

'No, nothing,' smirked Fitz.

'When I was in the military we had discipline.'

'So may I ask why we don't have discipline?' I couldn't hold back on this one. I could feel Fitz thinking *'oh no, not again'*.

'Look at your hair for a start.'

'Short hair gives you discipline does it?'

'Yes.'

'I'm not really sure it does to be honest.' Somehow, I felt I was going the wrong way about getting a favour. 'Look, we've come 4000 miles to do something for a good cause and you're undermining the whole thing because of my hair?'

'Well it ain't like a Marine's should be.'

'Were you a Marine?' I asked, trying to garner commonality.

'No.'

'Well what do you know then? Nobhead.' Oh God, I'd called him a nobhead. It seemed to suit, even though other nouns such as 'arsewipe', 'dickwad', 'bellend', could have sufficed. I could even have pretended I was a character in Bugsy Malone and called him a 'putz'. On this occasion nobhead seemed the most appropriate.

'What'you say?' he retorted.

'No bed. Seems there's no bed for us...'

Doing my petulant teenager impression, I picked up our folder and stormed out; my storming hampered somewhat by pushing on the pull door.

Fitz followed, laughing at my frustration. 'Good one Ty' he giggled. This brought me to fits of welcome laughter. I was now going to introduce myself as 'Ty McCharm - International Pimp'.

* Yes as a pseudonym the name may be fictitious but the true account is just as ridiculous...

***

The Rock Island Police Department were a lot friendlier and allowed us to use their car park but we felt guilty taking up two spaces in an already overcrowded parking lot.

We took a walk around 'The District' to discuss our next move. Famed for its nightlife, it looked like the shopping precinct dream of any 1960s council. Rigidly square concrete and glass in unimaginative harmony dictated the right angle turns between the dark brick of the streets and the lighter brick of the avenues. It reminded me of home.

Over a couple of social ones in the only open bar in town, I saw a sight that will live with me for the rest of my days. I have white hair from reliving it. Men back home shuddered in abstract disbelief when I told them on my return, thinking I was showing off and trying to win friends. Nobody believed me. I became a social outcast with only my thoughts for companionship.

It had just gone 5pm. The introduction to a familiar song came on. *"I'll tell you what I want what I really really want."*

"So tell me what you want what you really really want."

"I wanna huh, I wanna huh… etc… etc." I think you've guessed the rest.

Trying to get away from the Spice Girls was like trying to evade Stalin's secret police. Not that I've got anything against them, it's just having them as an omnipresent ear worm was a trifle too much and the Mid West seemed a great place to dodge them. Until that afternoon. Strangely, it was rather comforting to know we were still on the same planet as things around us were becoming strangely alien…

I admit, I rarely dance sober, and when I do it's a two footed shuffle with a niece at a wedding, so I'm the last to pour scorn on anyone dancing, but on this occasion I could not then, and cannot now, keep my silence.

I would find it difficult to imagine any male over the age of 15 getting up to dance to the Spice Girls, indeed when the first few bars of 'Wannabe' started a couple of young ladies got up to dance; again in the same style as they would to Tchaichovsky or Marilyn Manson. Yet it was with real astonishment when a man bigger and sweatier than the average Kodiak bear bounded onto the near empty dancefloor and bounced along to the bubbling vocals of Baby and Ginger. He was 6'8" if an inch. He dressed typically - red sweat stained vest, tight jeans faded on the knees, white baseball boots, and a back to front baseball cap over a classic mullet that was short and shaved over the ears, but long, straggly and unkempt at the back. He frequently spat baccy onto the polished floor, but still he thought himself a sex god. He climbed onto the stage next to the empty DJ booth and waved his arms to attract attention to the two ladies below. When he finally had his meagre audience, this cumbersome oaf then started his dance routine. He sweated, he toiled, he spat. His effort was phenomenal, double punching the air and pointing to a particularly alarmed woman on the words, *"if you wanna be my lover"*. Brad Pitt would struggle to win over a girl with over exaggerated dancing to the Spice Girls. Open mouthed, we couldn't even muster a word between the pair of us.

If it was a criminal offence to be a twat, this man was condemned and any respectable judge would, after little deliberation, sentence him to be shot at dawn. In the face. In front of his parents.

We came to the conclusion that we had to try Rock Island Arsenal and see if the Military could help us, if only it was to protect us from ursine Spice Girls fans.

***

Being a rather important military establishment, it was somewhat surprising to find that we could enter without any checks. I was accustomed to entering a military base and being searched and questioned by a portly civilian security guard with an annoying habit of re-telling his only mildly funny story from his time in the Cookery Corps. Accompanying him, a soldier so bored he'd rather be sticking red hot needles in his eyes than stood at the gate listening to the security guard's story that he'd heard 367 times.

Here at Rock Island, we drove straight past an empty sentry box into the heart of the camp. Then again, this was an era when the US, through its tactful diplomacy, had endeared itself to nearly every other nation and in pacifying all cultures didn't have any enemies that would want try and plant explosive devices inside camps.

Passing through the town sized arsenal, it had the hallmark of a base that had died and been embalmed. Our RV echoed along hallowed ground where Gunnery Sergeants would holler bellowed commands to a hundred knife-creased trouser legs that would stamp or turn about below glistening cap badges eddying to and fro across the glistening square from the wind of the instructor's voice.

In contrast to the sleepiness, we leapt in unbridled ecstasy as a pick up truck with Hawaiian plates overtook us. Unfortunately, in my delirium, it nearly ended up on the receiving end of our front bumper as I swerved maniacally craning my neck to get a better look.

We found a small USMC detachment and on entering the office were somewhat on tenterhooks, as there stood five gunnery sergeants, all smarter than guardsmen each tougher than a rough mutt's nuts.

Suspiciously eyeing my hair, one came over and asked what he could do for us. Before I could finish my sentence, one of the other 'Gunnies' exclaimed that he'd just been reading about us in the 'Marine Corps Times' and produced from an in-tray a picture of the four of us stood at ease behind the Klepper. This changed the whole atmosphere and they welcomed us in, disregarding my mop that hung limply in the need of a good wash. All introduced themselves by rank and surname, us returning with Christian names, surnames and a handshake. Even the captain, after the initial shock of seeing two junior ranks not addressing senior ranks in normal fashion, ended up calling us by our first

names. Whether he thought we had introduced ourselves in register mode i.e surname first, wasn't clear.
Fitzgerald Lee was probably a more common name in
the US than Lee Fitzgerald, but still their help was
graciously received and insisted upon us not staying in
the RV, but rather live in the junior ranks quarters
where the clerk would show us our rooms.

Like in all multi-service military establishments that
I've had the misfortune to spend any amount of time
in, the Marines barracks are always the old dilapidated
buildings out of the way, nowhere near the redeveloped
accommodation enjoyed by the other arms of the
services. Here was no exception - wooden huts, no
doubt constructed to house conscripts in training to
bravely fight evil in the fields of western Europe, sat
sadly behind the grander stone structures that were the
homes of the army contingent. Bill, the clerk, showed
us inside, and the state of disrepair was uncannily
similar to the spider blocks that had been my home
when based in Taunton for seven years.

We were to be here for the 4th July celebrations,
and thought it only right to seek out the better places to
indulge in star spangled Americana.

Bettendorf seemed too distant, plus there were far
too many low bridges to negotiate meaning we had to
detour via Denver to enter the city limits.

Moline, we'd already judged, was as pleasant as pe-
nile warts.

Bill had often found Davenport the most enjoyable
of the four, so taking him with us as a pub guide,
headed off on foot over the state line into Iowa passing
the many taxis that were waiting in ranks, much to Bill's
incomprehension.

We spent the majority of the night in a club whose
name I could never recall in a million years. It felt as

though I was on the set of some MTV show. Chauvinist idiots seemed to be everywhere, whooping and a hollering at any female with skirt length less than a metre. Embarrassing in the extreme, the music was stopped to provide a stage show where under aged imbeciles devoid of pride chosen from the rabid crowd had to think of an hilarious way to scream 'give me the money!!' to win $10, but lose credibility for the next millennium. Bill seemed to enjoy the thrill of seeing clowns perform like clubbed seals. We found it unbearable. At least they were enjoying themselves. We weren't, so our resistance to conformity meant we came out far worse. Bill ended the night with a woman who we'd noticed earlier giving her all on the dance floor to such classics as Duran Duran's 'Rio' and Dead or Alive's 'You Spin Me Round (Like A Record)'. Bill had obviously looked cool - he'd done the 'mashed potato'. The music thrust me back 15-20 years, me trying to get a snog in the local club trying to look cool with daffodils hanging out of the back pocket of my stretch stone-washed jeans.

Getting into the back of her two-seater jeep to drive to Denny's, Fitz and I huddled in the back squeezed in between the spare tyre and a wholesale box of *Tampax*. We talked until the wee hours. An amiable woman, Amy wore the face of a tired single mum. Unhappy that she'd never even been outside the States of Illinois or Iowa, she longed for the day when someone would take her away from her trailer home and show her a better life. This ominously sounded like a scene from an 'Officer and a Gentleman', and I could see her chameleon's tongue springing out and dragging Bill down the aisle of some back street registry office.

Our guts were now conditioned to intake large amounts of food at silly hours of the morning, so it was no problem tucking into griddled steaks at 3am. What we had failed to do was become real American in our eating. We still kept our pancakes and savouries separate, and upheld that great British tradition of using a knife for its intended purpose and not as ornamentation. It is beyond me how Americans, trailblazers in inventing anything to make life easier, rub and hack their dinners to death with a fork rather than simply cutting it. Maybe they try to save energy by using just one hand while eating, but that is often counterproductive as diners, tongues out in stern concentration, chase their food around the plate. I've even seen diners push their food along the table like a cloth wiping the surface, just to prong elusive food.

Wanting to stick around with our host, we arrived at Amy's trailer as the sun peaked over the horizon. Unjustly known as trailer trash, the inhabitants of these small communities of static caravans are the struggling working classes doing the best they can to make ends meet. They certainly looked after their properties. Most had small tidy touches of greenery surrounding their whitewashed trailer. Some had even bought next door and spanning the land between with wooden extensions had turned their abode into a landlubber's catamaran. These 'Super Trailers' were the homes of the upper echelons of trailer park life, those that had lived here since the park opened, and now were chair people of the park's committees and guilds.

Fitz and I were spending fourteen weeks in our mobile home. Some here would spend their whole lives banging their head on opened cupboards, catching their knees as they turned in two feet of cluttered space and forever readjusting their TV aerials when the latest gust knocked over their less than adequate extensions.

I slept on the couch, Fitz in Amy's seven year old daughter's bed. She was staying with her dad and so Fitz's 6'1" frame fitted perfectly onto her miniature mattress. It was Amy's revenge on Fitz for asking earlier if someone had nicked the wheels to her trailer.

***

We waited in the lockkeepers' office for the paddlers. The duty bod informed us that the lads had left L&D 13 around midday as per schedule. While there we asked if we could photocopy the few remaining pages of their Upper Mississippi charts to give to the lads, rather than spending $25 for them in the US Army Corps of Engineers Lock and Dam 15 viewing gallery. Typically, I had to ask the office jobsworth who'd just finished telling a party of uninterested looking kids how they were currently looking at the biggest basin on the river.

'I'd be breaking copyright rules if I photocopied them.' His wife must tear her hair out when he refuses to record the soaps while she's out down the bingo.

'We're hardly masterminding a big time counter-feiting operation,' said Fitz, hoping levity would assist.

'And we are doing it for a charitable cause,' I added.

'Well I'm not authorised to use the photocopier as it costs too much to copy.'

I often query excuses that change, so pressed him on it. 'We'll pay whatever costs are incurred.'

'I couldn't possibly profit from a private transaction.'

He'd worn me down. So with a $25 hole in my pocket, for a chart book that was 90% useless, it was with a rather less than sincere smile that I walked from Lock and Dam 15, not giving a damn that it was the largest basin on the river.

The night drew in and the paddlers were behind schedule. Any small light on the river caused me to flash my headlights ruining my night vision. By 11pm I was certain that they wouldn't arrive. If the darkness crept up too quickly they'd have set up camp. The river was a dangerous enough place in the day, but at night they were on a waterway fraught with hazards with peril lurking around every blind corner that could sweep the unknowing into the steely grip of menacing eddies. Virtually invisible to the giant barges that ploughed up and down the water, their kayak gave the same spurious radar signature as a floating tree that would be ignored by the officer of the watch who wouldn't even feel the lads being crushed and sucked under the vessel like brushwood.

In the event of them being caught in the dark they would tie on red and green cyalumes - luminous phials used in the military to guide troops in the night, hardly designed to attract the attentions of barge captains. It was these two luminescent specks that Fitz and I eventually saw just prior to midnight. Parked by the bank, we'd expected them to arrive the following morning, surprising then, they'd continued through the darkness. Determined not to paddle on the 4th of July, they'd defied common sense and continued. When they noticed the flashing headlights the two cyalumes changed course and hit the bank with a thud minutes later.

The bank wasn't the only thing that was close to getting a thud. Sean stepped out of the canoe. For the first time I'd seen in my life, he was livid.

'Why haven't we got any charts?' said Sean.

'Too busy pissing up?' added Rob.

Sean, to his credit, wanted to hear our side of the story before he tore off my head and kicked it into the river.

'We left the charts at L& D 13 as proposed. They said they'd give them to you,' explained Fitz, trying to hide indignation.

It was quite obvious to all that there had been a breakdown of communications between lockkeepers at shift change. Despite this, it was clear to me I'd been negligent. We even remarked that the lockkeeper who we'd handed the charts to, seemed like he was 1/2 man 1/2 idiot so we should have made doubly sure.

In hindsight, not ensuring the lads had received the charts was in all truth, laziness on our part and for this I could only apologise. Even if I was extremely pissed off at the lockkeepers, the buck topped with us. We were the support team and on this occasion hadn't supported them sufficiently. There wasn't any need to tell me the consequences should things have gone wrong. It was down to their skill and fortitude that they'd arrived here safely.

Sean, with his usual calm head, concluded the debate. 'Right, let's draw a line and move on. The only thing we're interested in now is to enjoy the 4th of July and forget about this river for the next two days. Where's the beer?'

That, we could organise.

Both waking up with bad backs from sleeping on soft beds, the paddlers had completed their admin, cleaned their kit, and done their laundry before Fitz and I rose from our slumber. Going to sleep soon after last light, and getting up at 5am every morning had turned their bodies into a different time zone to ours. They were three hours in front and were already hankering for elevenses as our bellies rumbled for breakfast.

Kicking us out of our all too comfortable beds they dragged us into the daylight reminding us the importance of the day.

On the 2nd of July 1776, the Second Continental Congress voted independence from England. John Adams, a lawyer and one of the American Revolution's most devoted patriots wrote:

The Second Day of July 1776 will be the most memorable epoch in the history of America. I am apt to believe that it will be celebrated by succeeding generations, as the great anniversary festival. It ought to be commemorated, as the Day of Deliverance by solemn acts of devotion to God Almighty. It ought to be solemnised with Pomp and Parade, with shews, games, sports, guns, bells, bonfires, and illuminations from one end of this continent to the other from this time forward forever more.'

Sorry John, the 2nd of July celebrations never took off. People were put off when you advertised they should enjoy the 'shews'.

So the signing, not the voting, got the nod and today, the 4th of July, was the one day the four of us wanted to be together.

The camp was deserted. Being a national holiday only essential staff worked, everyone else enjoying the sun with traditional trailer parties and barbecues. Bill had gone with some of his friends down river to a jazz festival but we decided the Quad Cities would be sufficient for us to sample the real flavour of America.

Despite pinging elastic bands of optimism from our fingers, the day lacked the expected patriotism. We longed for streets lined with Stars & Stripes, processions of glittery floats, interspersed with marching bands of toothless girls blue in the face from puffing infinite Sousa into their kazoos. What we got was a riverside Dixieland music festival of artists who may once had a small brush with fame but to us were just strangers in ill-fitting costumes.

It seemed as though we'd picked the place to go for all day drinking, which normally would have been fine and dandy, but today's significance meant we wanted to over indulge on hot dogs, wear Uncle Sam hats, and reminisce about the good old days of the Miami Dolphins, the Depression and the moral integrity of 'Operation Paperclip'.

The evening was like a normal Saturday night anywhere in the UK. At kicking out time, the precinct full of men offering equally inebriated women the chance of a fantastic five minutes, people vomiting in doorways that were the source of drying beds of urine streams, and fist fights around the hotdog stands.

'So what makes the 4th of July different to the other celebrations?' I asked one reveller who was undoubtedly pissed.

He burbled, 'It's a 24hour party, man,' before collapsing at just past 9pm.

I could hear the ghost of John Adams lament '…and they didn't even enjoy the shews.'

The paddlers admitted they weren't looking forward to getting back on the water. Elongating the time ashore, we ended up playing silly games on the dirty shale beach. Sean won everything. In the stone skimming, he got 11 bounces, although we reckon it was 10, and on the long range stone throwing contest, he nearly hit a passing barge. Rob was by far the outstanding competitor in our favourite game - the wrong handed throwing contest. We all looked pathetic throwing but Rob actually drew a crowd from passing bridge pedestrians not realising he was throwing with his wrong hand. Their suspicion that he was the worst athlete in history was confirmed when they heard his English accent.

It was a little too late to be setting off. There would only be a couple more hours of light. Where I'd have accepted that another night ashore wouldn't hurt, they were hewn from far sterner rock, their discipline (they had short hair) and determination dictated that they soldier on. I was impressed.

***

Nancy Halls had found time to take the job herself. From Iowa's oldest newspaper, 'The Hawkeye', she rattled on non-stop about just about every subject under the sun in a lively, carefree manner that made her a joy to be with. She'd suggested we meet at 'Big Muddy's', a restored freighthouse once owned by the Burlington Cedar Rapids and Northern Railroad, an industry that had put Burlington on the map. Now a popular watering hole and restaurant for locals and tourists alike, we'd meet Rob and Sean there at 6pm. Nancy bought us a couple of beers and introduced us to Jackie Brown, not the drug smuggling air stewardess, but the manageress of the place. Genuinely warm, Jackie also offered us a couple of free drinks to quench our thirst and promised that when the lads arrived, she'd cook up the river's most traditional meal - catfish.

Thanking her again, we waited on the outside seating, Nancy telling us about Missourians.

'What do you call a Missourian with no fur caught in his zipper?'

'Err don't know.'

'A virgin.'

Alright, you had to be there but she, like everyone else we'd met, couldn't resist taking a jovial swipe at the neighbouring States.

Rob and Sean pulled up at the bank at exactly 6pm. In front of Nancy, Fitz and I talking stupidly between ourselves about how they must have kept the strokes per hour at the correct rate. She asked us to explain and looked highly impressed when we concocted some improvised equation of strokes per hour x surface current flow x combined kinetic stroke joule output = distance covered.

The lads were tired, hungry, but happy. They'd found the current flow rather slow and their paddling therefore twice as laborious. After the interview, conducted over more free drinks, we dined on fried catfish, except for Rob who ordered half a cow. Being free, we'd accepted the catfish, but to be fair, Rob is a big lad, and a catfish ain't gonna satisfy a man of his appetite after a day on the river. As it turned out, when dinner was served we all sat doe eyed, tongues dripping at the biggest steak this side of the Mississippi that draped over the edges of his massive plate. The catfish was good, but every time I swallowed I could feel my taste buds water at the waft of steak juice running from Rob's fork. Jackie also offered a free dessert and we all gave Rob a *'don't do it look'* when he took an active interest in the menu when asked if ice cream was OK. Rob took the ice cream with the rest of us, and then ordered a great slab of chocolate mud pie.

We filled the following day with leisurely sight see-ing. Burlington, evidently no longer in its boom period, still maintained a charm that made the day pleasant. The downtown district was in need of a lick of paint but the quiet streets brought a relaxation that was appreciated by all. We even took a walk down the red cobbles of Snake Alley.

Lombard Street in San Francisco claims to be the world's most crooked road, but the locals here chal-lenge it with their own version. Having been down both I can't tell which is windier and I hadn't brought my crooked-street-o-meter. I noted the Burlington version wasn't a constant procession of open-windowed cars full of foreigners taking blurred pictures of magnolias. Both exuded curviness, but wanting a few more brown-ie points and free beers later in Big Muddy's I adjudicated that Snake Alley was far windier than the arrow-like Lombard Street.

Yet another financial crisis loomed. I was three weeks away from getting paid and I had £50 in my account. Phoning home, it appeared that my other half was hardly swimming in the pool of wealth. Every extra penny was being saved for our end of expedition holiday in Florida. Fitz faired hardly any better. His account just crept into three figures. We foresaw a month of scavenging in bins behind back street cafes. At the beginning of the trip we blithely bought pizzas, steaks, chocolate milk, and other extras that made living in the RV a joy. Now we scuffed our tattered shoes through the aisles of Burlington's cheapest supermarket looking for anything displaying the words 'extra value'. We found the God of all value foods - the humble ramen noodle. We even wrote a song about them. Dried Noodles are often the staple food of busy mums keen to get as much processed shit down their off-spring's neck with the least amount of time, effort and nutrition. We had plenty of time, and were always willing to try and cook something different, but the selling point of ramen noodles was their cheapness. Once we had sussed the ramen range, identified by the different serving suggestion that always included a fried egg, we could eat a hearty meal of re-hydrated noodles for 19c. By adding a tin of tuna and some sweetcorn we had something verging on palatable at a price where we could still afford to waste money on other things.

Looking in our rather sad looking pockets we needed cheering up, so taking Jackie's advice we did what many irresponsibly impoverished do, we tried our luck down at the local casino boat, the 'Catfish Bend'.

We drove towards the boat following advertising hoarding boards proclaiming in colourful writing 'loosest slots in town' that to made us giggle like childish perverts. Neither of us had visited such a place before, so Jackie and her brother escorted us down to the riverboat. Jackie was an ex croupier herself, and advised Fitz not to get into the business unless he was allergic to sunlight and wanted to work for pittance. She told us stories, however true, that the big Vegas casinos pumped oxygen through the air conditioning to keep insomniacs transfixed at the slot machines until they'd wasted all their money.

We walked around studying each game. Blackjack was straight forward, as was roulette. The one game that took our attention, as the cheers and shouting rang out, was the craps table. For the life of me, no matter how hard I tried I could not fathom this game of dice throwing. It looked fun, everyone their seemed to be animated, but the rules went right over my head, so I shouted along at any opportune moment and rather embarrassingly, at a very inopportune one.

The casino plied punters with free drinks as long as they were gambling. Noting this as a golden opportunity for freebies, we pretended to be big time Charlies. Each armed with $5, we were the ersatz Rockefellers. Scared to go on any of the games that presented us with decision-making we settled for a plastic cup full of quarters to squander on the endless variety of slots. Flashing lights pulled the serfs of the gambling hierarchy into their tractor beams. Sitting like battery hens, the slot addicts sat hour upon hour reaching into their cup, putting the quarter into the slot pulling the lever, never once taking their gaze from the spinning reels. It was enough to deter anyone from gambling. Anyone, that is, except us. Foolishly, we jumped on the machines.

Sitting down I pulled from my cup my lucky coin, placed it in the slot, pulled the arm and waited for the *thunk thunk thunk* of the reels to stop.

I didn't win. Never mind, try again. I inserted another lucky quarter.

Thunk cherry

Thunk lemon

Thunk orange. Bollocks. Try again.

Thunk orange

Thunk cherry

Thunk cherry. Knockers. The waterfall of winnings had dried up. Try again.

I lost count as to how many times I courted victory but it was quite a lot. I was now fishing for quarters in the bottom of my cup.

Thunk lemon

Thunk lemon

Thunk lemon. I couldn't believe it!

I spat a little 'yes' under my breath and watched with unashamed avarice at the $5 that spewed from the machine's metallic mouth. I'd broke even. It felt like a win.

I'm not sure whether eating a whole pack of bourbon biscuits would classify me as having an addictive personality, yet here I was addicted. I'd lose more often than not but the few not's more than made up for the losses. Fitz seemed to be having far more luck than me, his cup nearly half full of quarters. He'd won about $10. I had about $5. Together we could put down enough capital to do an aggressive takeover of a banana split.

Ten minutes later that was impossible. Greed had got the better of us. Fitz had burned out and lost his fortune. I just had one coin left. Kissing it, the last quarter was put in the slot.

Thunk orange

Thunk orange

Thunk orange.

This time I'd won a whopping $25 - enough to take ourselves out for a decent meal.

But $25 wasn't enough. We could win $50 and buy two decent meals. We sat again starry eyed at the reels, playing like the Vegas playboys we were, until I scratched around at the bottom of my cup for more coins. I found only plastic.

I need a quarter, I need a quarter. I must have more.

I scrounged around in my pockets. Despite over-loading myself with coke, my mouth had dried to parchment, my heart rapidly beating as a forewarning to cold turkey. I looked on the floor to see if anyone had been careless. Not finding one I unsteadily got to my feet, my legs taking me over to Fitz quicker than the rest of my body. I looked in his cup.

He's got quarters.

'Can I borrow a couple of quarters?

'You run out?'

I Don't want small talk, just give me the fucking quarters.

'Err yeah, just need a couple to, well you know, pass time.' My brow had started to sweat, palms were clammy like I'd been moulding clay.

He held out his mug and my heartbeat calmed to near normal. I took a few more than a couple but I didn't need too many. I could win back my fortune with five or six quarters. Taking a deep breath I exhaled in delirium as my quarter sank into the slot.

Thunk thunk thunk - music to my ears, but no win.

Fitz tapped me on the shoulder as I flipped in the last quarter again.

'This machine's a rip off,' I tutted.

'Well, why are you playing it?'

It was a question I couldn't answer. I looked around and saw in my despair the same people flipping in the same coins into the same machines that they had done when we'd arrived. It brought me to my senses.

'How much you got?' I asked.

'Nothing,' he laughed.

'Hmm about as much as me.' Getting off my chair, we wandered out of the casino, waved to the smiling doorman and retreated stony-broke back to the RV for a supper of ramen and sweetcorn. We'd now run out of tuna.

***

Driving back into Illinois we travelled down Highway 96 through wooded glades that cast shadows over the slate grey road. The river sparkled as the evening sun caught the tips of the wavelets like solar radar, specks of light flashing morse code from miniature beacons. The hills around the river now slowly caressed the water in a slow rolling slumber, towns and villages resting on their shoulders.

We passed through Nauvoo, the spiritual home of the Mormons. Sleepy, white spires looked over lush greens; church signs sat on every corner without a soul in sight to read them. We cruised round unable to find anywhere to park easily, so said our goodbyes and headed to Quincy.

We passed Lock and dam 19 at Keokuk. Once the largest on the river, it remained the ugliest - a set of giant rusting metal teeth spanning the river in an evil grin.

We entered Quincy. After ten minutes we left Quincy. I don't think the criminal pathologist named himself after this town. If he did he'd have been a dirty, scruffy, violent man with a drab exterior and insipid personality. The police station couldn't help us; it was a blessing in disguise as the town looked quite horrid.

Scooting through litter filled streets we looked for directions to find another rollercoaster of a metal bridge. We crossed over the river into Missouri.

After all the warning stories of Missouri, we crossed with trepidation. The grey storm clouds greeted us with a grumbling discontent threatening to wash the newly applied wax away from our gleaming RV. We now felt we were in the true Mid West. The landscape suddenly flattened to plains and the only visible breaks in the horizon were the passing road signs pointing in vague directions over the endless fields of corn swaying in rhythmic unison like a gospel choir. The sky looked angry and having the western edge of the State in 'Tornado Alley' we were close to donning our intrepid storm chaser outfits when we had a bout of wishful thinking we could witness a twister, hoping the pathetic cumuli nimbus above was a thunderhead brewing a spiral in the cauldron of its belly. Disappointed that the storm was a shower of British proportions, we continued to Hannibal, Missouri as the blanket of darkness was thrown over us.

***

Tourists don't bypass Hannibal. Near the welcoming bustle of fast food outlets and slow food diners, motels, and cloned gas stations, lies a town known for one thing - Mark Twain. And they wouldn't be disappointed.

Being such a small town of around 18,000, Hannibal hadn't much else to cling to and so Mark Twain, or Samuel Clemens as he was called in his formative years in this riverside backwater, got the full treatment. And a bit more.

We hadn't noticed anything untoward as we drove in under the cover of darkness into the police station car park on Broadway. The only thing to prick up our ears was the incessant throaty roar of muscle cars hurtling their reckless way up and down the street followed by whoops of joy from the local youths. The next morning we saw Hannibal in its full glory - a town squeezing Mark Twain for all its worth.

In the Mark Twain District, for instance, we could visit a plethora of gift shops with some tenuous attachment to his works - Betty Thatcher's Tampon Emporium or Indian Joe Curry Restaurant. We could fill up at the Huck Finn Gas Station, or get our washing done at the Tom Sawyer Laundromat. Ask directions to anywhere and the native's prefix to any answer was 'From Mark Twain...'

We walked downtown, passing the 'Mark Twain Museum' and gift shop, the 'Mark Twain Museum Annexe', which even though it was an annexe to the aforementioned museum still thought itself important enough to have its own title, before passing the 'New Mark Twain Museum' - a newer museum with a newer, more original title than the first Mark Twain Museum. We'd gorged until sick on Mark Twain after only three blocks, and I'm sure if he was looking down on Hannibal he would have drawn some droll quip he was famed for.

Commemorating a famous citizen is admirable, but here the sheer overkill displayed by Hannibal's sycophancy only outlined its own mediocrity.

After checking out possible landing areas for the paddlers, our over-ripe armpits dictated a shower. Our map showed a choice of Injun Joe's campground or Mark Twain's campground, just past Sawyer's creek. We opted for the latter as it was closer. We pulled up to the campground office all smiles. Unfortunately, my smile wasn't reciprocated. Noting them take a peek through the venetian blinds, I could see that the leather faced man and his two accomplices were going to need a hard sell. All three came out onto the porch to greet us. Handing over our portfolio, I kindly asked the man whether it would be OK to take a quick shower, fill up with water and dump our tanks.

'Ain't got no shower,' he answered, with a face like a slapped arse.

I turned my head quizzically towards a wooden building clearly marked "showers". 'What are those?'

'They'nt worken,' he replied curtly not taking his eyes from mine.

Feeling as though my request had been more than slightly refused, I said, 'Shouldn't you go tell the two men that have just gone in with their wash bags?'

Not bothering to answer, he flicked absently through the pages of our portfolio, the two male harpies behind each shoulder in a *'go on Hal, Giv't him'* pose.

'So can we dump and fill up with water?' I wanted now to see his temples burst.

'Ain't got no dump, got not warder.'

'Facilities are indeed scarce,' I replied glibly holding up a tourist guide. 'Are you sure your ad doesn't break some sort of advertising code? After all you say here…' I then called out the endless list of amenities that this 'friendliest campground' possessed before one of the younger men interrupted my flippancy.

'Look Mister, we don't know what dew want but w'aint god it.'

'Well I thought asking for shower, water and a dump was quite clear. I was also seeking some civility, but I see I've come to the wrong place.'

Fitz recognised my shortening fuse, so before I could say the word 'fucking' the word 'inbred' and the word 'bastards', he hustled me back to the RV.

Apart from Mrs Lindsay way back in northern Minnesota it was the first time we'd encountered any form of hostility. As sure as a middle aged couple will have a box of tissues on their car's parcel shelf, it was to happen sooner or later; many people harden to charity and see people such as us as freeloading pariahs, but it had shocked us all the same and it had put even the ever-optimistic Fitz in a slightly foul mood.

Still needing water, we pulled into a nearby gas station. The cashier was the spitting image of every other female cashier we'd thus come across. A green slide pushed her red hair to one side, her face glistening from perspiration soaked foundation. She wore a top so tight that you could see her bra cutting demarcated salt marks. And she chewed gum voraciously.

'There's an outside tap round the back. You god a container?' she muffled from behind a gum bubble the size of a pig's bladder. Yes, I've seen one. They're bigger than you'd think.

'It's for the RV.'

'Oh,' her tone changed. 'How much d'ya need?'

'About sixty gallons.'

'No way, uh uh, no siree, can't give ya that.'

'Bollocks.' I could say that here without censure.

Deciding subterfuge was the better option than overt honesty, I went back to Fitz to formulate a plan. After agreeing that we hated Hannibal and wished all its occupants were subjected to nerve agent trials, I returned with an empty water container.

'Would it be possible to fill this?' I asked holding up the five litres plastic bottle.

With her chipped nail varnish of far too much importance, she nodded.

Bottle in hand, I browsed amongst the aisles pretending to be interested in oil, melted chocolate and air fresheners designed to make your car smell like a public toilet. While I'd taken her attention, Fitz had sneakily driven to the rear, out of her sight. I joined him and we giggled like naughty schoolboys as we filled up the RV water tanks *and* our five litre bottle just to rub her nose in it. Laughing in a manner suited to the big time felons we now were, we retreated to the boat landing to cool ourselves on the water's breeze and to whine about Hannibal.

We couldn't be arsed to garner any PR, as we'd concluded most of Hannibal's inhabitants would be illiterate. The air, and our negativity, was starting to smother us and even sitting on the jetty couldn't dissipate the sweltering humidity that supressed our contentment. Unable to bear no more, we shuffled to the newspaper office with the sole purpose of sharing someone's air conditioning.

As expected, we were passed between uninterested journalists before finally being shunted to the city editor who thankfully had an air-conditioned office. He was going to get the full story whether he wanted it or not. We immediately struck up a rapport. Although his body and spectacles had similar sized frames, Leigh Bellinger was also a military man, having spent five years in the US Air Force. Quietly spoken, he seemed genuinely interested in our journey and asked questions others hadn't, keen to know about us as people as much as the expedition. We talked for an age, having a sense of humour we could relate to, we found time flew by, although he declined our request to castigate the owners of the Mark Twain campground on the grounds he couldn't print the sentence 'bunch of miserable wankers'. He scribbled ream upon ream of notes in calligraphy only he and a 99 year old General Practitioner could decipher, before becoming alarmed at the time. Interview over and late for his next schedule, he paused slightly before asking, 'Would you be interested in coming round for dinner?'

Humbled by his offer we readily agreed and returned to the furnace of the midday sun with lifted hearts. At the RV we fell into one of those contented snoozes granddad would have after Sunday lunch. Hannibal wasn't so bad after all.

***

Whether to appease the gods or just as punishment, sacrificing man for the 'good' of some fictional character, death in the name of religion has frequently been carried out in a hideously savage manner. The monks of the Spanish Inquisition were infamously world champion torturers. Whether to extract confession or just to satisfy the penalty of death; inquisitors found increasingly heinous ways to end someone's often god-fearing life. Just to be brought to the Holy House of Torture would draw confession from many a weak-willed heretic. Those with a stronger constitution or those totally bemused at their presence were subsequently half drowned by gallons of water forced down their throats, or raised from the ground by their arms wrenched up their back causing limbs to be slowly prised from their sockets - just as a warm up for a proper 'confession'.

One especially gruesome implement in the 'heat torture' category was the 'Brazen Bull'. The hollow bull's bronze stomach was just big enough to accommodate an adult. The bull would then be half filled of water and a fire would be lit underneath. Slowly, but definitely surely, the victim would simmer, bubble, then boil to a quite horrible death. To crank up the sadism level, the bull was usually the centrepiece for a banquet, the music aficionados of the banquet solved the victim's screaming problem by implanting reeds into the bull's nostril holes to turn the brazen bull into a giant steam organ to play a hideous background jingle to enhance the medieval dining experience.

I thought I'd never experience such a terrible noise, but my siesta was interrupted by a sonic cheese grater attack to my ears - the blood curdling whistle of the musical calliope on board the steamboat 'Mark Twain' as it docked nearby. The calliope's steam power pushed out similarly strangled yowls of boiling flesh in a dreadful improvisation of what is commonly called 'music'.

As we didn't want to fill the Bellingers' pristine home with bleeding ears and the stench of crusty BO, we suggested a shower might be the best option, Leigh's wife Michelle agreeing far too readily. Washing the remnants of calliope music from our grimy ears, we felt and smelled a hundred times better. Michelle waited on us hand and foot offering fresh lemonade and iced fruit to cool down our overheated bodies.

They lived in American suburbia where white wooden houses slept in the shade of the falling sun. Small but cosy, their home seemed rather British. I had visions of every American house being the size of a small country with Bald Eagle statuettes adorning every mahogany item, but it seemed western homes spoke in a universal language of decoration. Equally, our shared humour became the propagator to friendship and just being able to vegetate in their all-too comfortable chairs and channel hop for hours, watching 'Renegade' or something similarly shite elicited a happiness that taught us a valuable lesson in hasty perception.

We waited by the Mark Twain Riverboat to welcome the familiar shaped speck of the kayak. I ventured onto the spit where sat two attractive women. Not wanting to sound like I held the patent on the worst chat up line in history, I asked, 'Have you seen a kayak go past?'

Looking at each other with look that said '*that's the worst chat up line in history*' one, shading her eyes, said, 'No.'

As if by a miracle, the lads came into view. I pointed out to the girls that indeed I didn't have the worst chat up line in history, although my 'can I plait your hair with my feet?' comes close.

Accepting me in an altogether different context, they were then keen to hear of our daring deeds. 'Yes we drink beer,' we said. 'Yes we play pool,' and 'yes we'd love to join you later at the pool hall.'

The lads landed. Rob winced in agony. His back was 'in bits' and was fearful his role on the river was at an end. As reserve, Fitz would take up arms to paddle the duration - a worst-case scenario that Fitz had taken philosophically, Rob with dread. Although nights of disjointed sleeping on sand bars would be replaced by deep slumber on soft beds, and the monotony of counting mileage markers exchanged with exploring the towns' river folk and listening to my drivel, Rob saw not completing the paddle as failure. And failure was something he didn't take kindly to.

We joined the two girls, Chrissy and Gjetta, the latter of Native American descent, for a quick beer and a game of pool. Worried about Rob, we took our leave to see how he felt after his post-paddle siesta, just as their suspicious boyfriends arrived.

Rob's glass back was giving him some serious grief. As low as I'd ever seen him, he lay there quietly pondering his future. Unable to humour him, we thought it best to let him have some solitary rest so took Sean to Leigh's ambient office via the Tom and Huck statue, the 'J.M Clemens Law Office', and a shop displaying gingerbread cut to the shape of Mark Twain's penis and bottles of Sawyer Milk. I've made some of these up just in case you're wondering.

The best course of action was to rest an extra day in Hannibal. The paddlers were well ahead of schedule and to rush things for the sake of an extra couple of days enjoying New Orleans would be madness. We took up Leigh's invitation to use his living room floor as a hard base for Rob to lie on.

Miraculously, sleeping on the wooden floor had done wonders for Rob's back. While not 100%, witnessing his animalistic gorging at breakfast suggested a significant rise in spirits. Michelle must have thought she was feeding the 5000, Rob eating enough for 4997, but she generously turned down our offer of replacing what we'd consumed, which was fortunate as I didn't have the $500 that it would need to refill her cupboards.

Two days ago we'd dipped our toes warily into social etiquette by talking about the weather. Now Fitz had Michelle in stitches at the kitchen table, as the conversation had somehow meandered into how Michelle's friend would look dressed in a rubber suit and gimp mask swinging from the ceiling by nipple clamps. I was as confused as everyone else how we'd got onto the subject, but it reinforced our affinity for them.

Leigh finally satisfied the paddlers with photographs that were splashed onto the front page of the Hannibal Courier Post. It was the first time Leigh had seen the kayak and was even more impressed with our venture. Just as impressive was the wooden boat that berthed alongside the kayak as the paddlers were set to leave. Painted in the brightest white, it was an old fashioned vessel skippered by Captain Birdseye himself. His life was a marine version of the RV couples we had met back in Wisconsin, his solitary life revolving around boating around the waterways of North America, his healthy tanned cheeks showing his last three years were well spent. He proudly showed us around his beautiful 1920's vessel, a floating homage to art deco, even his portaloo of polished wood was maintained with love and affection. He spun the walnut pilot's wheel as we entered the small bridge space furnished in the finest mahogany. It was a trip back in time and a welcome change from the modern craft that ploughed like torpedoes through the water. We were approximately a thousand miles from the sea and despite living in Poole, I'd never seen so many boats in my life as I had in the past nine weeks. The Mississippi was just a berth for most this far down. Many didn't see its muddy waters as pleasurable, so would scoot off onto of its more 'enjoyable' tributaries but Nils, the skipper, loved the river and used it as the backbone for his touring.

Saying our goodbyes, we returned to the RV where we found a note held in the windscreen wipers from the police staff inviting us to an evening out the following night. Unfortunately, we were due in St Louis but were advised our last night here should be spent at a bar called 'Sippi's'.

We bumped into Gjetta, enjoying her evening with an elderly married couple who weren't her parents as suspected, but her drinking partners. And drink they could.

'You ever had Jagermeister?' Gjetta asked.

I had, Fitz hadn't. He gurned as he downed his first, and last. I feel nauseous after a couple. Gjetta, on the other hand, didn't. She was an efficient Jagermeister processing machine, sinking shot after shot, dragging me with her on a downward spiral into not losing at drinking games. Forgetting I get absolutely shit faced with a suck of a barmaid's apron, I found myself getting the all too familiar shudder, the body's alarm signalling me to quit forthwith. But ignoring sense, I soldiered on. I matched her shot for shot, feeling more nauseous, yet refusing to be psyched out by each small shot glass that increased in size with every gulp. Defeat was as unpalatable as the Jagermeister, yet Gjetta knocked it back like lemonade. Making my excuses that I needed a pee, I calmly walked to the toilet before my stomach pushed out a spray of vomit that would have covered Mark Twain Square. I think the ferocity of the jet cracked the urinal, but it gave instant relief. My stomach now spent of alcohol, I wiped the elastic dribble from my chin and exhaled into my hand just to confirm it stank of vomit. I returned with the tell tale signs of watery eyes, and making the excuse that I couldn't afford another bottle of Jagermeister, conceded defeat.

'Defeat?' she asked quizzically.

'Were we not just having a drinking competition?' I asked, slurring 'competition' into 12 syllables.

'No we weren't. I don't do that sort of shit. It gets you too drunk.'

The night over, I stumbled out into the warm night without even a cooling breeze to knock me to my senses. Gjetta offered us a lift in her pick up.

'You fit to drive?' asked Fitz.

She looked indignant, struggling to find the lock with a swaying key. 'Course I am, not hardly had drop of it to drinking.'

Fitz snatched the keys from her. Not at all happy, she eventually listened to reason and directed Fitz where to head.

I once saw a T-shirt that read, 'Instant arsehole - just add alcohol' which, although not funny enough to purchase, was rather apt. Gjetta was being a real arsehole. She kept grabbing hold of the wheel pulling the pick up onto the sidewalk.

Fitz's orders to stop were ignored. Dulled with alcohol, I didn't really comprehend the danger she was putting everyone in.

In my alcoholic haze, I didn't particularly care where she was taking us, but we drove for what seemed an eternity. My head jolted wildly as the pick up swerved off the road into a field of man-high corn. Fitz slammed on the brakes, throwing Gjetta into the windscreen. The water of a reservoir was 5 yards to our front.

Fitz wasn't impressed. 'I'll drive you back handcuffed to the door.'

Gjetta giggled. Fitz shook his head then joined her.

More coherent, I braced my legs under the dashboard until we stopped at a gravel car park in the middle of nowhere.

Gjetta took us to where she came to reflect when stressed. I could see why. It was alluring under the shining full moon that cast a silver sheen over the darkness of the river. The river soothingly lapped against the bank in slow mellifluous kisses that pecked our feet as we dangled them over the edge of a lonely rowing boat. She'd grown up on a farm near here and used its tranquillity as her therapist. I lay back in the bowels of the rowing boat, slowly rocked by the sway of the river. The dopamine of serenity pulsed through my veins, the stars, bright in the sky, smiled down upon me. The still night air interrupted in its repose by the chattering of the crickets and the occasional buzz of a mosquito. I thought of England and its dour skies. *I could die here,* I thought, and I wouldn't give a shit.

I woke up with a start, Fitz shaking my arm like a rag doll's. I'd been asleep for over an hour and felt as rough as a badger's arse and not quite as attractive. Fitz drove steadily back, Gjetta asleep on his shoulder. She'd pushed through her halcyon fix and wore a contented smile. It was a shame to wake her when we reached the RV but she had to exit the pick up. To be behind the wheel of a vehicle in her state was suicide enough but while in a police car park it was taking a bottle of cyanide tablets with your feet encased in concrete while driving over a cliff into the sea. When we awoke next morning, the only proof of her existence was the note left on the crumpled bed sheet. *'Thanks for looking after me. Good luck on the river G x'.*

After Leigh humiliated us by giving us both a good thrashing at putt putt golf, he took us for a farewell lunch at Sawyer's Creek. Seriously warning us of the perils of East St Louis, we felt like we were driving into an episode of Scooby Doo.

'Let's not focus on the crumb that falls on our lap.
Enjoy the many we eat.'

~ Nije Thorpe, satirist

We still hadn't discovered the clearing height of the RV, so winced approaching every low bridge into St Louis. They couldn't be that low, trucks had to pass under them. The worrying lack of trucks on this particular road did suggest that the position of our air conditioning unit remaining on top was somewhat in jeopardy.

Reaching the city centre with the top of the vehicle intact, we dawdled around the empty streets to find the St Louis Metropolitan Police Department Headquarters. Our steps echoed in the grand polished stone entrance hall aesthetically injured by airport style x-ray portals. We were in the big city.

Sgt David Calloway from the Prisoner Processing Division met us. An advert for 'Soul Glo', his terrible hairstyle couldn't detract from him being the most helpful man we'd met so far.

Unlike the tosspot in Moline, this police officer was of the opinion that our cause deserved help. Limited space restricted us from staying at headquarters, and despite several knock backs from other departments, he took us to the mechanical workshop. While we looked over a sparkling Harley Davidson, the chief mechanic passed on the good news that there was available space. The bad news was that the bays weren't secure.

'Only last week, the police commissioner's vehicle was stolen from here.'

It would have been hilarious but for the fact it didn't solve our parking issue. Eventually, we received permission through Sgt Calloway to park in City Hall car park opposite Police Headquarters. Although secure behind fencing, it didn't feel safe, so double-checked every lock before walking to the riverfront.

When it comes to modern construction I used to fall short on interest. But the more I travel, the more I see an architect's certifiable imagination reflected in structures that make me gasp, and here in St Louis was one of them - The Gateway Arch.

Designed by Finnish genius Eero Saarinen, the 'Arch' stands glistening in a 630ft elliptic loop of stainless steel as a symbol of St Louis's position as the gateway to the New World, the last staging post before westward expansion. Invisible from many angles, the Riverfront Park hid the Jefferson Memorial Museum of Westward Expansion. We followed the gradual incline directly under the Arch down to the museum entrance. Once out of natural light, our eyes adjusted to the underground atrium with space that deceived like a TARDIS. We browsed the different sections that chronicled the sweep across North America starting from the earliest expeditions to the construction of the Arch above. Not surprisingly, the main butt of the displays concerned the impact of expansion on the Native Americans. It was handled objectively and informatively, causing parents brought up on a diet of John Wayne and Rawhide to leave decidedly confused. We spent an informative hour examining original chuck wagons, tepee interiors and the bloomers of 19th century mannequins, before taking note of our grumbling bellies and looked for somewhere to eat.

Downtown was unerringly quiet. It was in gradual decline. The money was now being siphoned from the centre and being disseminated to the suburbs, where the middle classes lived. This seemed rather sad, seeing this ailing patient coughing and spluttering through its final years, its strength being sucked away by its younger siblings rising in new residential districts, complete with their own commercial infrastructure, to take over the next era. Going the opposite way towards the centre, the low cost housing complexes complete with its own infrastructure of crime and addiction. The big boys remained - the banks, the communications conglomerates and in this particular city, the brewery, the biggest in the world.

As we hadn't managed to find any decent street maps or tour guides, not wanting to tempt fate and wander into a rough neighbourhood we spent the evening playing cards in the RV. The night was interrupted every so often with the sirens of police, and a gunshot too close for comfort was heard more than once.

With a night combining noise with humidity, we awoke less than refreshed and grumbled through breakfast trying to figure out our next move. We reverted back to plan A, which was to go to Granite City, Illinois. We'd originally poo-pooed plan A upon realising it was next to East St Louis. Having being told that it was one of the worst areas in the Mid West for violent crime (car-jacking's a speciality), we looked back over the river for a place to stay. But here, in the City Hall car park, options were no better.

As it transpired, we found the Illinois side rather less hassle than the Missouri side, possibly because we were out of the hustle and bustle of St Louis. Hoping not to get car jacked by some modern day dandy highwayman, rather than go straight over the Poplar Street Bridge into East St Louis, we took a long cut going north out of town up to the bridge on I270 towards Granite City.

We hadn't realised our destination Lock and Dam was within a US Army base. Comforted by the fact we may at last have the necessary security, we were confronted by a barrack policeman who, not understanding our accents, thought it best we report to his headquarters where we were introduced to Lt Ronnie Spiroff - a veteran of policing and, by his welcome, party hosting.

There are not many occasions where you can boast of spending an enjoyable evening in a police station reception but this was one. Most of the watch stopped to chat in between their patrol, and our stomachs bulged on the constant stream of coffees and snacks. Retiring relaxed back to the RV, a couple of officers invited themselves in to share a 12 pack of beers. Both of Irish decent they immediately turned the conversation to the 'Troubles' in Northern Ireland, us trying as impartially as possible to wipe clean their rose tinted glasses. Once we'd got that sorted, our interest turned to them. Jake, the elder of the two was a hunting fanatic. Hoping we weren't to be again subjected to hours of stories of blowing away stationary animals with Uzi's, we ended up being fascinated by his slant on blood sports as he hunted with a bow and arrow. I was staunchly unconvinced that hunting with a bow and arrow was a quick way of killing the deer that he so often hunted. Quicker than a bullet, I was told, a bolt aimed in the correct place killed a deer instantly. I could hold no real grudge as long as the animals are killed with minimum of suffering. Once my doubt was removed, we sat enthralled by the art of bow hunting. Stalking is a highly specialised skill within the military, and the Royal Marines hold possibly one of the most professional sniper's school's in the world where stalking is a inherent part of passing the course. Stalking a human target 400 metres away before slotting it with a high velocity 7.62 round is one thing. But to sneak up to within 20 metres on a hyper sensitive white tailed deer, before shooting a bolt straight in between its forelegs was an immense skill, one that had to be admired - and anyway those bastards were the most dangerous animals in America so needed sorting.

We managed to pass the couple of days in the army camp itself. Although virtually empty, it sported its own golf course and state-of-the-art gymnasium to keep us occupied. We made friends with Steve Grant, Special Agent in charge of the local agency of the Army Criminal Investigation Command, his PA's office being nominated to supply the hook up point. His access to the internet allowed us to contact various authorities to gain certain information, and to contact the Embassy in DC to notify the relevant agencies of our arrival further down river. He was a lexicon of knowledge on the areas to avoid on the way down, East St Louis at the top of his list. He had first hand knowledge of the UK having been on a presidential bodyguard team. Without egotistical tales, he impressed us with stories of his experiences.

We waited at Lock & Dam 27. Incorrectly noted as the final Lock and dam on the river, it is actually on the 10 mile long lateral canal that runs as a short cut for traffic just off the main flow of the Mississippi.

The river now ran ferociously as its big brother, the Missouri River, was now in cahoots. Starting 2714 miles away in Montana, the Missouri is the single longest river in North America. Some suggest the Mississippi should be its tributary but as the Big Muddy is the artery of a drainage basin covering over half of the USA's landmass, the Mississippi is the daddy, and as the floods of 1993 proved, a rather volatile one at that.

In the fall of 1992, soil moisture levels were already high. Winter rains and snow further saturated the ground so the following spring precipitation and snow melt, instead of soaking into the soil, could only run off into streams and rivers.

In March 1993, the national weather service, in true Michael Fish style, predicted below normal precipitation for the summer, which would allow the soils to dry out.

Exactly two months after that survey, 8inch rainstorms hit the Dakotas, Wisconsin, and Minnesota, bursting the first dam ten days later submerging one hundred homes up to their rooftops.

By July 15th every area in the drainage basin had at least twice its normal rainfall, some areas six times as much. There were twelve major storms with rainfall up to 12 inches in the wettest June and July since 1895.

On August 2nd the river was at its highest, cresting in St Louis an outrageous 49ft 7in higher than normal - 19ft over what is considered 'flood stage'. The water passing under Eads Bridge was eleven times the volume of Niagara Falls, and enough to fill the nearby Busch Stadium every 65 seconds.

Over 1000 of the 1300 levees, designed specifically to hold back flood waters, failed along the Upper and Middle Mississippi leaving 16,000 square miles of farmland submerged, displacing 70,000 people and 50,000 homes. Damages to surface and river transportation were the worst ever incurred in the US and in total damage was estimated between $15-20 billion. Although many of the losses could be repaired, some things could never be replaced - 52 people lost their lives.

***

As I strained my eyes down the straight of the canal, I started talking to a man waiting for the same people. He introduced himself as Dr Jerard Bonbrake from the small town of Alton just up river. Sean and Rob had stayed at his marina the previous night and they'd whetted his appetite for adventure. As an active member of the Make-A-Wish foundation, that gives terminally ill children the chance to fulfil their last wishes, he was keen to help our charity in any way he could. He'd promised Rob and Sean an evening to remember when they arrived and cordially invited us as well.

It certainly was an evening to remember. He asked us whether we minded going to 'tittie bars'. We didn't. Fitz and I agreeing so long as our intended destination wasn't as crumby as that fleapit on East Dubuque. Jerard assured us that the place we were going was anything but crumby.

He picked us up with his son, Jeff, in tow. We pulled up outside the glitziest, showiest building outside of Las Vegas.

'Guys,' said Dr Bonbrake as we stood at the entrance, 'Tonight is on me. No arguments. Just enjoy.'

Despite feeling guilty about him wanting to splash his cash, he furthered by saying we were doing him a favour. Not knowing what that favour was we entered nonetheless. Once past the sizeable entrance fee, I was amazed what affluence frequented the place. Despite the beautiful naked women dancing lithely on the various stages around lighted poles, 'PT's' didn't feel at all sleazy, and the prices once inside prevented all but the rich from coming and enjoying themselves. We were continually plied with beers as we sat around a large table before ordering the finest in steaks, and seafood, I received a strange 'no' from the waiter when I asked if they served ramen noodles, and had to settle with lobster as the wadding for my beer.

Full to the sinuses, I found my waistline and my bladder bursting. We hadn't even sat goggle-eyed at the stages yet. Jerard sensed our embarrassment, not by the cavorting girls but by his generosity. He did nothing to quell it when he ordered cognac and cigars thinking it would put us at ease. Now as already mentioned, I've always maintained an anti smoking stance, I'd never even taking a crafty drag with the scrotes around the back of the bike sheds at school. But for once I allowed my guard to drop, after all cigars are nearly as healthy as bananas, so said my Uncle Frank.

'Do you want straight or French?' asked Jerard.

'Err which are the best?' I asked, naively thinking a French cigar might only work for a bit then go on strike.

'No it's not the cigar, it's the cut. French cut is at an angle like this.' He cut his own with his silver clippers. He had a silver cigar clipper. I didn't even own a nail clipper. I took the French option, after all I was drinking cognac. They all looked on giggling at my inability to light it. I sucked and sucked until my lungs filled with smoke coughing out plumes of spit and tobacco all over the table to the delight of the rest. But at least it was alight, and I had to admit it didn't taste bad, not great, but not bad. Looking extremely cosmopolitan I followed Jerard's example dipping the end in the Cognac before sitting back in my plush armchair choking on my cigar the size of an RPG watching some of the most beautiful women I'd ever seen getting their kit off. Life couldn't get much better than this. But it did. Jerard came back from the in-house ATM machine and put a hundred one dollar bills in front of each of us. Looking twice seeing if it was real we were instructed to stop being fannies and get some money spent.

Never having watched Noel's House Party for pleasure, but for research, I always seemed to turn over when the 'Gotcha's' were on - tricks played on the rich and famous, hilarious to people who bought coats for their dogs in the winter. I was in such pleasure, I expected someone from the TV to similarly come and spoil my fun. With equal delight, Sean decided to play a 'bite' on Rob. A bite is a joke or prank, usually played on gullible novices - think of sending someone for a long weight or stripey paint, and you get the idea. In the military, sprogs on ships are often pinged to stand on the bow of a ship with a broom handle for hours on end undertaking the important task of 'iceberg pusher'.

Rob, as I've mentioned, is a good looking bloke, and although not vain, he knows it. So Sean's idea was to pay $25 for a girl to do a private dance for Rob and say it was free as he was the best looking guy in the club. Sean's train of thought was that upon completion Rob would return thinking he could get private dances for free, only to brought crashing down by Sean admitting he'd actually paid her to say it. Somehow I didn't this would particularly bother him.

'Can't you play that bite on me instead?' I asked.

Even so, Sean went ahead with it and was in raptures when Rob returned and told him of his jolly jape. Rob didn't give two shits as he had just had a fantastic five minutes. We decided we would organise the expedition's bites from now on.

Once we'd spent up, we talked to some of the girls. A few were working their way through college, a number did it as a career, none had been forced into it nor did any regret doing it. The rules here were strict, definitely no touching and the girls could order someone to be ejected if they were being subjected to verbal abuse. One of the girls Gerry, was a massive English music fan and a keen keyboard player. With Fitz now able to strum the chords behind 'Abide with Me' and I, a descant recorder winner at the 1981 Pontefract Music Festival, we felt we could take the charts by storm with my fantastic Match Of The Day recital, especially if Gerry got her kit off in the videos.

I woke up feeling like someone had defecated in my mouth and smeared axle grease around my teeth. My throat felt as though I'd swallowed barbed wire and my head as though I'd met a quartet of violent skinheads. In short, I had a hangover and the residue of a cigar necessitated me to head for Steve Grant's toilet and pay homage to Huey. Never again would I smoke, whether it was a cigar or haddock.

What was worse was that creeping feeling of my dark twin. I thought I'd left him locked in a cupboard in the UK, but it seemed he had stowed away in my luggage and managed to get into the USA without an appropriate visa and here it sat inside my brain living rent free, not even having the decency to chip in for the RV. It was a bad day for him to arrive.

Parked in the Casino Queen's Car Park in East St Louis, we had to run round like blue arsed flies to film the lads canoeing past the Gateway Arch and get back over the river in time for the Mayor of St Louis to greet us. It was a ball ache of a job trying to compose myself while hot and bothered. I stripped down to just my shorts. Once I'd got video footage and some stills withholding that ominous sobbing feeling that stuck in my throat, I had to rush to catch the train over the bridge to Laclede's Landing, some surly train attendant saying I couldn't travel without a top on. With a crimpled lip I just gave a sardonic answer that I didn't have a shirt. He then ordered me to leave at the next stop, which suited me as it was where I intended to alight anyway. Running to the guys, when all I wanted to do was run away, they were now joined by a small camera crew at the Riverfront. It was all I needed, more people to veer away from. Sean confronted me with a train attendant's voice ordering me to get a shirt on. Self pity turned to silent seething.

'I've been running about for you in the midday heat, after all we've done you're complaining that I have no shirt on?

'I haven't got one,' I returned angrily.

'Well you won't be able to meet the mayor,' he replied.

While this may have been a good thing considering my state, Sean's words twisted inside. *Who the fuck are you to tell me what I can do?*

Fortunately, the mayor phoned to inform us he couldn't make it which meant the news crew had no story, so made their excuses and left.

Sean was not a happy camper. Neither was I. The dark twin's selfishness had manifested itself upon me. To make up for the disappointment we were visited by the pop star sounding Rick Skinner from the organisation 'United Cerebal Palsy' who kindly handed over a cheque for our cause. In my state, I hardly acknowledged his presence, preferring just to sit to one side and build the barricade for my solace.

They dined at the world's only floating MacDonald's. With no money, I declined. I wanted no communication, even with the smell of fat encouraging primordial salivation. Fitz saw my predicament and offered me a meal that I refused with what must have looked like ingratitude.

I sat sweating like a pornstar, declining the offer to go to the St Louis Cardinals Major League baseball game that night. I had a Major league cloud above me so just sat sullen in the humidity of the Casino Queen's car park. Having time to reflect, I ruminated upon the down sides that were of far more interest than the good points.

Welsh flags, wrong RV's, wrong meeting points, women with scabby faces, no shirt, no family, what the fuck will I do when I leave the Corps, where will we get a three bedroom house if we have more children, still no tuna.

I rattled on conveying my thoughts to my darker side, until I saw the Hannibal Courier Post laying there on the table. The word 'Hannibal' brought up images of the A-Team, and my thoughts then strayed onto their escapades. God knows why, but my mood again lifted as I reminisced about how bad the programme was - Mr T building, but refusing to fly awake in, a Microlight made from a washing up bottle and dog leads, then waking to join the rest in getting the job before returning Murdoch to the institute in time for his evening sedative. It was now from a blithe overview that the dark twin took a quite surreal decision to leave as quickly as it had arrived. I could have wondered why, but was fearful that he may return upon my introspection, so sat confused as to my surroundings. My personal GPS kicked in. I was being paid to travel for three months away from work down the Mississippi, with three of the best bloke I'd ever known. That was all I needed to know.

***

A reporter from Alton's newspaper had promised to leave a package at the Museum of Westward Expansion's reception containing a copy of the newspaper report and tickets to see the films showing in the museum and the escalator to go to the top of the Arch.

Collecting the package, we read the report, Fitz and I feigning abhorrence that Rob and Sean hadn't even mentioned our names whilst in interview. Biting, they took offence and what was meant to be a joke turned into a bit of a stand off, which in the middle of a museum was pathetic. We split up, having seen the museum already it was pointless going round again, so with time to kill, Fitz and I did the only thing two mature commandos would do in a museum, play tig.

We again met up with Jerard and Jeff at the River-front, Jerard kindly donating a cheque for $500 for our cause.

He'd previously confessed his disdain at the thought of Jeff getting married so young without really seeing much of the world as a single man. So it was more of a forthright question than a hint when he suggested it would be good for Jeff to do something similar to us, such as taking a road trip down the river. He had relatives in Memphis so a short trip with a bunch of guys may do him some good. So this was the favour he needed. Taking up on his camouflaged request we invited Jeff to join us on our way down to Memphis. With his bags already packed, Jeff readily accepted, so bundling him into the RV we said our goodbyes to both the wonderfully benevolent Jerard and the paddlers, promising to meet them a few days later.

Thinking it best to leave St Louis as soon as possible, we took to the highways boasting truck stops offering free laundry facilities with every fifty gallons of diesel, not planning on our next destination.

'Man was made to assist man.'

~ Prof Pangloss, Candide, Voltaire

Waking in a mall car park in St Genevieve, we took breakfast and stretched our legs taking a walk up and down the main drag before setting off to Cape Girardeau.

We had given Jeff the usual interrogation - his life, aspirations, hobbies, likes and dislikes. We rarely found commonality, which was only to be expected. He was half a generation younger and from the Midwest. Our taste in music, for instance, happened to be worlds apart. We played a veritable smorgasbord of Manchester classics all the way down to Cape Girardeau. Rather than a verse of Morrissey being an epiphany, he showed his appreciation by donning his Walkman headphones and listening to his own vibes at a volume loud enough to know it was ear cack.

Jeff did share certain habits with his American brethren in so much that he had a penchant for chewing baccy. We tried to ignore it at first, we would have stopped him smoking immediately but as there was no foul odour we gave him the benefit of the doubt. However, the human mind can only take so many repetitive spits and ultimately seeing the cohesive swill of sticky brown spit and bits of tobacco in a clear plastic bottle, we could take no more. We eventually asked him to stop or at least not spit into something transparent that increasingly looked like a chain smoker's plastic lung. He agreed on the latter and so turned his attention to an empty Coke can. This was only slightly better. I've since given up drinking Coke, not due it being nutritionally empty, but for fear of gulping someone's baccy infused phlegm.

***

Growing up on a coal mining town's council estate means I have the occasional craving for tinned ravioli. Sitting next to the Cape Girardeau floodwall on Water Street was such an occasion. Just before licking the plate clean of remaining sauce, I noticed a bespectacled old man shuffle slowly from behind the floodwall trying to attract attention by waving a quivering stick held in his knurled hand. Being inside the RV we couldn't make out what he was saying, but he was obviously distressed. It was a slow motion panic, in contrast to those that I'd previously seen, such as a fellow Royal Marine recruit called Andy, who in his last minute preparation for the adjutant's inspection, ironed out a small crease his stone shirt - while still wearing it, resulting in a lovely iron shaped blister.

Disembarking from the RV we immediately heard the screaming from behind the floodwall. Running through the gap to the river we were confronted by a teenage girl. Half clinging to the boulders up to her shins in water, her face was luminous scarlet through the strain of her incessant wailing, her hands cupping her cheeks and tears ran in torrents to her mouth where saliva carried on down her chin.

The old guy behind mumbled, 'The boy, the boy.'

Autopilot took over. It was obvious her friend had gone into the water and not returned. We sprinted as fast as we could along the bank hopeful to see a speck of hair or the flailing of a weakened arm. Fitz returned from the RV with a spare lifejacket hopeful we might need it. The bobbing of deadwood caught our attention but only floated into the bank with an inanimate thud.

We searched again not knowing really where to look. Would he be at the edge, the middle, or dragged far downstream? Wherever we looked, we saw nothing.

We felt useless, totally and utterly useless. Submerged where we stood not more than two minutes ago, by now he was probably passing under the Cape Girardeau bridge 400 metres away, entrapped in the undercurrent like a kitten in a washing machine spin cycle.

The fire crews were first on scene, followed by the press, then the police.

Still looking out for any sign of life, we watched the rescue boat launch, accelerating through the water in figure of eights around certain objects. It was now out of our hands, not that the situation had ever been in them. The fire fighters questioned us, but apart from running up and down the bank in vain there was little we could tell them. The old man mumbled incomprehensible sentences, the girl too distraught, head in hands still screamed into a police officer's bosom. Only now when surveying the water, it was blatantly clear to see why he'd fallen into such difficulty. The current was strong enough to carry a dead tree past at the speed of a prize-winning greyhound with an even quicker undercurrent, as this lad's feet had just found out.

Speaking to a fire fighter he pronounced that the body would probably pop up south of Memphis. Some shrimping boats had even spotted bloated corpses from the north on their way out into the Gulf of Mexico. What state they'd be in by then was anyone's guess but presumably they'd be appetising to the many hungry river creatures.

Not really the time to promote our venture, the radio interviewer still managed to take the conversation away from the accident in a conscientious bid to streamline a double story. The only apt thing we could say was that the people had to respect the river, not openly conveying that the deceased clearly had not.

It had saved us a trip to the radio station. We aimed straight for the office of the South East Missourian newspaper, collected our thoughts and spoke to a journo keen to add spice to the real time account of the incident and a résumé of the expedition so far. Not knowing what we could offer, we resorted to default mode and hit a bar to raise a glass for the recently departed.

We'd intended to spend only one night in Cape Girardeau. As Mickey gave Fitz doe eyes all evening it seemed, for his sake, we should stay longer.

We'd met Mickey a couple of hours before in a bar where she'd approached a surprised Fitz with the chat up line, 'You got change?'

Mickey was undeniably pretty and whether this caused Fitz to clam up, I don't know. Mickey's overt 'come to bed' body language was blatant to everyone but Fitz, who nodded quietly to her every word accentuated by a sultry lick of the lips. Despite sitting on a rather open table, Mickey was huddled as close to Fitz as humanly possible without actually wearing his clothes.

When the conversation turned to our sleeping arrangements, I denied knowledge of our plush beds kindly reserved for us at the fire station. Instead, I gave the poor excuse of, 'The RV is a tip, the paddlers have only just left and it smells of filth and frogspawn and isn't fit to sleep humans.'

Mickey scrunched her face in disgust.

'So can we sleep at yours?'

Totally shocked by such a forward request, she stumbled to a yes. At least it saved her begging for Fitz to go back with her.

Jeff seemed quite impressed with the luck that we seemed to make for ourselves. It was undeniably hard for him as we were the novelties that people would want to talk to, and not necessarily a fellow Mid Westerner, but to his credit he didn't seem to deny us our status as the 'attractions'.

Mickey's housemates must have perceived my incessant nods and winks to Fitz as a nervous twitch. He still didn't seem to notice Mickey's flirting and her libido must have been at boiling point when she retired to bed at 5am. As I'd been on water for the evening I was still fresh as a daisy. Fully de-toxed, I was feeling a million dollars and decided to treat myself to a small make over, painting my finger and toe nails with the nearby bottles of glittery blues and greens. It wasn't the first time my painted hands had raised eyebrows. I'd woken up a few years previously after a real bender, with silver hands. Quizzical as to my predicament, I shook my head with self pity as it transpired that I'd washed my hands in a small tin of silver Hammerite paint to add authenticity to my Tin Man for a Wizard of Oz run ashore. The sergeant major told me he'd kick me all the way back to Kansas if I didn't sort them out pronto.

Even without sleep, we felt fresh taking breakfast at the Greek restaurant where Mickey worked. Fitz, still oblivious to Mickey's usage of the words 'jugs', 'nice round buns' and 'take me over the hot plate big boy', looked through the newspaper report of the previous day's incident. Being there as the crisis unfolded, assistance was all that mattered and there was no time for feelings of sensitivity. But when reflecting upon the drama, we felt a huge sense of sadness. Here, smiling from the front page, sat a school photograph of a boy with a full life in front of him leaving family and friends behind. He still hadn't been found.

Cape Girardeau, despite the best efforts of the genteel lady at the tourism office to turn a day into a unique experience, didn't have a great deal to offer such cultural lepers, so instead took the opportunity to indulge in the local people. We introduced ourselves to Mickey's fellow trainee teachers, amongst whom was a white Rastafarian named Jason, an English music freak. Brought up by a teenage mother, he'd grown up on a diet of The Beatles and Led Zeppelin, the latter the topic of his conversation for the majority of the day. Interspersed between 'Fuck'n A man' and 'Jeez', he glowed in his admiration for John Bonham's fateful drinking binges while downing double Jack Daniels like a basking shark to reinforce his ethics of live fast, die young. He shared these passions with Tony, his best buddy. It was the first time on the trip we'd seen white and black people out together as friends. Tony, equally as pleasant, talked about his heroin addiction as you or I would about eating crisps, which was both enlightening yet disturbing.

I often thought when I'd been mugged in New Orleans all those years ago how the news would be conveyed should I have been murdered. Although tragic, the British Forces I'm sure would have constructed an obituary around the fact that I had enjoyed life to the hilt and that it had eventually brought my downfall. Being murdered in a mugging wasn't something the M.O.D would be ashamed of. But how would they react if two of their own were to die in a road accident caused by someone driving under the influence? Could they make respectability from this?

Especially when it transpired the deceased were amongst ten others crammed into a small jeep driven by a man totally off his face on questionable substances, thinking he was Michael Schumacher around the tight streets of suburban Cape Girardeau. Immediately realising it had been a bad idea to get a lift to a party, we cringed while attempting to inhale titbits of oxygen. We couldn't exactly exit as we were at the bottom of the pile of bodies cramped around the rear roll bars, so hoped that the jeep could survive impact with a stationary object being hit at 70mph. We could only laugh at sinking into yet another unfortunate predicament.

Arriving at the party we were immediately recognised by the many strangers. Our accents had caught their attention the previous day when speaking on the radio at the scene of the drowning. Feeling like radio stars we soon engaged in numerous conversations to small groups within the masses, ranging from 'Is Mrs Thatcher still president?' to 'Do you think I should take out my twelve face piercings once I start teaching grade 1 classes?'

They were all trainee teachers. The majority seemed to enjoy illegal substances, Tony totally spaced in the corner. Not knowing what the hell was being consumed we kept ourselves close to the pile of beer cans and guzzled merrily on things that wouldn't cause us to end the trip on our knees scrubbing floors in front of Mr Big of E wing. This was a party where we were becoming increasingly alien and decided we should retire. Mickey agreed, her only intent being to jump on Fitz's bones. Mickey had earlier approached me concerned that Fitz didn't like her. I reassured her that it was Fitz upholding the British tradition of chivalry. While I'm hardly a modern day cupid, I had to force feed Fitz the belief that he'd definitely trapped.

He was surprised, so breaking down the brick wall of ambivalence, he humped her to a near death, Mickey selfishly keeping me awake with her moaning, and it wasn't about me finishing her nail polish.

***

Present day Cairo, Illinois looked like a slum of present day Cairo, Egypt. It certainly looked as though they'd forgotten to clean up after the 1967 civil rights riots that had left a racial scar deeper than the garbage on the sidewalk.

We drove slowly along Washington Avenue, Cairo's one and only main street, surveying the post-apocalyptic rubble of a third world town. It belied belief that we were now in a once prosperous area; by far it was the worst place we'd passed through and I sighed relief upon finding the fire station.

After the hospitality we'd received at the hands of Cape Girardeau Fire Department we now looked to the fire rather than police department as a prospective host. While the police had been gracious, their added security implications sometimes made us feel intrusive. The 'fireys' also had spare beds.

Cairo's early history revolves around the civil war, both northern and southern strategists realised its importance, as it stood at the confluence of the mighty Mississippi and the equally awesome Ohio River. Here, as we stood in Fort Defiance Park from the observation platform of the neglected tower, we admired nature at its most impressive. In a perfect wishbone, we followed the water on our right - the dirty brown flow of the Big Muddy; on our left - the wider bluer waters of the Ohio. On days of heavy rain or high flow, the two crash into each other like tectonic plates forming ruptures of waves perilous to all but the larger craft. But today, as had happened on the majority of the trip, the weather was clear and the vista took in a happy confluence, the clear demarcation line where the colours mixed like a conscientious child's painting, to form the gargantuan stretch of river that now ran away from us.

We'd been expecting Rob and Sean early morning. Having missed our last radio contact, as the afternoon furnace burned on we became slightly tense. But in the best traditions of fretting, they arrived just as we were contemplating contingency plans. While their skin pallor was proof of their weariness, Sean dragged the Klepper sucking in his lips evidently trying to suppress a smile directing his eyes in the same direction of his nodded head.

Having paddled 60 miles through the heat of the Mid West I'd hardly expect Rob to salsa up the bank like Carmen Miranda, but he looked like he'd lost a pound and found a penny. Which was rather apt as he'd lost a very expensive pair of sunglasses and seemingly found a pair of very shit ones.

Fitz broached the subject delicately, 'What the fuck are those on your head?'

Rob had bought some rather beautiful expedition quality sunglasses prior to the trip, advisable when paddling through the sunnier parts of the globe. However, what he now wore could only be won on a shit game at a fairground.

The paddlers had run out of water. Severely dehydrated, they pulled up at a sandbar party to ask whether they could be spared some. As true partygoers they had no water but plenty of cheap, boxed wine made especially for alcoholics and teenagers. It was liquid so they happily gorged. The party leader was so impressed with the paddlers' tales upon the river he offered Sean a St Christopher necklace hoping the Patron Saint of travels would keep them safe. Sean swapped an old baseball cap in appreciation. Bereft of equally profound gifts, the party leader offered Rob his shit sunglasses. Not wanting to offend his generosity, and with a certain amount of encouragement from Sean, Rob offered his own sunglasses in return. With more wine consumed they got back into the kayak and immediately capsized. Sean found it funny, especially when looking at Rob's sunnies. Rob hadn't found the experience so humorous and now, as they dragged the Klepper up the bank to meet us he was hungover with burnt corneas.

Jeff was looking forward to the following day's paddle accompanying Fitz in a spare Klepper. Excitement led to apprehension as Sean ran through the myriad of equipment that was now laid out before him. The threat of incidence never far from Sean's mind, capsize drills had to be ditched due to the rapid flow of the river, reluctantly leaving Sean and Rob to paddle as close as possible to aid any accident.

The local newspaper came, interviewed, and took pictures; Sean ensuring that I hid my painted nails. He'd not been impressed with my make over, labelling me an idiot and bringing the Corps' good name into question on a newspaper photograph. I found holding my hands behind my back solved this issue.

Waving off the two kayaks, we'd next meet at Dorena's landing near New Madrid, my next stop off point. I now found myself alone for the first time in over two months..

New Madrid is famed in these parts for two things. The first is that it sits on the biggest oxbow bend on the Mississippi River. To travel the half a mile between the neck of the oxbow, the lads would paddle a full 20 miles around the near perfect teardrop curve. At this stage it could be soul destroying to paddle north, but to portage the shorter distance could be deemed a short cut, so the New Madrid bend became a character-building demon. The lads would just laugh in its face.

New Madrid is also famous for the earthquakes of 1811-1812. At around 2am on the 16 December 1811, witnesses reported that the land around New Madrid peaked and troughed like waves on the ocean. The river spewed up its bed discharging mud and water to the outlying lands leaving trees bent like old men and boats stranded on dry land thus generally spoiling everyone's Christmas. Believed to be around 8.6 on the Richter scale it was followed by another on 23 January 1812 of around 8.4. It again swallowed houses whole as the soil was shaken into liquification dropping the land 20ft. Just when the locals feared things could not get any worse, fifteen days later the final and largest quake ever to ever hit continental North American smashed the town. Calculated to be 8.9 it released energy equivalent to 150,000,000 tons of TNT. As not many of us can imagine such an amount unless they know someone who lives solely on baked beans, cabbage, and prunes, it is 3750 times the combined strength of the two atomic bombs of Japan in World War 2. Over 400 miles away, windows in Chicago were shattered and people in twenty States felt the earth move, quite welcome to some I imagine. The river not only changed course due to the disruption of its topography, but stories spread far and wide that it actually started flowing in the opposite direction.

Driving into New Madrid, it was pretty clear that the present town dined on this event like Hannibal consumed Mark Twain. A diner, a gas station, and a skyline of industrial parks welcomed me. With a spec-tacular array of signposts, none of which pointing to Dorena's landing, I visited the diner in the hope that the waitresses were as much as part of the furniture as, well, the furniture. Having a face as leathered as the upholstery, one particularly skilful lady simultaneously tried to impress the US javelin selectors and anger her boss by throwing cutlery and condiments onto my table from a great distance. In between chews of never ending gum, she garbled unfollowable instructions enhanced by an improvised map scribbled onto a pink napkin.

She'd made it seem like a couple of blocks around the corner when explaining the route, but the difference in mileage appreciation between a simple Englishman and a simple American is such that the drive down the levee was a full seventeen miles before I hit the first bridge.

76miles later, signposts had become virtually non-existent. Feeling totally displaced from the modern world on a small road hemmed in by mature cornfields with only trepidation to guide me, I felt as though I was in a hedge maze, but doubted there'd be a smug ice cream vendor at the end.

I feared running out of petrol and food and would survive on eating my arms (choosing the right one first as it was slightly more cooked from constantly hanging it out of the passenger window and, if I'm perfectly honest, it's only there for symmetry). Once I'd consumed my spleen, some hillbilly family would rescue me from my hunger-induced coma then enslave me into a world of impregnating the chlamydia ravaged uteruses of family members named Betty Lou. Possibly.

In my slightly clouded state, I thought I'd imagined a bungalow. Like most mirages, it was truly in the middle of nowhere, totally on its own, miles from the last building seen. Thankfully, it was real. Trying to turn the 27ft RV around in a 15ft turning circle, I caught the attention of what I assumed to be the woman of the house. Half hidden under the swathe of a Korean market dog's hair, her face was so disfigured I didn't know whether it was a pooey bum or she had chocolate round her mouth. Following her trailed a procession of ragbag children, all sporting very similar features in different stages of deformity. I counted seventeen, all seemingly fertilised in a petri dish mix of Frankenstein's sperm and Dorothy Flange's ovum then inseminated into a chimp's vagina. I was sure I heard 'Deliverance' banjos.

Thinking I had stumbled upon a crèche for the unwanted she shouted at them, 'Get back'n the fucking house.'

I wondered in what context she meant 'fucking house'.

She approached warily, but that could have been her limp and asked me through bleeding, chapped lips, 'Whad up?'

Closing my eyes to prevent being blinded by her breath that could have been bottled as skunk musk, I asked for directions.

Dorena was now virtually obsolete, only hers and a couple of houses still remained. The boat landing was 30 miles down the road I was on and should arrive without let or hindrance (my words not hers) within the hour. Thanking her I sped off hoping I wouldn't run over two scabby dogs fucking on the unkempt verge.

The molten sun dripped heat like treacle onto my sweaty body wrapping me in the cling film of humidity, the natural rotation of the Earth my only escape. Outside the RV was even worse. Not only would I have to endure the same heat and humidity but also spectate the annual midge contest designed to test which midge could most annoy an irritable human. It's not often you dream of a dreary English day.

I'd lost around 4kg in sweat by the time the lads arrived. Peeling my nakedness from the driver's seat impressing the upholstery with a perfect sweat formed 'Shroud of Dorena', I ventured out, trying unsuccessfully to ignore the whirling midges. At the water's edge there felt the most welcome of breezes, which, apart from the coolness, allowed me a midge free interlude. If I'd lost 4kg, Fitz had lost 10. Doing a fantastic impression of 'Skeletor' from 'He-Man', he paddled in, his reddened face smiling, which fattened his face to the width of a goldfish's. Behind, Jeff was as pale as a Glaswegian submariner. The ordeal had been noticeably difficult, his paddle hanging in the water creating more drag for Fitz to paddle against. He coasted into the bank letting Fitz pull the last few strokes until they slid against the shingle bank. Wearily Jeff hauled himself from the kayak, Fitz already out waiting to drag the hull from the water. Sean and Rob smoothly glided in behind, not a hair on Rob's head was out of place, Sean so chilled he looked as though he's just ordered a piña colada (without umbrella) rather than paddling thirty miles.

'A few miles too far,' Jeff's wheezed - about twenty nine miles too far by the look of him.

To his credit, although too exhausted to co-ordinate his breathing and blinking, he helped dismantle the Klepper rather than sit on his arse and watch, like many I've seen in similar states. He'd paddled thirty miles, something he should have been extremely proud of. I was to tell him this, but by the time we'd started the engine, he was fast asleep sleeping in the comfort of his sweat.

***

'AAAAGGGGHHHH.' Although a fictitious word, it is the only way to convey my screams just before I peeled myself from the ceiling. I honestly thought a bomb had gone off by the side of the RV and my ears rang like the bells of St Clements.

Humidity had compressed the previous evening when we'd pulled into a lay-by on the outskirts of Memphis, accompanied by angry thunder and the occasional flash of lightning. Five hours later the storm had hunted us down. Outside, a smoking tree told us that a lightening bolt had earthed just a few feet from us. Never being so close before, the shock had turned my shorts a browner shade of yellow. Near miss lightning bolts in the Mid West are as common as dog shit on a council field, therefore, Jeff managed only to murmur from his slumber to ask how close it was.

There was another, more painful, explosion that morning. I couldn't locate the normal cigarette lighter to light the gas hob when cooking our breakfast of eggs over easy, so used matches to light under the pan. I should really have taken the pan off. Cooking in my normal state of nakedness that Jeff couldn't get his head round and thought was 'gay', I fried merrily until 'whoosh' - a flame tore up my hairy torso scorching a singed path up my 'crab ladder' and chest hair. It appeared the lighter was next to the hob and had turned into a micro BLEVE. Jeff thought there was some divine intervention involved. I knew it was my shit sniper skills.

'Nothing behind me, everything ahead of me,
as is ever so on the road'

~ *Sal Paradise, On the Road, Kerouac*

Memphis, the biggest city in Tennessee and globally famous for its musical heritage, welcomed us as we journeyed into its city limits. We'd been into many places thus far on our journey but none were quite as impressive as the drive over the Jackson Memorial Bridge, the Mississippi living up to its Big Muddy nickname below. To our right, the city's harbour boats glinted in the sunlight like iron filings in a flame. Ahead, the tallest pyramid in the world. Named simply 'The Pyramid' it stood gracious and triumphant in a shimmering homage of what could be done with a bit of glass and steel.

By now we'd been to more visitor centers than the occupants of an elderly coaching holiday, ensuring the RV was littered with piles of handouts and souvenir brochures big enough to prevent the Amazon rainforest ever taking root again. Visitors centers for towns, visitors centres for attractions. Religious organisations had visitors centers, polystyrene cup manufacturers had them, selected supermarkets boasted them. I'm pretty sure we even found a visitors center with its own visitors center.

As we visited the Memphis version, while speaking to one particularly friendly member of staff who explained with great zest the 'hilarious' ducks of the Peabody Hotel, we received a call from a lady from ETA. For the second time in five hours I kecked my pants. Was this anonymous voice from a disgruntled Basque terrorist issuing a threat on behalf of some foreign active service unit? Unfortunately not, it was from an organisation far worse, one that struck fear into the heart of even the most battle hardened veteran. It was someone from The English Tea Association. The local radio had done a feature on our trip from the networking we'd previously done up river and the caller, Lynette, a great fan of the English, had been so impressed with the trip that she wanted to meet us. We arranged to meet, puzzled as how she'd got our number.

By default, we ended up at Fire Headquarters on Front Street. They welcomed us like every other fire station we'd visited, but as they only commanded a tiny real estate footprint they could only accommodate us that evening, but kindly contacted Station 2, opposite the pyramid, to book us a space in their car park for the coming week.

The majority of midtown Memphis's tourism revolves around Beale Street. Such stars as Carl Perkins, Jerry Lee Lewis and, of course, Elvis plied their early trade here. But Beale Street wasn't founded just because WC Handy decided to play his trumpet there, it was a catalyst for free black expansion.

Way before slavery was abolished, Beale Street was home to many free black families, and has since been the cornerstone of the civil rights movement especially as Dr Martin Luther King was assassinated a stone's throw away (admittedly by a very good stone thrower). Even now, it seemed Beale Street bridged the racial divide. For the first time since the Cape Girardeau teachers I witnessed blacks and whites mingle affably. Conversely, we could travel five minutes in any direction and revisit the distortion of bigotry and be in a solely white or black neighbourhood.

Maybe it was because it was a weekday but Beale Street seemed quite subdued. Now home to clubs named in honour of such legends as BB King's for die hard Blues fans and 'Elvis Presley's' for anything to do with the King including, it appeared, songs by Kajagoogoo, we bimbled down the street peeking through steamy windows vibrating to the sound of rock 'n' roll, jazz, blues and more American heartbeat. Disturbing memories of M Street in Washington DC flooded back as men who should know better belted out Hall and Oates classics.

Outside on the sidewalks, the entertainment continued as young teenagers dazzled us with their agility as they tumbled like Olympic gymnasts, flick-flacking and somersaulting their scruffy way amongst the crowds who would either ignore their back and forward somersaults, double pikes with triple trouts or give them a bit of loose change. Gladly pulling out some notes I thought I'd join in and impress them with my amazing double cartwheel. I say 'amazing' I should say 'abysmal'. Not quite Tom Cruise in the film 'The Firm', more Mark Time P.E remedial class. It was instantly regrettable as I didn't quite pull a double cartwheel I pulled a hamstring and to add insult to injury my right hand had landed in a nice juicy patch of tobacco phlegm.

The music from an Irish Bar tempted us in - some Irish guy on a piano eulogising over the young ladies in the bar, who he volunteered up to dance to his renditions. He sang with such gusto that if had been a soprano rather than a tenor the windows would have been blown all the way down Beale Street. The beer, however, left a lot to be desired. Thankful to get a proper pint rather than a bottle of American beer, I explained to Jeff the different ways that British beer was served, going into great detail about head retention, clarity and temperature. I bought one of each of lager, bitter, and stout on tap and after picking my chin up off the deck, I begrudgingly handed over $30. The barman confirmed they served traditional British beers at the correct temperature. Their version of correct temperature was similar to that you would drink cocoa. As well as scolding my mouth, the taste of the bitter was like dirty dishwater, but without the lumps. The lager was no better and by the time I'd sipped the stout, I felt ill.

'How can you drink this shit?' Jeff quite rightly asked.

Trying to explain that we didn't, he ordered three bottles of Miller and undeniably the relief in drinking something cold enough to shatter teeth was as genuine as the beer.

***

Jeff's family lived in the Memphis 'burbs, out along a multitude of identical dual carriageways. And back up the same ones in the opposite direction where we'd become lost. And then back down another that we thought we'd been down, over a flyover that we thought we'd been over before realising we may have been under one very similar. Eventually, we drove into a small cul-de-sac, more Knots Landing than Brookside. The house we pulled up outside was nice, real nice if I was to talk like Jeff. His uncle was evidently a rather successful lawyer. By the time I'd gone the length of the hallway I needed a rest.

Jeff's aunt greeted him and, as all aunts do, talked to him as though he was still a candy-covered kid with freckles, not a 6ft brute with a penchant for Death Metal. My eyes scanned the palace I now stood in. I'd been in less religious churches. The home had more crosses than a dyslexic child's spelling test paper and adorned on virtually every wall a psalm or biblical proverb reminded us not to do anything mildly enjoyable.

We never did meet the man of the house. It appeared he worked all the hours god sent, which begged the question I imagine many wealthy overworked people think at sometime or other *'Why the hell am I working all these hours when I can never enjoy any of the things I've strived to buy?*

Rob and Sean impressed again by arriving at our pre-designated point exactly at the prescribed time. Although extremely knackered due to the hideous heat, being bootnecks, they wanted to digest a belly full of Beale Street.

Not being a travel guide I'll refrain from recommending any Memphis attractions, but because of its amenability we took a trip to Mud Island. The 52 acre man-made misnomer boasts upon its peninsular the Mississippi River Museum that, surprisingly enough, traces the river's history. The Memphis Belle, the famed WWII B17 bomber and film title, and a 5000 seat amphitheatre are also spectacles situated amongst the oddly placed new housing developments. What did tickle our fancy was the River Walk, a scaled down version of the Lower Mississippi. Each 30" stride (which is a military regulation marching pace) is equivalent to 1 mile. We could have mimicked Guardsmen in Bearskin hats marching the thousand paces along the 1.3 million gallons of water to the end of the model to check its accuracy, but we realised there would be more enjoyment in genital self-mutilation, so instead followed a genius guide who made water and mud hilarious for his 30 minute tour. The last time so much mud and water had been involved was as a Royal Marines recruit and that certainly wasn't funny…

We'd been turfed out of Fire Station 1 and were now squatting at Station 2. Picked up that evening by Lynette from the ETA, she drove us all up to a diner in the Mid America Mall. We listened to her, covered in barbecue sauce from sharing eight chicken wings between the five of us, as she launched into an infinite monologue about tea. After an hour of the benefits of Darjeeling over Assam she strangely turned to the lack of elocution within the British working classes, driving us all into a silent anger. Her viewpoint spawned from her English professor friend who considered ignorance being a working class trait. It was quite clear that ETA was a colonialist refuge where ex-pats of varied generations talked about the Raj, thick rind lime marmalade, and Lord Kitchener, sneering at anyone who'd had a free education. Lynette seemed genuinely nice, but wholly gullible, absorbing this class-based crap and still thought the British as bowler hatted businessmen, and we were only negative monocles due to our pursuit of rowing excellence down the river. Not withstanding the fact she was in the company of an East Londoner, two Yorkshiremen, and a Welshman who wouldn't recognise the Queen's English if she lifted up her skirt and showed him her 'The rain in Spain stays mainly on the plane' motif on her knickers, Lynette still relayed her friend's snobbish preaching. As she could only stay for the starter as she was chairing a meeting at the local 'Women With Lice Society', an air of relief washed over us as she left. It was blown back by her insistence on meeting us the following day to meet her friends.

'Bring your professor friend,' said Sean busily sharpening his butter knife under the table.

'What a splendid idea,' Lynette replied in here best Anglophile accent.

'Yes, splendid,' we replied in ours.

***

A place you must go when in Memphis, toilet apart, is Graceland, the home of Elvis. Not that you must go because it's memorable, but in Memphis you must go. That is an order.

People snub you in the street in Memphis if you claim not to have seen Graceland. The first thing the fire station guys asked us was 'When are you going to Graceland?'

Serial Killer's have been given 30 hours community service after telling the judge they only murdered the orphans, (orphaned due to their reluctance to visit Graceland) because they were in a bad mood due to Graceland being closed for refurbishment. Elvis over-load is everywhere. Hannibal was bad enough, Mark Twain however, was the only reasonably interesting character from that region, but Memphis has so much more to offer than just the 'King'. But orders are orders and it wasn't long after 9am that we travelled down an already packed Elvis Presley Boulevard, in a part of town that is called simply 'Elvis'. It was my intention to turn Graceland into Disgraceland.

At the attraction entrance, gangs of chiffon scarfed women barged their way to the front of the huge queue to make sure they could get in every attraction on offer. We plumped for the basic mansion tour. Not being an Elvis fan, (I know, kill me), I was rather happy not having to traipse around Elvis' plane or his automobile collection, both covered in swarms of tourists like flies round shite. Shite would actually have been quite the money spinner. It would have been quite feasible to set up a stall on the Boulevard, fill up a few jars with poo and ethanol and sell them off as 'Stools of Elvis' to the gullible hordes. You could even scent them so the more intrusive purchaser could have boasted that Elvis was so perfect his shit did indeed smell of roses.

The mansion tour was a painless experience, even if I did get told off for taking a photo of a 'no photography' sign. A shrine to 70's kitsch, Graceland from the outside is quite beautiful. Graceland on the inside looks like the set of 'George and Mildred'. I was surprised not to feel car sick as the place was just another bandwagon being jumped on by hungry entrepreneurs squeezing the last cent out of a corpse, which as it happened, was the last thing on the tour. In the Meditation Garden people stood silently behind the fence that separated them from Elvis' grave in solemn reverence unless you accidentally stood in the way of their photographic opportunity. I tried to comprehend what impact Elvis had on public life. I was too young to appreciate the man, but here as they grieved with annoying, exaggerated sobs, it dawned on me he was a deity above godliness, after all, despite me being only knee high to a grasshopper, I remember where I was when I heard he'd died. I was on the loo as well.

Lynette thankfully didn't show up. We wondered whether she'd been abducted by a hit squad of the infamous TCP, - Tennessee Coffee Protectorate, an evil band of highly skilled militia intent on death and destruction to all tea drinkers on the planet. Or was it that she'd been informed that anyone called Sean or Lee was working class. We hoped it was the former and her professor friend had also met a slow, timely death.

Free to choose our own entertainment, we resorted to a laid back evening. It was Rob and Sean's last in Memphis. They were paddling a big leg the following day and after a day looking at Elvis toilet roll holders and walnut finished boxed sets of 'pomegranates in the shape of Elvis' head', a restful evening was in order. It was also Jeff's last evening with us and after so much gobbing off how big drinkers us Brits were, Jeff spent his final night around a group of big girl's blouses drinking water, although Fitz went totally crazy and had a diet Coke.

Not that we begrudged Jeff being with us for the past few weeks but it was a relief to get back to being just the two of us in the RV. Moreover, there was no further need to check our cans of drinks for signs of it being a baccy receptacle.

By now we'd built up a rapport with our fire fighter hosts and their ethos reminded me somewhat of life in the Royal Marines.

Never one to sit down for more than a second, Jim's bubbly nature got to some of the other fire fighters who couldn't relax for a second without fear of being hosed down, or branded with a boiling hot spoon or being splattered with rotten fruit. His practical jokes enamoured us to him, so happily accepted his invitation to stay with his family on the city limits. He promised there would be no fruit thrown.

Fire fighting is rightly revered as a rather macho occupation. Many a boy grows up with the burning ambition to climb ladders and pluck a stricken damsel from a 36th floor furnace. Here in Memphis and in many parts of the US, men and women of the Fire department risk life and limb every day not only through the actions of fire fighting, but being target practice for many street delinquents. These were some of the changes that now made Jim a weary and disenchanted fire fighter. After 21 years service, he and his colleagues had noticed the general decline in the respect shown to the department. Over a beer, he explained how the guys on a 'shout' were more scared of taking a bullet in some areas than going into a burning building. He'd been a target in many shootings; some fires were started deliberately just so hoodlums could ambush a fire truck.

'Fighting fires and fire fights?' said Fitz.

'Yup,' he replied, shaking his head, wallowing with his bottled therapist. 'Not like the old days,' he murmured repetitively to a rather worrying extent.

We'd expected to have a rollicking good time at Jim's but his melancholy ramblings could stop a conversation at twenty paces and it seemed an eternity before a different subject was introduced, finally drowning out the ticking of the wall clock.

With Jim on night shift, Fitz and I spent a blissful evening in the company of his wife Dayna and daughter Debbie eating ribs and watching cable TV. Debbie obviously had the hots for Fitz, taking sneaky glances at every opportunity, totally oblivious to Fitz of course who was far more interested in the movie. Their eyes did meet on one occasion, Debbie smiling showing a chunk of meat the size of a pig's leg hanging from her front teeth much to my inner amusement and to Fitz's horror.

Other than lamenting on days gone by, Jim's other speciality was drinking badly. After a morning in bed he made us a traditional Tennessee breakfast: sausage, gravy and scones with a side pile of cindered bacon so charred they could only be recognised by dental records. We then hit the beer. Within twenty minutes he was a gibbering wreck, slurring his words far better than any emotional pub singer. He retained that state for the rest of the afternoon while Fitz and I felt slightly tipsy as if we'd had a Babycham shandy. The down side of his inebriation (if there could be an upside) was his insistence on showing off his firearms, loaded and some even made ready while stumbling round his bedroom/armoury. We hid behind his wardrobe as he swung round a double barrelled shotgun in a deadly arc praising its body stopping capability.

'I stoppedamoose, I did. I stoppedamoose.' he slurred, raising his index finger slowly. 'With one shot.'

'Must have been a good shot,' said Fitz, hoping to pacify him.

'Nooo, they too small to get a second shot off,' he slurred before sliding a bedside cabinet across to show us the hole in the skirting where he'd claimed his prey.

It seemed accents had reduced his kill to a scurrying rodent.

He started to laugh, not quite manically, but enough for us to change the subject to something more gentile like rabid dog fighting.

The night was still young but a return home was preferable to enduring Jim swearing at his wife behind the wheel of the car. Fitz, Debbie and I sat quietly in the back cringing at every 'f' word that flew from Jim. We had known from the start it was a bad idea to go out for a night drinking.

'Fuck'n get'the way you fuck'n fuck,' he screamed at some pedestrian waiting patiently for a signal to cross the road. 'Where you fuck'n fuck gown ye fuck?'

Dayna ignored his constant abuse and drove unhindered like a saint, to a lap dancing club which under the circumstances wasn't a particularly good idea.

The sight of scantily clad women writhing around polished steel poles actually calmed Jim, but for us it was a strange experience. For you see, Dayna didn't drop us off for a 'boys night out'. No, she and Debbie joined us and watched the girls doing their thing. I tried to pass off my unease by chatting to Dayna about any subject that had no link to dancing girls. My cheeks burnt with discomfort as if I was watching hardcore porn in front of the vicar, especially as Dayna asked me my opinion of the dancing girls.

'Errm lovely, yes very nice,' I fumbled in my best Hugh Grant voice.

Fitz felt the same, and despite having seen and done things that could get me arrested in half the western world, I suddenly felt rather prudish, rather British.

After leaving the lap dancing club that I think was called 'El Squirm', we ended up in a bar where I drank a ridiculous amount of alcohol that would do me no good whatsoever. The little I recalled involved a cage. As a memory that can't be good.

'What?' I exclaimed through the pain of a tortured head.

'Yeah, you and Fitz were gonna get may-ried,' explained Dayna over a tray of coffee.

After a welcome sip of early morning scolding black sludge, the idea seemed ridiculous. Ridiculous, but funny. Sod the sanctity of marriage, it would have been a great story to tell the lads back home.

'Yeah the trip was fantastic and to top it off, Fitz and I got married.'

I revelled in the anger from the corridors of power when it emerged that two Royal Marines Commandos had married each other. The thought of consummating the marriage brought me back to sanity. He's a good looking lad, but his hairy ball sac that frequently dangled over the edge of the over-cab bed had somewhat put me off.

Dayna added while searching for a 24 hour drive-thru church, she and Jim had again got into an almighty argument, so Fitz called off the wedding saying, I quote, 'I want to feel special! I can't get married with all this bickering.'

***

We took a couple of runs up and down Greenville's main drag to make sure we hadn't missed anything. We hadn't. It had the outward appearance of a deadbeat town where the deads outnumbered the beats by 10 to 1. Even tourist brochures, which are renowned for being economical with the truth, couldn't find any laudable way of turning Greenville, Mississippi into anything that would constitute attraction.

'Boasts Indian Mounds as well as commerce,' was the whole sum of what one brochure could muster in its defence. The only reason it was a planned paddle steamer stop was so affluent tourists could see what poverty looked like.

The beaming smile of the woman behind the counter of the Tourist Information Center belied the fact that she struggled to offer anything remotely interesting, apart her name. I thought I'd misread her name badge but no, on second glance she was actually called Fanny Trump.

'There's the Mississippi River to look at,' she smiled knowing we had just seen the previous 2000 miles of it. 'A casino, and some Indian mounds.' A supermarket car park to view various coloured vehicles, and a newly painted warehouse were the only other things Fanny could pull from an empty bin labelled 'Points of Interest'

I did feel sorry for her, plaiting diarrhoea would be far easier. Greenville had nothing. She knew it, and we knew it.

We drove to the casino for some air-conditioned coolness, as the Mississippi summer was becoming an energy sapping experience. After an hour, we'd seen enough. Unfortunately the guy on the roulette wheel next to us hadn't. Only his mullet was as ludicrous as the amount of money he placed on the roulette table only for the wheel to invariably stop on the wrong number. Knocking ourselves from our morbid voyeurism we left watching his emotionless face steel itself as he piled another column of chips onto the same number to vainly recoup his losses.

We spent the next five days inside the RV in Greenville. It could have been worse. We could have spent the next 5 days outside the RV in Greenville. Our home was the casino car park. Having first persuaded the armed security to let us stay he kindly hooked us up with electricity after an amazing amount of brown nosing on our part and the odd crate of beer.

To establish an indication of how bored we were, throughout the trip thus far we'd played one of those card games where the loser is the first to get to a certain amount of points. Usually we played until the loser hit 100 points. This would take up a couple of hours when waiting for the paddlers' arrival. Here, in the casino car park in Greenville Mississippi, the loser was the first to get to 10,000. And of course, I lost.

We clinched Rob and Sean like long lost brothers as they stepped from the kayak. How glad we would be to leave this town, and how glad we could now continue down to the beautiful towns that lay further down the river and 'who the fuck is that?'

'That' was Greg. The lads had met him just after Memphis. From California, his story was a melancholy but inspiring one. Alone after his Mom had passed away, he sold his sole possession, his car, and bought with the proceeds an ultra modern kayak and all the gubbins to go with it. He'd started his trip at the mouth of the Missouri River four months previously meaning his trip length doubled ours. He was continuing on to the Intra coastal waterways down to Florida where he hoped he would get some bar work, 'or something.' I loved him immediately.

In his late forties, Greg had the look of a seasoned expeditionary, with a tanned body slimmed down to sinewy muscle. Despite this, he was a man with all the gear and no idea. He didn't have the slightest clue what he was doing. On his own, he had drifted down river before following the lads for a couple of miles until he plucked up the courage to ask where they were going.

'All the way from source t'sea.' Rob, I imagine, answered.

Somewhere in the conversation Greg asked how they knew how far they'd gone.

'By looking at the mile markers on the river.'

Although he'd travelled nearly 3000 miles he'd never noticed one. 'How did you know what towns you're passing?'

'Your charts will tell you.' It'd be hard not to sound facetious.

He didn't have any charts.

'So how do you know where to stop and where to feed?'

'I just set off in the morning and stop at night,' was his simple answer.

There was a certain romance about how Greg travelled. He had no deadlines to meet, no support crew to liaise and argue with. In fact he had no worries whatsoever. He, in his own words, just 'followed the river'.

This lack of knowledge, unfortunately turned Greg into a self styled survival guru trying to impress us with gems such as matches were best kept dry and not to drink toilet water *unless it was life or death.*

Sean woke everyone the following the morning, including Greg who, despite our invitation to sleep in the RV, insisted on being at one with nature in his tent outside.

'Greg, it's 8 o'clock mate. Get up.'

Greg peered outside his flysheet. 'No it's not.'

'Not what?' asked Fitz, already on the grass outside with a cup of coffee wrapped within his hands.

'It's not 8am.'

Fitz at first was going to say that Greg's watch was wrong until he realised he wasn't wearing one. 'What time is it then?'

Greg took another look at the sullen sky, 'Around seven.'

'Mine and Sean's watches say eight, look.' Fitz offered his wrist to Greg but was brushed aside.

'Nah, I think you'll find both your watches are wrong.'

'I don't think we will,' answered Fitz.

'Oh I think you will,' retorted Greg equally sarcastically.

There is a proverb that says 'a man with one watch always knows the time but a man with two is never sure'. However, I've yet to hear of a proverb reflecting 'a fool who looks at a cloudy sky from a tent knows the time better than two Swiss chronographs'.

'Well whatever the time it is, we need to get our shit together and make a move,' placated Sean.

And move they did. Sean and Rob as always gliding smoothly into the deep water, kit stowed as immaculately as Rob's hair, equipment tied securely in its rightful place, hardly a foam of white as their paddles cut gracefully through the water. Greg followed looking like a tinker of the river. Self-washing pots and pans trailed in his wake, the clothing draped over his stern comically got caught in his paddle as he battered the water into submission. Despite this, Greg still insisted he could circumnavigate the globe using a stick and a hock of out-of-date ham.

***

The Unionists were on the offensive as their flotilla and land forces overran the Confederates to give them their first major victory of the Civil War. Now with a foot-

296

hold in the south, the Unionists, led by Ulysses S Grant, realised that to split the Confederacy, the Mississippi River would have to be controlled. In strategic terms the place most suited was on the eastern banks of Vicksburg, Mississippi.

The first attacks on the heavily fortified Vicksburg were, to say the least, suicidal. The high bluffs overlooking the river gave defending Confederate troops a clear vantage point to ward off attacks from the river. After several unsuccessful attempts, Grant took the bold decision to attack Vicksburg from the east. The Unionists beat off Confederacy positions south and to the east of Vicksburg to set up a final push on the town itself.

After many failed Unionist attacks, siege operations commenced on the town; now an unbreakable Confederate fortress.

The people of Vicksburg in their ensuing hunger resorted to eating horses, rats and, in desperation, even shoe leather. One can only eat so much of this and in complete desperation on July 4th 1863 Pemberton, the Commander of Vicksburg, surrendered.

With the Confederacy now split it was only a matter of time before the Unionists recouped the southern lands to end the war. Vicksburg was indeed the activator for the downfall of the Confederacy.

Being such an evocative date to surrender, some people of Vicksburg scorned, up until very recently, the 4th of July celebrations. In fact some hardy Southerners still dismiss the festivities and refuse to park next to any vehicle displaying an Illinois licence plate due to its links with Abraham Lincoln.

Vicksburg still lives and breathes the war. The National Military Park welcomes tourists from either allegiance and as military men it was only right we take a look. We watched small re-enactments of Confederate soldiers in their gun pits on the hill overlooking the woods that once contained Unionist troops. Dressed in original clothing these actors cleaned their original rifles looking at their unoriginal digital watches to notify them of their shift change. Steep though the bank below us was, we couldn't resist having a roly-poly race down the 50m slope into the gully below. The sight of four fully grown idiots rolling speedily down the hill brought a round of applause from certain quarters as we wobbled to our feet festooned with grass and mud. The park warden wasn't so amused and sternly warned us not to roll down the hill. It was a little late.

Sighted where the battles took place, the park itself took us sixteen miles around an immaculately preserved route of shrines to each and every State taking part on both sides of the conflict. Their navies, armies, and people all commemorated amongst the 1300 monuments, markers, reconstructed trenches, 125 cannon emplacements, one antebellum structure, a restored Union Gunboat USS Cairo, and the Vicksburg Military Cemetery. We reflected on the scenes while cruising around the park giving out our own misguided advice on what the generals should have done. It was abundantly clear, with the amount of tourists en route, the US still holds the conflict amazingly close.

'Space Monkey' Greg was still with us and spent most of his time on the craps table in the casino. The four of us, however, thought exercise was in order so spent a day at a small amusement park playing more crazy golf.

My hand was fully recovered from my previous injury and so I played straight out of a tricky water trap on the 14th, underneath a large plastic volcano. Unfortunately, my unskilled swipe led to my hand muscles being ripped again in exactly the same way as before. Having an important industrial abseiling course in less than a month's time, needing to be dextrous was quite helpful, so in a flash of unbridled anger I spun round like an Olympic hammer thrower and launched my putter high over the volcano, across a miniature windmill on the 9th hole, before landing it twenty metres away on the 6th narrowly missing the head of a small child who waited patiently for his father to putt. The other three found this particularly hilarious as I cursed and swore in concentrated fury - the father on the 6th hole blissfully unaware that his son had narrowly missed decapitation from a flying putter.

With the finish still three weeks away, money was chronically short, a trip to the supermarket now a balancing act between bankruptcy and starvation. Even eating ramen noodles was getting monotonous (and how often does that happen?) How apt that it was in Vicksburg, a place famous for its residents nearly starving, that we eventually had to formulate an action plan to forecast our dietary consumption ensuring we didn't over budget or die. On the first day of the trial I served to the lads:

Breakfast

Light flakes of sawdust enhanced with rabbit droppings in a bowl of diluted pond water

Lunch

A compote of finest scum scraped from the Vicksburg marine engineering plant on the banks of the historic Mississippi River, spread thickly on thinly sliced toasted cardboard

Dinner

Finest cut of outdoor raised dog accompanied by thickest wallpaper paste, with a side of nuts and bolts. Dessert is a selection of street residue freshly collected on the day.

Other than that it was ramen noodles and grits, and for anyone who has tasted grits, the above menu is ambrosia itself.

The National Waterways Experimentation Station is located in Vicksburg. It's where Army Corps of Engineer boffins think of ways to stem tidal flows, redirect a river's intentions and play river god for the benefit of the American people. Being on the banks of the Mississippi River we had a vested interest in its work, but as the flood of '93 showed, the river is an all-powerful animal and trying to muzzle it only served as a sticking plaster for a mental patient. Considering these profound findings, we didn't take the trip, instead going to a bar to spend a couple of hours on a foosball table.

The final day in Vicksburg was, as per usual, a day of shopping, administration and route checking, all with Greg peering inquisitively at our actions. Leaving the shore was sadly to be the last we saw of Greg. He'd decided he was going to spend a few days chilling on the river rather than pushing out the miles like Sean and Rob. So it was with handshakes and best wishes that Greg set off - in the wrong direction. Oh how we laughed as he struggled to paddle upstream for a minute before we couldn't see him struggle anymore. We called him round to realise his mistake. Sean and Rob followed shortly after and within half a mile they were all paddling together again.

God knows where Space Monkey Greg is now. He's probably managed to paddle south all the way to Alaska...

'One loyal friend is worth ten thousand relatives'

~ Euripides, tragic playwright

After experiencing ever-changing scenery, driving through the flat Mississippi Delta was somewhat monotonous. Even so, there is something hypnotic about travelling along an ironing board of land. Passing through cotton fields must have felt like a pilgrimage for my clothes and the roadside plantations ran into the far horizon taking with them some of the worst of North American history.

The paddlers had felt slightly underwhelmed since leaving Cairo. The Upper Mississippi was a river holding surprises around every slow curve. Now on the wide expanse of the Lower Mississippi the only scenery was the high levees that protected either bank. From having the company of recreational craft, mad swimmers and party boats, this section only hosted monsters barges, their salutary greeting being two warning blasts to get out of the way or be crushed like small gerbils under one of those bowling balls with the really big finger holes. This fear was tangible enough for them to paddle outside the main channel and ride out the bow waves as if in the Australian surf.

They were now paddling 50-60 miles a day, the flow pushing them along to a speed where they could have lunch in the canoe and still cover a couple of miles. Paddling, by admission, had become a chore. Long days, through dazzling heat with only a tented night on a sand bar to look forward to, both Sean and Rob were now just counting the miles rather than enjoying the experience. However, the mark of these guys was such that they overcame these mental and physical hurdles and paddled on regardless, determined to reach their goal like the intrepid voyagers they'd become.

Although our lives were far easier, this shoulder phase of the trip had turned excitement into disinterest, even driving straight through Natchez, one of the most historic places on the route, foregoing its romanticism in favour of apathy, deciding we could see many of the antebellum houses in fifty years time on a virtual reality Wallace Arnold cyber sex interactive coach trip.com.

After a night in a St Francisville trailer park listening to the evening chorus of crickets, birds and overly loud arguments about drinking all the money away and *'how we supposed to pay for Mikey's diapers,'* our journey through Louisiana was one of overhanging weeping cypress trees, heat haze jumping from the road into the sodden atmosphere, and of tortuous sweating and brow wiping as our decreasing fuel budget meant we had to conserve fuel.

Into Baton Rouge we swept like an Indie music-blaring broom, hopeful of soon being in air-conditioned pastures, only these were pastures for cows that consumed oil. At the head of Louisiana's oil industry, refineries pleasantly scorched indelible scratches of black piping onto the skyline. Thankfully nearing the centre of Baton Rouge the view became easier on the eye mainly thanks to the State Capitol Building.

One of the most charismatic figures of the 20th Century Huey P. Long was elected Governor of Louisiana in 1929 and immediately set out to promote the State into being the superpower of the south. The capital, Baton Rouge was in decline, so Long's far reaching plans included building a bridge across the Mississippi River with a clearing height too low for the ocean-going freight ships ploughing north. Once built, the port of Baton Rouge overnight became the principal port on the river, much to the pleasure of the locals. Obviously it didn't sit too well with the commercial powers of Mississippi, Arkansas, Tennessee, and Missouri, and Long's name became synonymous with corruption, so much so that within a year of being elected he was impeached on charges of bribery and misappropriation of State funds. These outlandish charges were mysteriously dropped after some infighting within certain circles. Long subsequently became a cult figure in his homeland despite his despotic regime.

Like most men of self importance, Huey found it essential to have phallic related trinkets. To drive a muscle car with a 6ft bonnet is to have round your neck a sign saying 'look at the size of my nob'. Wear chunky jewellery and you are inferring 'the contents of my underpants would fill a fruit bowl'. But Huey P. Long went one better. He built a 450ft appendage and called it the State Capitol Building and it was here, at the base of its shaft near some overgrown bush next to some testicular shaped gardens, that we parked the RV.

Taller than any other State capitol building, this huge striking erection, finished in Long's final year as Governor in 1932, is a limestone laudation to Art-deco architecture. Through its 50ft high main entrance, we were welcomed by the vast walnut lined atrium that cooled the air like a blast of liquid nitrogen. Amongst the decorative reliefs, murals, paintings and quotations sat proud the colourful State seal, a Mother Pelican at nest feeding her three offspring, Union, Justice, and Confidence. There had originally been five but Wit, we'd decided, had died at birth and Honesty had flown the coop to set up a second-hand car business in Wichita.

We hadn't called in to discuss 20th century styles and influences but to call in at the tourist info booth situated in another grand hall. But the building itself was so impressive that one had to take a more in depth look. Like two childish explorers we followed signposts to anything that sounded interesting. We were astounded that in a country renowned for its secretive nature, we were able, I think, to freely walk through the working hive of parliament between the Executive, Judicial, and Legislative branches of government. Even the courts were on the tourist trail, access only denied during trials. We stopped short of walking into the governor's office to ask for a happy snappy and a raspberry snow cone. These corridors exuded an air of power, of past and present. We could imagine that behind the frosted glass doors we now passed, briefcases full of unmarked bills were being carelessly left under a planning developer's desk, funny handshakes exchanged across crowded chambers and senators asking what colour knickers their secretaries preferred.

Up the building urethra in the elevator we were propelled like two sperm cells to the glans of the 27th floor observation deck. Not quite the view that one gets from the Empire State Building, we did find it an excellent vantage point from which to view the river that had now become a family member. It didn't so much as curve its way, like a lithe girl, as it did in Minnesota; now an obese couch potato, it just did her own thing, gorging on the land it passed through. Impressive too were the gardens that surrounded the building as if these penis obsessed designers had purposely designed the area to be well maintained pubic hair of Capability Brown proportions.

Satisfied spending the day in the building's cool air, we headed to Fire Station 7 near Louisiana State University. With its propensity for promiscuous nightlife, LSU was nicknamed NSU. With students on their summer vacation, the clubs and bars, normally throbbing with the sound of youthful optimism, were filled with cynical old men.

The tasks of newspaper exposure and kayak stowage were completed the first morning, the latter of the two chores being a rather wholesome experience.

On a parcel of land on the Baton Rouge riverfront lies the USS Kidd, a WWII destroyer berthed for the benefit of tourists. It is the main attraction of the Baton Rouge USS Kidd Naval Museum. Being from a nautical background on a nautical voyage we thought we may get some help from within. Bypassing most links in the chain of command, we headed straight for the main man. Adorned upon the corridor walls towards his office were paintings of famous sea battles, iconic vessels and nautical figures mostly from the 'golden age' of British Imperialism. We could see this man liked naval history so were confident we'd be warmly greeted. His P.A. wasn't so sure.

'Do you have an appointment?' he asked nervously. 'Mr Drummond won't see anyone without an appointment.'

'Can you please tell him that two Royal Marines Commandos from the UK are here. We're on an expedition paddling the length of the Mississippi and require a place to berth our kayak,' I postured, as if I'd just informed him of an impeding visit by the President of Jupiter.

He shrugged his paper wide shoulders and got from his chair, 'I don't know if he'll be happy, he sure is busy. You really should make an appointment.'

He scurried to the door displaying 'Maury Drummond Executive Director', and knocked meekly, cautiously entering on command. Literally shaking with fear the P.A, who by the second was metamorphosing into Dr Frankenstein's assistant Igor, repeated a Chinese whisper that two UK guys from the Marines were here to berth a Mississippi canoe for some Commandos.

'The hell you talking about, boy?' boomed a voice from within.

Fitz and I both gulped. Was this wise? Was this man as fearsome as he sounded? If so we were going to run.

'Two British marines, Sir,' the P.A started again.

'Two Royal Marines? Hell, why didn't ya say, boy?'

And from that, the doorway darkened as we saw for the first time Mr Maury Drummond. Looking like a Texan oil baron, at 6'5" in his socks and a voice that carried a 8.5 pressure wave on the Richter scale he stood there with the self-assuredness of a man eating a pie at a public urinal. He shook our hands with a verve that made my arm pop from its socket, his gargantuan paw making mine feel like a child's. He told us how much admired the Royal Marines, before inviting us into his office, where hopefully they had an A&E department to push my shoulder back in. The P.A stared with disbelief as these two scruffy individuals walked into the hallowed ground of Maury Drummond's office - without an appointment.

With coffee firmly in hand we told our tales of high jinx on the river, lengthening the inhospitable conditions the lads in the kayak were facing and shortening our own comfort, yes your coffee is lovely and could we stow our kayak somewhere safe while we stayed at the fire station? Of course this wouldn't be a problem, Maury couldn't do enough for us. We felt quite humbled that he thought so much of our trip, his authority on everything naval was in no doubt which made us feel even more privileged for him to laud us so.

A private tour of the museum was immensely interesting, his boundless energy and knowledge enhancing the visual display. Although small, it retained interest until the early evening when we bade farewell to Maury. We wouldn't see him again as he was away for the weekend but his personality had left an indelible mark on our journey.

A tropical monsoon of Bangladeshi proportions greeted the guys as they pulled alongside the USS Kidd. The clouds had thickened considerably between our new fire station home and the riverfront and the air had a tad more water content than I'd initially expected. By the time we'd reached the river's edge I was drenched from the neck up, saturated from the neck down and Fitz had to hide under a pier to prevent the video camera from shorting in his hand. The fact they'd paddled the whole day through lightening strikes and rain so torrential it had restricted visibility heightening the chance of being run over by super barges bolstered my already saturated admiration for them. They arrived in a state befitting such a journey - exhausted, bedraggled and saturated, yet energised the RV with their smiles and were ready to tame Baton Rouge's nightlife. Unfortunately, with half the local population indoors on such a miserable evening the nightlife was not so much in need of taming but coaxing from behind the sofa after a slightly scary episode of 'Dr Who'.

Maybe it was the inclement weather that directed everyone, including us, to wait for the premiere of a new film. Not since I waited for 40 minutes to see 'Grease' had I seen such a queue for the cinema. Even so, this eagerness to be able to black cat friends by reciting the day of first seeing John and Olivia shaping up must pale into insignificance against the reports that people queued for six weeks to see the first Star Wars episode. I heard on the radio one particular geek from the warmth of his cardboard box at the head of a significant line of similar obstructions on the sidewalk, hoping that after his unrequited commitment his reward would be to get his stinking, grimy, unwashed backside sat in seat 107 in row 8, the best seat in the auditorium. Oh how I wished I could have seen his face when the 6'7" bloke in seat 107 row 7 refused to remove his top hat. I needn't traipse to the local milliner for tremendously high headwear. Due to being skint I waited in the car park while the lads watched 'Face Off'. Sustenance is always high on Rob's list so the following day we wandered around a shopping mall food court - a United Nations of diasporic food franchises. Unable to locate my favourite 'Antarctic Penguin Grill', a man invited us to pick some Bourbon chicken from a delicious smelling tray he held to our faces. We all took a chunk. It was bloody lovely. So lovely, in fact, Fitz took another.

The man lightly slapped Fitz's wrist. 'Only one piece.' He must have been a former military chef.

'Ow!' screamed Fitz, falling to the floor like a professional footballer and rolled around holding his arm. 'Medic! Medic!!!'

The man froze in fear. In such a litigious society as the US where a contestant on 'Who wants to be a Millionaire' can sue for distress caused by a question that was a 'bit hard', he could see his life turn into some terrible daytime soap opera of bankruptcy, jail and contrite clichés to his long suffering wife. 'Here have as many as you want,' he said, lowering the tray.

'Ooh don't mind if I do,' replied Fitz, leaping up like Lazarus, taking a handful of chicken.

Fuelled with bourbon chicken, we decided to recapture our youth and play some video games. Fitz decided he wanted to play a driving game because:

a) Two consoles meant we could race each other

b) I was a driving biff and would kill a virtual spectator if I accelerated past 35mph. I sincerely hoped not. I didn't want to be sued by a virtual family member for reckless virtual driving and spend time in prison with a Bourbon chicken salesman.

It was fun being humiliated in consecutive games until a small child decided he wanted a go and tried to wrestle the steering wheel from my grasp. I wasn't having any of that; no pre-school bully was going to take over Timey's position at the wheel.

I wrestled it back, crashing into a tunnel wall in the process.

He pulled it right. I careered into the opposite wall.

Left I pulled. Crash.

Right he pulled. Skid.

Harder I pulled left. Oh no, virtual spectator!

Previously intended to incapacitate Special Forces enemies, my unarmed combat skills now were being used on this little shit. Twisting his thumb from the wheel took me into an uncontrollable spin past a pit stop lane. He was determined. He attacked from a more acute angle distracting me in my concentration to turn my AS Cobra the right way round. Clever for someone so young, he knew I couldn't gain optimum power in first gear, so lunging at the wheel he purposely knocked the gear into first with his knee. Enough was enough. I could take no more. It was with super human effort that I finally found the strength to flick his ear, telling him 'to fuck off' and 'find mummy.'

This did the trick. He left clutching his ear, pulling a string of transparent snot between his wavering shirtsleeve and his nostril. While all this commotion was going on, Fitz had won the race handsomely. I didn't care. I'd lost the battle, but won the war.

The night was spent talking to locals about our trip. We weren't so much celebrities but we'd commanded a front page picture on the Baton Rouge edition of the Louisiana Advocate Newspaper, the picture itself didn't do any of us any justice catching us all in a moment of sucking lemons. Despite this we'd been recognised, and Rob and Sean were correctly the heroes of the hour. They retold stories of swashbuckling grandeur on the dangerous waters of the river, showing scars of their time wrestling 30ft snakes, swimming to safety seconds before being dragged over waterfalls and the very real dangers of surviving collapsing sand bars, paddling around deadly craft-swallowing whirlpools and trying to understand people in Kentucky. Often sounding patronising, the American's coos of "wow" and "gee" were genuine and Rob's already massive head was having trouble fitting through the double doors on exiting the club.

***

When one leaves the Royal Marines there are skills learnt that prove invaluable to potential employers. Which financial institution would be stupid enough to turn down the application of a man who can skin most animals and eat worms? Wouldn't any corporation like to boast that one of their employees can lie in an observation post for weeks on end and shit in plastic bags? The truth is that men who leave the Royal Marines are a in the main a special kind of person (like any walk of life it has its share of 'tubes'). They can adapt to work in any environment, doing extraordinary things that the normal thinking layperson wouldn't dream of doing. And that is exactly where the problem lies when these guys leave. Mainstream employers seek lobotomised brand-defined process monkeys and not those who choose to do extraordinary things, and the laziness of HR departments translates 'transferable skills' as 'extra work' much preferring to employ those who fit easily into their tick box pigeon hole. That's why many intelligent ex-service people end up in far off countries doing specialised security work, hanging from oil rigs 200ft over the North Sea, setting up their own commercial ventures, and doing time. A comfortable life in civvy street isn't really enough for the 'average' Royal Marine.

Phil had left the Royal Marines with nothing other than a strong bond with Sean and Rob, a reputation for extreme shagging and a commercial diving qualification. Although he'd had an offer to pursue a career in the former he decided to dive in Saudi Arabia. After being on a dive barge for three months at a time with not so much as an 'FHM' to read due to Saudi's strict censorship laws it was hardly surprising his time off would be used to fritter away all his hard earned money on booze, women, and skydiving. The rest he would waste. Unfortunately, his penchant for jumping from aeroplanes had recently left him with a broken arm and so was currently on sick leave. With time to kill, money in his pocket, and two close mate 3/4 the way down the Mississippi River, he'd managed to persuade one of the two air stewardesses he was dating to get him a free flight to New York. From there he'd taken the bus with the dog ends of US society down to New Orleans where he was currently awaiting our arrival.

I'd been impatient to return to the 'Big Easy', Fitz more than anyone relieved to arrive to prevent me spinning any more N'Awlins dits. He'd already warned me that on no account would I be able to start a sentence with the words, 'This is where...'

We entered on the I10, the massive expanse of Lake Pontchartrain on either side of us. Wild fowl escorted us in, the waters rippling underneath giving indication of mysterious underwater activities. The slow build up of urbanisation gradually fed us into the city's heart. As the concrete landscape shrouded us, it dawned that I didn't recognise a single thing. We took the main feeder route to the French Quarter by way of Tulane Avenue and took our RV through the narrowing streets to the Fire Department HQ on Decatur Street at the riverside of the Quarter. To meet us there was the Assistant Superintendent Darryl J Delatte. The highest ranking fire officer we'd yet met, Mr Delatte was 2ic of the whole City Fire Department, so it was even more of a surprise how laid back and amiable he was. Taking us into his office with iced tea on tap he laughed and joked with us for over an hour. He'd pre-arranged accommodation for us at Task Force 5 on Magazine Street over towards the Arts District. The kayak, he added, could be stowed here, as Task Force 5 was too far away from the river.

Thoroughly thankful, we left happy in the knowledge that the majority of our administration had been done within an hour of arriving, leaving more time for enjoying the pleasures of the Big Easy.

Task Force 5 was not as it sounded - a Squadron of intergalactic space fighter pilots from the Battle Star Galactica, but a fire station full of equally brave and welcoming crewmen.

Before even sitting down, we had a cup of coffee in hand and were led to a four berth ready-room usually allocated for duty fire fighters. Again we'd fallen on our feet. This time, rather than us making our own luck through a bit of neck, it was down to the hospitality of the locals.

I hadn't seen Phil for at least two years, Fitz had never even met him, so it was typical of the espirit de corps that is inherent within the Royal Marines that within two minutes we were giggling like pigtailed schoolgirls laughing at nothing in particular apart form each other's hair, me with my terrible 70's sitcom mop and Phil with his flowing golden locks straight from Bondi Beach.

We met in Pat O'Brien's. Easily recognisable, well known, and my old haunt. At 6.30pm it was pretty quiet, so to soak away the quietness we began drinking the infamous 'Hurricanes'. As I'd downed a copious amount of these previously I had all the confidence in the world that I could stomach more than a couple. How wrong I was. Either they'd become increasingly stronger or my drinking capability considerably weaker. To my own admission I am gratefully pathetic now in the drinking stakes, pour me a schooner of sweet sherry and you will find me sleeping off a hangover for the next three days. Fitz, on the other hand, can down 'em like the thirstiest alcoholic known to humankind. But as I had witnessed in DC, Fitz's behaviour after a few drinks can sometimes take on a somewhat strange form.

Usually you can see a person slide slowly from being a bright intellectual in sobriety, through often witty in merriment, then perhaps down into introverted stares or becoming annoyingly extroverted before collapsing into incoherent mumblings. Fitz missed all the interim stages. From intelligent, witty conversation, within the blink of an eye he was upholding the Corps tradition of being a drunken idiot. Having seen my 'Hurricanes' splash against the toilet bowl in a multi-coloured spray of vomit, I was feeling quite sober, sober enough to realise that Fitz was not. His amorous advances were repeatedly revoked, and before his ears rang with the sound of a whip crack palm I pulled him away. As per usual, Phil spent the night beating off women with a shitty stick. Rather than see Fitz's more than swift deterioration lead to arrest for gross indecency, Phil thought it wise to stay with us and try and help me control Fitz who by now was a burbling wreck of foetal proportions.

Unbelievably, Fitz was up at the crack of dawn, fresh as a gambolling lamb. I on the other hand nursed a headache liable to make a hypochondriac migraine sufferer green with envy. To make matters worse we had to drive over the river to a military air base - the NAS New Orleans to blag a freight flight back to Washington DC for all the equipment. With all the best will in the world we still hadn't managed to organise how to get all stores back to the RAF air-head at Dulles Airport in DC. We were thirteen days from flying home, best we get started.

'No cuff too tough,' said Phil as we drove to the air base with a name in my pocket that may be able to help us.

*'You cannot surprise an individual more than twice
with the same marvel.'*

~ Mark Twain, Writer

With my head thumping, I was hardly going to be the
best negotiator yet my sniper skills were sharp. As we
crossed the Crescent City Connection I spotted a
colourful plate two lanes over that I didn't recognise.
Hungry to finally tick off Connecticut and taste number
plate victory, I notified Fitz, whose hunger burned as
strong as mine. He swerved recklessly into the adjacent
lane of our prey. Stalking the vehicle at 55mph we were
barricaded by four cars, obscuring the view. My palms
sweated, my throat dried. I needed to see it. Directing
Fitz to divert our 27ft beast into gaps a mini would
struggle to squeeze into, he accelerated, braked, turned,
swerved, throwing Phil from his seat into the kitchenette. Getting on his feet he was ceremonially thrown
back across the table and back onto the floor as Fitz
skidded in between a Cadillac and a huge juggernaut,
receiving honks and horns in stereo. Fitz now had fire
in his eyes, encouraged by the devil on his back, as we
closed on for the kill. Now only one car delayed victory.
Caught in our vehicular crossfire, if it didn't move
quickly it would unfortunately be bulldozed off the
bridge into the river below, another innocent casualty
of number plate spotting, subsequent court action a
mere inconvenience. The driver must have sensed
danger, possibly due to Fitz's demonic stares boring
into him, and moved over into a space he couldn't fit
comfortably into. Wiping the sweat from our eyes we
closed on our prey. The smell, not of the blood of
victory, but the burnt rubber of spotting filled our

nostril There it was, in all its glory - a jazzed up Missouri plate. Bollocks.

Arriving at our destination, we introduced ourselves to a corporal of cerebral limitations. 'No, never heard of him,' he insisted from behind the reception office glass when I'd asked to see Chief Heinkel.

'Look mate, we have been given this name by the RAF dispatch team at Washington DC Dulles and they're pretty certain he's here,' I said between patronising head tilts. 'They spoke to him only yesterday and we were to meet him here.'

He was obviously getting tired of me thinking I was correct. 'Look buddy, your guys at DC have got it wrong. There's no Chief Heinkel here, got it?' reciprocating the word 'look' to suggest equal irritation.

Even Fitz, usually calm as a millpond, was now pissed off. These guys didn't even know their own personnel.

'We have it here.' I pulled from my shorts a piece of paper with the same name and number, just to show how fucking stupid this guy was. 'Chief Heinkel H-E-I-N-K-E-L, freight depot NAS New Orleans,' I added, assertively pushing the screwed up paper to the glass.

The corporal's face lurched from anger to delight. 'Well you better go to NAS New Orleans then,' he said in a tone so smug it would have made Shirley Temple vomit over her lollipop.

To us it only confused matters. We looked at each other but in our case two heads were no better than one and returned our quizzical looks to the glass.

'You are at NSA New Orleans, he said as though talking to two deaf old ladies lost at the tube station.

'Err yes we know.' God I was going to punch this twat if he hadn't been behind the glass. And 6'1" and 15 stone.

'You need to go to NAS New Orleans.' Mimicking me, he added, 'N-A-S New Orleans.'

'You mean…?'

'You're at the wrong airbase. The one you want is thirty miles out of town, that way,' pointing in a manner that said he really wanted us to follow his finger, and fast.

We scurried away red with embarrassment, sheepish in gait and dishevelled in appearance. Phil, who we'd smuggled into the base as he held no a military ID card, asked us what was wrong. After repairing his split sides, he reminded us that we were tossers. Realisation that he was absolutely correct followed, along with us bursting into raptures of uncontrollable laughter.

Once we did find N-A-S New Orleans, it was with frightening swiftness that we met Chief Heinkel, sunk a couple of Mountain Dews, and before we could say 'Bob's you uncle' had booked space on a forthcoming freight flight heading for Dulles. We were back in the city in time for tea and medals, congratulating ourselves on a job well done, even upholding the time honoured British tradition of being buffoons abroad.

Whether I just wanted the trip to end, or disappointed that the trip *was* about to end it made it difficult for me to enjoy the surroundings as before. Fitz and Phil were brilliant company, but the fact that I was meeting my girlfriend in Florida when returning the RV meant I had to refrain from anything requiring a financial transaction. I couldn't meet her for a week's holiday in the sun and say, 'Sorry, could you sub me a few hundred dollars, I've spent all mine pissing up with the lads,' unless I wanted my gonads fed to hyenas. I stayed in wallowing in self-pity as Fitz and Phil painted the town red. I felt like a walk but my paranoia of walking uncharted areas kept me imprisoned indoors reading tourism brochures on a New Orleans that I couldn't afford to enjoy.

It was dark by the time the paddlers arrived. With port and starboard cyalumes dangling from the Klepper's side, they paddled overtly in the river's blackness, reflected in the dazzling city lights like a spacecraft cruising its shimmering path along the Milky Way. We pulled them from the rocky riverbank, Phil, especially glad to see them. It was only right that they chewed the fat for a few minutes to catch up on the gossip, i.e. how many women Phil had slept with in the last month. With their chins wagging at ten to the dozen it was left to us to de-rig the kayak and throw all the equipment, sand, mud and all, into the immaculate RV.

Built on the foundation of intoxicated frenzy, you may witness many things in the French Quarter. The year-round party atmosphere ensures never a day goes by without some form of novelty, whether it be the florid iron lacework typical of any New Orleans tourist poster, street entertainers, or lots and lots of tits. Once done only during Mardi Gras, now it'd be rare not to cop an eyeful of bead craving women exposing their mammary glands on any given day. Rarer still is the sight of two half-naked men carrying a mud covered Special Forces kayak through its crowded streets. So it was only natural that, as Fitz and I carried the kayak the 300 yards or so to the Fire Department, we were the recipients of odd stares, photography flashes to blind us, and the occasional unanswered question, as it isn't easy to reply with a rudder prodding into one's cheek. Admin completed, we set off to New Orleans Task Force 5.

On our initial arrival we'd been warned by the fire fighters not to go into the area behind the station. These were some of the most dangerous streets in the city. Riddled with drugs, endemic with crime; the projects were no place for the tourist. With memories flooding back from my personal experience years before, the warning was heeded to the letter. We'd discussed the issue with Sean and Rob as we approached the front of the station only to meet a police 'DO NOT CROSS' line of tape. Dazzled by revolving police lights through the windscreen, portable floodlights on the forecourt of the station illuminated the grass verge. Around the spotlights huddled uniformed police, fire fighters, paramedics, and forensics personnel wearing white coveralls, either that or they were bootnecks dressed as a tampon on a silly rig run. I got out to see what was happening. Luckily one of the fire fighters we knew was held at the cordon and greeted me with a chuckle, 'A typical night on Magazine Street.'

'What happened?' I pointed to the area of interest.

'A druggy carrying a load of shit just got shot. Made a real mess of the road too.'

'Dead?'

'Oh yeah, real dead. We heard four or five shots, ran out and there he was, his bike and drugs thrown across the street, his head all fucked up. Yeah he ain't goin' anywhere 'part from hell.'

I looked at the scene. Crime dramas soften the impact of death, but I couldn't help thinking that the blood I watched dribbling into the drain was a sad allegory of the victim's life.

Local radio brought the previous night's murder into perspective; it was one of sixteen that'd happened in five hours. The one on our doorstep was listed only 12th. Murder on one's doorstep is a pretty big deal yet conversation in the fire station was still about the up and coming football season, last night's film and the fire up on St Charles Avenue. Perhaps some would find this nonchalance uncomfortable yet working in this area had hardened the fire fighters to it, ironically, like those same people would to third world death.

Uniquely a quintet, communal sight seeing seemed appropriate. Walking across the single lane carriageway of Magazine North towards St Charles Avenue to start our day, the ideal of 'have's and have not's' was all too real. Not more than 100 yards behind us sat the projects, a rat riddled tip of human degradation where you couldn't tell whether you were in the bad streets of New Orleans or Nairobi. Here, as we walked larch lined pathways, we passed huge ornate gates secured by CCTV, the odd guard and warning signs of impending doom to anyone wanting to gain entrance without a specific invite. These were the homes of New Orleans super affluent, the lawmen, business leaders and sports stars, all within a pathetic ball throw of abject poverty. Would I be comfortable living here? Whether it was from fear of crime or just being guilty of living on the doorstep of this poverty, I felt that this extreme paradox tarnished my view of what I'd loved about the USA.

After a $1 tram ride from St Charles Avenue we did the normal thing of traipsing Bourbon Street, trying on silly hats and visiting voodoo and sex shops, the latter being a lot more frightening. A scuba mask with 7" dildo attachment to the nose interested Rob far too much for my liking, and Fitz being Fitz tried on a crotch-less PVC thong, which just didn't do him justice.

Since my last visit it seemed that street begging had become a growth industry. I'd often noted their dusk arrival to poach money from the pub crawl crowd but now dayshift beggars were plentiful in the searing heat of the city's midday sun, squinting vacantly at passers-by, holding out a pathetic hand in the hope of sympathy change. One could see how this could be upsetting to many a visitor. We, however, reciprocated their humorous advances. I felt like a freak show visitor rewarding a performing animal should they want to perform something more original than a 'have you got a spare dollar' sketch. A few even offered us something for our money, but since it tended to be illegal narcotics, their kind offer was gracefully declined.

One particular space cadet bumped into Fitz with his tumbling gait looking as though he was still suffering the effects of something particularly strong. Even from my withdrawn position his acrid B.O was overpowering, so Fitz was rather nonplussed at him falling into his arms. As thanks for Fitz holding him up, he opened his clenched palm and offered him the contents. Should Fitz have been the most clucking crack addict imaginable he would still turn down the mucus in this fellow's sweaty palm that he claimed was 'top shit'. It certainly looked like shit. Fitz explained that *he* would have to pay *him* to take it off his hands. The beggar was now dangerously agitated, pushing Fitz from him as if it had been Fitz trying to molest him. I suppose he could have taken his threats further but being surrounded by five sober chaps of varying degrees of fighting ability seemed to bring some clarity to his thought, so he stumbled off to try and sell his shit to someone desperate enough to inject Vim into their penis.

It was to be a busy final couple of days. Not only was it Sean's birthday, but the British Embassy was sending both David Wilson, the Royal Marines Liaison Officer and the British Naval Attaché, Colonel Andy Pillar to visit us. We debated whether in the presence of such a senior military figure we should get haircuts, but being Royal Marines Officers we hoped they'd probably see through our unkempt appearance and be more concerned with the substance of our trip.

Probably a less wise decision was to let Sean buy 'Golden Grain'. The owner of the liquor store warned us not to drink it neat and was only to be used heavily diluted in a punch. He may as well have put a gun to our heads and said *only* drink it neat. It would make an ideal aperitif before meeting the highest-ranking Royal Marine on the continent that evening.

There were five men and one innocent looking half-bottle of 'Golden Grain'. I should have erred more to the side of caution when Phil piped up that he'd drunk it before and no way was he going to touch a drop, admitting that it 'blew yer tits off.'

I have stupidly imbibed diesel-based rum with indigenous villagers in the Belizean jungle, idiotically drunk Thai whiskey containing formaldehyde in the fields of Northern Thailand, and happily shared a bottle of 'Bucky' with the homeless in London, but nothing could prepare me for this.

Rob took the first small sip. After swallowing, he immediately convulsed into spasms, much to our delight. His vomiting made us laugh even more, and his shaking like a shitting dog was only slightly less amusing.

Fitz next swigged from the poisoned chalice. He managed to conjure up such facial gymnastics I honestly thought his head was suffering from a severe bout of lycanthropy, even managing an animalistic howl of pain as his insides rejected the liquor.

Sean, as usual was as cool as a polar bear's arse. Nonchalantly taking a sip, then a gulp, he left the liquor in his mouth before smiling calmly, then swallowed before grinning. He could handle it easily. He was Welsh. He stood there in triumph, master of the devil drink. We stood there both impressed and worried that he wasn't actually human before he hiccoughed then promptly ran behind the RV to throw his ring up.

Peer pressure is a strange phenomenon. Surely only the weak succumb to the encouragement of others. The strong would never do as others wanted, man (or woman) enough to make up his (or her) own judgements he (or she) may do as he (or she) see fit and travel along his (or her) chosen path. Or so I thought. All these principles I wanted to hand down to my children were now cast aside as the fire fighters were now out in force to watch us play silly buggers. They stood there in hysterics as Fitz continued to wretch by the RV on his knees coughing like a dog eating grass. How could I now say no?

I took the bottle and slowly took a sniff. Big mistake, even the smell shot a bolt down my spine, pure alcohol distilled from Satan's piss. I closed my eyes and put the bottle to my lips. The liquor stung as it hit my tongue. Only a quarter full, my mouth felt like it was on fire. So swiftly did the burning commence, I swallowed immediately. The fire followed its journey down my throat to the pit of my stomach. Fire alarms were triggered everywhere inside, my head a flashing distress beacon. My mouth instantly filled with saliva. Overflowing with spittle, I dribbled like a teething baby. My stomach raised the vomit alert to red as it took a countdown to throw this unwanted visitor out. But no, I had to keep face. I swallowed hard, belching in baritone to keep the liquid fire down. My stomach tried again but the peristalsis of falling phlegm helped dilute and dowse the conflagration in my stomach. Now only the burning embers of 'Golden Grain' lay uncomfortably in my gut. I still dribbled. I still belched, my face contorted as convulsion after convulsion waved through my bones. What an absolute wanker, giving in to peer pressure. But I had done it. With everyone's laughter ringing in my ears, I took a few steps past Fitz's puke and scrambled inside to 'take a shower'.

Laughter was also the next thing I heard as Rob pointed in exclamation at the sight of me heaving bile into the shower basin. The proliferation of dribbling led me past the point of no return. Without the presence of an audience, my will had waned and had puked. And boy did I puke; not quite the three pints I managed to evacuate at Beaufort Rugby Club after Wales defeated England that consequently my mate Paul ended up drinking, alarmingly without himself being sick. Not only did I bring up the 'Golden Grain', but that day's lunch, last night's dinner, a couple of Tonka toys, a magician's never ending line of bunting and the whole of my duodenum were thrown up in a series of ever increasingly painful wretches. My wanker rating was still high.

It was Sean's birthday and hardly anyone was drinking. Colonel Pillar had invited us all to a very posh seafood restaurant in the Quarter, where the extortionate prices were graciously irrelevant as he was paying. I realised I wouldn't be able to drink or eat. My stomach had taken such a battering that it needed sufficient time to convalesce. Rob didn't have such a dilemma. This allowed him to scrounge the many leftovers I had available. Rob can eat. When we'd breakfast together at any eatery, I would be shocked at the amount he would put away, even the waitresses would looked puzzled when he'd ask for another breakfast. Refills of coffee were one thing, refills of breakfast another. Mind you, a body his size needs fuel. With a back of a world champion body builder, and a belly of a world champion beer drinker, Rob was often the butt of our name-calling teasing him about his so-called baggy body, which was rich coming from me. With a body of a weak young boy I was hardly in any position to take the piss out of anyone.

Colonel Pillar had now taken leave for the night, probably aware of the ensuing carnage. After thanking him for his support, we showed David Wilson the Quarter. Whether he saw too much is debatable, as his eyes were increasingly akin to piss holes in the snow. We attempted to have a sociable beer but it wasn't going down particularly well. David, on the other hand, was knocking them back like a park bench tramp and by the time we'd gone halfway round the Quarter (an eighth you may quip) he was pissed as a fart. Leaving us every so often, he'd return from the toilets with tell tale tears in his eyes and as far I was aware they weren't any Lassie films being played in there.

By now I had become slightly aggrieved by the constant badgering from street beggars. They'd cleaned me out of dollar bills and my patience was now wearing thin.

He only had one eye, bless him. He was 6ft tall with a body that would make Mr Burns look like the Incredible Hulk. He was onto a loser straight away. He walked in front of me boasting of his magical voodoo powers.

'Yeah yeah go on.' I lazily challenged.

'I bit you twen'y darllers I know where you got doze shoes.'

Having bought them in Taunton I very much doubted it. 'Go on, try me.'

'OK, so you're betting me I can tell you where you got doze shoes?'

'Yes,' I sighed with audible impatience.

'OK, you got doze shoes in Bourbon Street, N'Awlins, right here right now.'

Knowing I had been hoodwinked by an anomaly of the English language or a woeful piece of grammar I decided to get my own back.

'No I got them in Taunton, Somerset.'

'No you got dem here in N'Awlins.'

'I *have* them here in Bourbon Street. But the question you posed was where I *got* my shoes. You seem to have failed to include the second person singular of the verb 'to have' misleading you to incorrectly use the past participle of the verb 'to get' in your original question in turn misleading you to give a grammatically incorrect statement.' I didn't know whether I was talking bollocks or not but with an English accent it must have sounded good.

It was difficult to ascertain a confused expression with his one eye but he mused before replying. 'You owe me twen'y darllers.'

Having survived the armed mugging several years before, fuckdust here wasn't going to get much change from me - quite literally. His pursuance was the last straw. To his surprise I turned on him, chasing him down the crowded street gesticulating with a pointed finger. I let rip a barrage of Yorkshire dialect as grammatically poor as his. Usually it was tourists being harassed by beggars, but the worm had turned. Onlookers wondered how destitute I must have been to harass a beggar.

Even worse was to come. I'd passed the guy a few times. He stood motionless painted grey in a statuesque pose. He was good, granted. I'd yet to see even his nose twitch in spite of the fact he stood in a rather unorthodox pose in between a pepper factory and a field of newly mown grass. I dug deep into my pockets, and almost skint from the night out, emptied all my small change into the shoebox at his feet.

'Is that it?' he asked moving his lips like a bad ventriloquist.

'Sorry?' I asked, thinking I'd misheard.

'Is that all you're gonna give me? That ain't much.'

It was even less once I'd reached into the shoebox and retrieved my handful of coins, and a few more for being an ungrateful shit, what was he going to do, chase me? What sort of statue would he be then? With abuse from a pissed up Fitz and a glazed stare from David Wilson, we continued our way to the taxi rank hardly surprised that we were refused by countless taxi drivers to take us to Magazine Street as they feared for their lives.

With the morning sunshine burning our faces, we took some photographs in front of the Steamboat Natchez with Colonel Pillar before bidding farewell to both him and David Wilson. David was in poor form, and took on a rather lime green pallor, promising never to drink again.

Although sad to see him go, Phil was also leaving. He was also disappointed, but had a prior arrangement with an air stewardess in Atlantic City. All things considered, I'm sure he'd prefer to get up with her wrapped around him rather than waking up to the sight and smell of Sean's hairy arse poking out of a duvet in the morning.

Now back to the original quartet, we launched the kayak for one last time. As we dodged the crowds who wondered what these idiots were doing in the busy streets of the French Quarter, we found ourselves reminiscing already about the trip. How Rob had been a muppet with the radio back in Minnesota, how I'd thrown my teddy out over anything that couldn't be solved with a smile, and Sean when losing his Welsh flag. Fitz got shit for being Fitz, but it was camaraderie that had brought us all together and it was camaraderie that had kept us together. While totting up plenty of arguments, our common goal was the most important thing. Here, as we carried 110lbs of 18ft canvas and metal through the streets of our favourite city, we felt as one. The day was bright and alive with the hustle and bustle of New Orleans. The cafés were full, the street stalls busy, the wafting smell of beignets and coffee carried on their backs the sound of live jazz, the pressure of the humidity licking our bodies, the taste of the Big Easy lingered satisfyingly on our tongues.

We reached the bank at the spot from where they'd come ashore. This time rather than a quiet stealth-like landing in pitch darkness, we stood amongst a crowd of tourists and locals, alike in their inquisitiveness of our trip. We felt like film stars at the Oscars as question after question was thrown upon us, we tried to give informative answers where we could and lied when we couldn't. By the time Rob and Sean were ready to leave, the crowd had swelled to around fifty people including a street saxophonist who offered to play us off. The lads entered the kayak, Fitz and I helping them off with a push as the saxophonist played Sousa's 'Stars and Stripes'. The crowd burst into a spontaneous round of applause as the lads paddled away on their last leg of the trip. My nostrils flared with pride, We sat on the wet rocks and basked in our fleeting glory. Fitz then informed me that he'd shit himself.

'The journey not the arrival matters'

~ T.S Eliot, poet

The 70-odd miles to Venice were impatient ones. It was as if we'd been bought a new toy and were returning home on the bus, frustrated at the driver stopping at empty bus shelters. We'd come so far, the light was blinding us at the end of the tunnel. The route wasn't the most invigorating ever but its locality gave it a sentimental appearance. After all, it wouldn't be long before these single story wooden houses bordering on shacks nestled in groves of oranges would be long distant memories. Even the gargantuan oil refineries bordering highway 23, eyesores to even the most progressive eco-terrorist, couldn't spoil the scenery or dampen our spirits. We'd done it. Well nearly. They had a day's paddling left, or as the case may be a day paddling to the end and then another day paddling the ten miles back upriver to Venice if they couldn't hitch a lift from Pilotstown. That wasn't a concern at present. For once we didn't have any.

I remember not having such eagerness on a vehicle trip since the age of six or seven, when we'd go to Yorkshire coast to the resorts of Bridlington or if we were extra adventurous all the way to Scarborough. 10p would be offered for the first one to see the sea, all us kids in the back straining our necks like vigilant Meerkats as soon as we'd left the A1 into the East Riding looking for the tiniest modicum of translucent green. Sometimes we'd hallucinate in desperation for monetary gain and scream wildly that we'd seen it. But alas it would be a mirage, the clears blue sky low in a break in the skyline. Being the youngest and therefore the smallest I rarely won, but it didn't matter. Once one of us had seen it, we could all then see it, the 10p became irrelevant as stares fixated on the smallest speck of reflected water. We'd then the squabble about who saw it second.

As we mounted the crown of a bridge, we realised how near we actually were to completing our quest. The whole delta opened before us as if on an ultra-wide cinema screen. To our front, the marshland of the swamps and bayous lay, a junkyard of TV aerials sticking out from the greenness to show life inside the forest shroud. We'd heard 70% of the nation's fugitives hid here, a figure that could shake the spine of the newly travelled, yet our interests were firmly on the vista. To our right ran an estuary separated by a small causeway to the sea; magnificent in its enormity, it was the holy grail of water that we had longed to see. We didn't need a 10p reward. The panorama was priceless. Like a couple of pricks we gave a Texan 'Yeehaa' and suggested filming the view would be a good way of reliving the memory. We headed back north and gave ourselves a mile to steel ourselves before reaching the bridge. As we approached we played Kula Shaker's 'Hollow Man', singing along to the lyrics 'it's a long, long, long, long lonely road' hoping it would take us to celestial heights. Coming over the apex again, the view was still magnificent, the music fantastic, but the moment had gone. A surprise of this magnitude is a profit of human nature, only the first of a thousand skydives leaves you breathless. We now just cherished the view.

Venice, Italy and Venice, La, as far as we could see, had two things in common. The first was their proximity to the sea. The second, and most obvious as we now drove past run-down trailer parks and derelict shops, was that they both stink in the summer.

I'd read that over a third of the USA's water passed by the town but I didn't realise half of its sewage did as well. The place was indeed grim. Nothing to see but the pipes and smoke of the refineries, built on the back of the oil industry to cater for its commuting workers, Venice, La looked like the disowned garden of a derelict house.

We passed a café called 'The Last Stop' before passing another. Admittedly, 'The Second-To-Last Stop' doesn't have quite the same ring.

Our agenda was to find the coast guard compound. Cruising further along the unkempt carriageway we passed marinas full of resting shrimping boats of varying age and condition, some receiving the attention of heavily tanned chandlers restoring the stilted boats to a sailable standard. Screaming gulls swarmed above, scavenging for the contents of emptied tanks. Nets limply hung high in the air made a skyline of monofilament spider webs drying in the midday heat. The road gradually reducing, the yellow line separated oncoming vehicles now into passing wing mirror to wing mirror. Further and thinner still, it became a small causeway bridging the swampland only wide enough for two vehicles to pass if one waited on the boggy verge. Buildings became rarities. The map suggested we'd come to the end of the road about five miles back but we continued to see if we could fall off the Earth. Old knotted fingers of swamp tree roots rose out of the murky waters to the shrubbery that provided safe haven to the wildlife. The water on the passenger side rippled into concentric circles, Fitz exclaiming in his usual four letter manner that he'd just seen an alligator. Checking the doors were securely locked, as modern 'gators apparently have evolved the capability to open vehicle doors, we scoured the area to catch a glimpse of one, but to no avail. Only small rodents scurrying about in the undergrowth and a couple of knock-kneed Herons caught the eye. The road was now a track, until it abruptly stopped by a car park fence. A few rusting pick-ups and an old Cadillac filled the small space.

Was this the end of The Great River Road? Over 3000 miles covering the widest spectrum of history, scenery, and society, all to end in this crumbling car park? Hope masked reality. It was. We were as far south as anyone could go on four wheels.

There was only one way in and one way out, and I would only want to take the 'out' option. Two partly boarded-up grey huts that sheltered small boats needed bulldozing out of their misery. Travelling with such unyielding optimism, we'd foolishly believed the end would be paved with gold, a sunbeam shrouded sign would praise our feat, angels would sing harp-based muzak from on high to welcome us. Pixies adorned in brightly coloured spandex suits and pointy boots of finest velvet would dance in adoration handing us ambrosia sandwiches and a box of assorted biscuits before carving our names into the marble obelisk commemorating all fellows brave and dashing who had completed the route. Not so. We lamely got out of the RV and scuffed our feet around the dusty surface inspecting anything subsurface that could have been gold but now covered with the debris of decay.

***

The Coast Guard HQ was a typical government building designed by uncreative architects to be the most boring, cheap structure that they could think of, functionality an afterthought.

Speaking into the gate intercom we struggled to find an opening line that didn't sound ludicrous. 'Excuse me we're two Brits who've just come all the way down the Mississippi River following a kayak. Can we stay here? We're not murderers, honest.'

Just satisfied to ask for someone from the duty crew, we were met by a young officer who studied our paperwork with suspicion before cagily leading us up to a senior figure's office. Amazingly, he'd heard on the New Orleans grapevine about our expedition. He waved away our paperwork and sat us down and offered us his dinner. We loved the Deep South.

The duty crew were surprisingly young considering their responsibilities and eyed us up like children first seeing a lion at the zoo. They silently gave us the occasional quick peek and would jump when we spoke, but once confidence was gained, conversation blossomed.

They could have been characters in a sitcom:

The redneck, who spat baccy into a plastic cup while boasting of his prowess with a gun.

The bespectacled nerd, who insisted we play him at table tennis.

The petite woman, who looked more at home playing with Barbie dolls but sat with a modicum of social intelligence. Being called Annie and having a gun, our presence renewed the opportunity for the redneck to quip 'Annie get you gun'. Having heard it countless times we could have sympathised with her putting cyanide in his baccy.

Venice, Annie told us, was the posting everyone dreaded. It was easy to see why. Between here and New Orleans was a no man's land of social outcasts rotting in their trailers spending their social security cheques drinking in the seedy one light bars. She lived in the romantically sounding Port Sulphur in a Coast Guard provided house. Imprisoned in her home, scared to go out in case she was accosted by some jerk and his brother/father, she actually looked forward to being re-interned in the duty room with the nerd and Johnny Ten Men. I pitied her situation. She was desperate to do well in the service but her enthusiasm had taken a dramatic downturn when posted here. She could have had been posted to Miami, San Diego, US Virgin Islands, but no, she got Venice. She didn't even know whom she'd upset.

Sean phoned as we simultaneously played table tennis and watched WWF at the redneck's insistence. We were to meet them in a couple of hours at a small marina upriver. They seemed upbeat, only another ten miles before Pilotstown.

Pilotstown is a floating village of pontoons, shrimping boats and fat gulls living well from the overspill of shellfish dropped onto the decks. The lads still had no sure-fire way of getting back but felt confident they could get a lift. Only a few hours earlier we'd bumped into a seaman who informed us there was always steady traffic heading upstream and it shouldn't being a problem to hitch a ride. Good job too, it was one thing paddling the last ten miles to complete the trip, something else entirely to paddle ten miles back upstream after they'd finished. Happy things were going to plan, we lazed around in the damp sunshine.

Thirsty, I drove out to collect a six-pack of sodas. Stopping at a small convenience store, three suspicious characters eyed me braking into the car park. As I got out, they kept their eyes on the RV. My stare didn't budge from them as I collected the drinks. They surveyed the RV closely looking underneath, inside and out. Hurriedly handing over my cash, not bothering to check the change like a true Yorkshireman, I stepped bravely into the sunlight. Butterflies anticipating conflict, I asked them if they were OK.

'Yeah sure,' smiled the first.

Hispanic in appearance he wore a gold necklace thicker than the hawsers that secured the nearby shrimpers.

'Nice vehicle,' said the second, similarly dressed with a crop of peroxide hair. His Spanish accent was much harder than the first.

'Yeah it's OK.'

'You from Australia?' asked the first.

'Yes,' I sighed.

'How much is it worth?' Asked the first guy, looking at my soda.

'$1.99.'

'No, the RV.'

'Oh,' I smiled knowingly. 'About $80,000. But it's rented.'

'Yeah I know, I can see the rental sticker.'

'You wanna get rid of it?' said the second guy.

This stumped me for a second and with a confused look answered, 'It's rented.'

'Yeah I know, I can still see the rental sticker.'

I liked him - a sarcastic twat. 'So, it's not mine to get rid of.'

'It's insured, no?'

'Yes.' I was getting more confused.

'Well if you lose it it'll get paid for.'

I now understood. They were going to rob me in broad daylight, in the shithole of the universe. I wasn't even wearing clean underwear. I could imagine the RV company shrugging their shoulders at the news of my death.

Yeah pity him dying from a sucking chest wound. At least we'll get the insurance money. He deserved it anyway, he didn't even know what VDK stood for.

The bile of fear erupted in my chest. My sphincter started to twitch like a Hare's nostril. I went ghostly white.

'I'll give you $30,000 cash,' offered the third guy. The strong quiet one, he waved a wad of notes as thick as an ice cream wafer sandwich.

The knot of fear loosened to a half hitch of interest. 'I can't sell it now. I'm picking up some kayakers in a few hours then going back to New Orleans tonight.'

'That's cool. We didn't want it until tomorrow, anyway.'

It was like a dream, these three crooks outlining their plan. In films, the baddies would mystifyingly disclose the plan before failing to kill the hero. Unfortunately, I was no James Bond, and only armed with six cans of soda my chances were slim.

I was to park it in a car park just off Tulane and South Liberty. I'd meet them under a nearby tree where they'd hand me the money or kill me. Fitz would be there, so at least I wouldn't be the only one murdered if things went pear shaped. I'd then leave for about six hours returning to find the RV gone. By the time I reported the theft they'd be in Texas, well on their way to the Mexican border crossing point of Laredo/Nuevo Laredo. By the time officials were notified they'd be back home in Monterrey.

Just one thing nagged me. It just didn't make sense. Either I was being set up or they were the most illogical criminals in a long history of motiveless crime.

'Why don't you buy one, you know, legally?'

'You can't get anything for $30,000. We could live in this.'

There was merit in his statement, but after only three months I was longing for more static lodgings.

'$30K man,' said the leader waving the wad around. The sight of hard cash can do things to a weak man. At this precise moment I was so weak I would have struggled to lift my eyelids.

'How do I know this is for real?' I thought it only fair to ask.

'You don't,' blunt but to the point. 'But when you ever gonna make 30K if you don't take a gamble.'

He was like a Mexican Yoda. Thinking back to Chicago and the woman gleefully handing me a bill for $1800 worth of extras I wouldn't need. Where was the moral difference in them robbing me of nearly two grand? Fuck them. It was time for revenge. Legality aside, who'd suffer, an avaricious insurance executive's bank balance?

'OK I'll do it.'

With further instructions for the following day, I returned to the Coast Guard.

'Frigging hell Fitz guess what…'

'…What about Sean and Rob?' he replied after I'd told him of the plan.

It was the first time I'd thought of them. 'Well as long as they haven't got anything important like passports and stuff, they'll be OK. The kit's coming out tomorrow anyway to de-rig it all.'

'We gonna to share it with them?'

'Bollocks to that, they won't go for it. Anyhow it's only twenty grand English. Divide that by four and it only be five each, it won't be worth it.'

His silence turned to an evil grin. 'Lets do it.'

The guys finished late. Our minds weren't on what they should have been, other matters were far more important and we didn't even acknowledge their feat.

Luckily, they were too tired to notice and so kayak folded roughly and packed we returned to neon lit New Orleans and bedded straight down back at Task Force 5. I don't think I slept a wink but got out of bed at 8am feeling quite refreshed. I started unpacking the RV, purposely taking out Rob and Sean's personal belongings on the pretence that I was going to give the place a good once over.

I'd already mentioned a PR contact I needed to see so took it as the perfect opportunity to leave while the paddlers did their admin in the late morning sun. We started her up for the last time. We felt rather sorry for her. She'd been blindly faithful and now we were repaying that loyalty by discarding her to a life of crime. If there'd been such an organisation I'm sure we'd have been hounded by the RSPCRV.

'You sure you want to do this?'

'Too right.' For some reason, it seemed the most natural thing in the world.

There was still the niggling doubt that the three amigos were going to do us over. Driving up Magazine onto Common I felt all eyes looking at us. Everyone turned, some pointing, paranoia telling me they weren't looking at the Aquarium of the Americas but yelling that we were selling the RV. My blood started to pump harder, harder, my heart was thumping its way out of my chest. My hands clammy to the touch gripped the steering wheel blanching my knuckles. Pulling into the car park, I automatically spotted the trio dressed in the same garb as the previous day. Brazen on the sidewalk as if waiting for a bus, they held a solitary vanity case. One budged the other to alert him of our presence, and they retreated to the shade of a nearby tree. Throat resisting a dry swallow I inhaled deeply to calm my electric nerves. My hands shook, a hot surge spread like wildfire vibrating through my body, curdling my bile into nausea, and indeed I did want to pass stools.

'You shitting yourself?' asked Fitz.

'Yeah, you?'

'Filled 'em twice already.'

The laughter eased the tension. Once we left the RV we returned to the land of jelly legs.

The middle guy put his fingers to his lips and handed us the vanity case. On opening it all we saw was a row of six $20 notes stacked high in the frilly interior.

'Check it if you want, but it'll take forever. You don't wanna hang around do you?

'No, no I agree.'

Quickly closing the case, we walked hurriedly trying to look normal with smiles smirking under a reddened blush. It had been the easiest $30K ever made.

I was on cloud nine. In our hands we had $30,000, enough to keep us stocked on ramen noodles for the next 432 years. We sat on a nearby bench and watched the California Flyer speed off. Slowly opening the case I took out the first wad. Still as thick as an ice cream wafer sandwich, the wad started to melt. Creamy vanilla ran down my wrist. Looking closely at the note on top then at the one on the bottom, they were both made from a wafer. In between was a wad of ice cream as thick as $5000.

I stepped out of the shower and sat down to dry naturally. Fitz walked in, a globule of white in his hair.

'What you been doing?' I said, looking at the gunk.

'God knows, woke up with it in my barnet,' he replied wiping his hair.

'Did you not wake up? I bought you an ice cream, gave you a shake and put it next to you. You picked it up so I thought you were awake.'

'Did you?' Fitz asked quizzically.

'You not remember?'

'No, first thing I know is waking up drowning in vanilla ice cream. I had a hoofing dream though. I was you and we sold the RV for six ice cream wafer sandwiches.'

'What? That's what I bought you, an ice cream wafer sandwich.'

'That must have triggered it. It was mega realistic. We sold it to three Mexican dudes for $30,000 but they saw us off and gave us six ice creams instead.'

'Oh bargain, sounds like something we'd do.'

'Yeah, you organised it all.'

I laughed. 'Sounds like me. Who got the extra ice creams?

'What you mean?'

'Four of us, six ice creams. Did I get the extra ones for setting it up?'

'No you left Sean and Rob out of it.'

'Oh cheers, so not only am I the worlds' worst car criminal, I'm a complete wanker as well.'

'Well no I was, but then again, I was you.'

I'd been awoken myself by a phone call from a jubilant Sean twenty minutes earlier. They'd done it. They'd completed their quest and reached the Head of Passes at mile 0, just past Pilotstown. As the Gods were truly smiling on us, they'd managed to organise a lift back to boot, but wouldn't be back until 10pm. Congratulating them, I had stolen into the canteen freezer, nicked a couple of ice cream wafer sandwiches before giving one to Fitz who was still snoozing but now wearing it as a hair clip.

The next four hours seemed like forty. Every boat that chugged its way up Tiger Pass made us jump from the RV, camcorder at the ready to welcome back the heroes. One after the other they passed. Hoping it wouldn't be a case of the boy who cried wolf and we ignore the boat that carried them, we sat as vigilant as the stars above. This perseverance paid off as we eventually heard the familiar shouts of the Welshman, and saw the familiar grin of Rob. Jubilant as though he'd won a F1 Grand Prix, Sean waved, whooped and hollered. We responded as though we'd been buggered in the bayou. Rob, more reserved, just wore a smile of contented satisfaction, which on his huge head looked like a chipolata sausage on a 12" dinner plate.

It was over. After all the trials and tribulations of the past few months, they could turn round and say that they'd paddled the length of 'Big Muddy' the 'Great Provider' 'Ol' Man River' and the most frequent name - 'this fucking river' - the Mississippi.

Relief now washed over them. They'd confessed a feeling of anti-climax at the red triangle marker signifying mile 0, but now back on terra firma, the realisation had set in. No more would they wake up with sand in their mouths. No more would they have to stretch and warm up for twenty minutes before they could sit down to a cup of tea. They would now be able to feel that they had a backside. They could now dream of things other than being washed away by a raging river or being stung to death by swarms of killer bees.

All shaking hands in an overly British manner we revelled in happiness. I brought the champagne and classy plastic flutes and passed the bottle to Sean, after all, it had been his idea and it was only right he pop the cork.

Annie kindly took the video footage of Sean shaking, popping, and spraying the bubbly over us all, then sharing the 25ml of bubbles left in the bottom of the bottle. Even Sean's dire release of Sean the Sheep trotting off to pee on the wheel hubs went without the usual groans.

The collapsing of the Klepper was done with reckless abandon, as we were desperate to return to civilisation. When asked whether they'd like to kick or kiss the kayak they chose the latter. It had served them well and respect was due to Klepper.

Thanking Annie, we left Venice and cruised back to N'Awlins to the lullabies of the Beatles that sent both Rob and Sean into deep sleeps. We cruised, basking in our achievements. A car overtook us. I nudged Fitz. It was a Connecticut plate. We didn't yelp like sugar-fuelled children, a contented nod of victory was far more appropriate.

The next day, I left the group. Although sad to leave, I was looking forward to the forthcoming week. They had to endure another week in N'Awlins. I pitied their livers.

The trip to meet my girlfriend in Orlando had, at first, filled me with trepidation, but after looking at the map, with 4956 miles in the RV already covered, another 450 would seem like a walk round the corner to post a letter.

***

I was sixty miles south east of Tallahassee, Florida. It was dark, and darkness tends to bring on reflection. I felt a rare permeating warmth emerging from within. I remember feeling it on my passing out parade as a newly qualified Royal Marines Commando at the age of seventeen. The strongest and most recent times were witnessing the birth of my children. It's the most wonderful flush anyone can experience. You want to grab strangers in the street and tell them your news. You want to punch the air, break the silence with shouts of joy. You want to laugh outwardly and giggle inwardly.

Yes, pride truly is a wonderful feeling, and I was full of it.

Epilogue

I stood in front of the Commanding Officer for the very last time. As is procedure, it is he who presides over the final act of military theatre. I stood there in my smart civvies - long-sleeved shirt, trousers, polished shoes and no fucking cleverness, according to the RSM, to be handed my 'Testimonial' - a brief summary of my achievements in the Royal Marines, resplendent within a marbled green faux leather book cover that looked more like a menu holder. In return, I handed over my military ID card. The CO asked why I had chosen to leave. I didn't want to sound profoundly churlish like the marine before me who boasted he would reply 'I joined the Royal Marines to become a man, so why do I still feel as if I am treated like a child?'

All I could be was be thankful. Being profound didn't seem appropriate at such a time. I only could offer thanks to the men of Corps for giving me the best years of my life. While it may not have been the smoothest journey, I could leave with my integrity intact, my head held high, and with testicles looking like a pair of space hoppers inside Santa's sack, I was ready to take on the world with a confidence that would knock over anyone willing to shake my hand.

I exited the main gate for the last time. There was no fanfare to see me off, no white doves released from the gloves of a troop of Royal Marines bedecked in ceremonial uniforms, no gilded sunset to walk towards, just a bored-looking baggy arsed bootneck wondering if there was to be any toast left when relieved. I wondered whether leaving was the right thing to do. The weight lifting from shoulders told me all I needed to know.

A new chapter was about to open. While I knew my intrinsic character would lead me to new adventures, I couldn't foresee it taking me to some of the most bizarre and dangerous places on the planet, challenges I would relish when opportunity knocked.

What I couldn't prepare for were the personal battles I would fight, against an enemy far more formidable than I could ever imagine.

Printed in Great Britain
by Amazon